DAVID J. BREWER

THE LIFE OF A
SUPREME COURT
JUSTICE

1837–1910

Michael J. Brodhead

Southern Illinois University Press

Carbondale and Edwardsville

Library of Congress Cataloging-in-Publication Data

Brodhead, Michael J.
David J. Brewer : the life of a Supreme Court justice, 1837–
1910 / Michael J. Brodhead.
p.   cm.
Includes bibliographical references and index.
1. Brewer, David J. (David Josiah), 1837–1910. 2. Judges—
United States—Biography. 3. United States. Supreme
Court—Biography.
I. Title.
KF8745.B7B76   1994
347.73′2634—dc20 [B]
[347.3073534] [B]   93-16866
ISBN 0-8093-1909-8   CIP

Frontispiece: David J. Brewer. Courtesy of the Kansas State
Historical Society, Topeka, Kansas.

The paper used in this publication meets the minimum requirements of American National Standard for Information Sciences—
Permanence of Paper for Printed Library Materials, ANSI Z39.48-1984. ∞

For my brother and sisters
Dan, Karen, and Molly

CONTENTS

ACKNOWLEDGMENTS

MANY KIND AND knowledgeable persons have contributed substantially to the completion of this study. I much appreciate the encouragement of Donald R. McCoy of the University of Kansas, the late F. C. ("Tim") Bannon of Leavenworth, Kansas, and members of the Department of History of the University of Nevada, Reno, most notably Jerome E. Edwards, Russell R. Elliott, William D. Rowley, and Wilbur S. Shepperson. The departmental secretary, Margaret McCracken, assisted in innumerable ways. So too did colleagues elsewhere in the university: Jake Highton, William L. Eubank, and especially Nicholas M. Cady. Steven D. Zink's information retrieval wizardry is unmatched. Nancy Taylor helped in the preparation of the manuscript. A grant from the university's Research Advisory Board made travel for research possible.

Heartfelt thanks go to those who read parts of the manuscript and supplied much needed corrections and suggestions for improvement: Jack H. Crouchet, Denver; Charles W. McCurdy, University of Virginia; and David W. Wheeler, Marion, Kansas. John E. Semonche of the University of North Carolina gave the entire manuscript the benefit of his thorough and authoritative reading. My valued friend David L. Harvey, Department of Sociology, University of Nevada, Reno, also read it in its entirety and contributed many sound insights and recommendations.

Help with specific legal points came from Donald J. Pisani, University of Oklahoma; James E. Sherow, Southwest Texas State University; and Felix Stumpf, National Judicial College, Reno. David Bianchi and Margaret E. Winter, both of Northwestern Mutual Life, kindly provided me with materials relative to Brewer's association with that company. Clara Kelly and the late John Mohler, librarians of the National Judicial College, were unfailingly helpful. So too were the archivists and librarians at the National Archives, the University of Kansas, the University of California, Berkeley, Yale University, and the University of Nevada, Reno. I am much indebted to several staff members of the Kansas State Historical Society, an institution justly esteemed by a multitude of grateful scholars. My wife, Hwa-di, has been patient and supportive and has furnished more than a few good thoughts about my subject and his times.

INTRODUCTION

In January of 1893, at the beginning of his fourth year as an associate justice of the United States Supreme Court, David Josiah Brewer addressed the Kansas Bar Association. With understandable pride, he pointed to his professional life as a judge of a court of record for thirty years. "Few men in the United States have had as long, and I think it is very doubtful if there is a single one who has had a more varied career on the bench than I. There is scarcely any judicial position which I have not filled; scarcely any service in the profession which I have not been called upon to discharge." He had been a judge of a county criminal and probate court, and of a state district court and a federal circuit court, as well as a justice of the supreme court of Kansas. "In addition, I served on a petit jury, was once foreman of a grand jury, have been U.S. Commissioner, and prosecuting attorney, to say nothing of filling up odd times with such little services as master in chancery, and the like."[1]

No member of the Supreme Court has ever come to the High Bench with a richer judicial background. Previous service as a jurist is not a prerequisite for appointment to the Court nor a guarantee of success as a member of it; several of its most notable justices had no prior judicial experience. But in Brewer's case, a long career on other tribunals was an asset, both for himself and the Court presided over by Chief Justice Melville W. Fuller. His life presents a unique opportunity for viewing the American judicial system and one man's passage from its lowest to its highest levels.

Brewer became the member of the Fuller Court best known to the American people at the time, not merely by virtue of his long tenure on it but largely because of his many off-the-bench statements as an orator and writer. His public visibility did not translate into popularity in all quarters. Several of his judicial opinions and nonjudicial utterances stirred up controversy, particularly when he confronted the reform issues of his day.

Historical treatments of the Fuller Court have readily dismissed it as a pack of reactionaries, hell-bent on infusing the law with social

Darwinism and laissez-faire ideology. Only Justices John Marshall Harlan and Oliver Wendell Holmes, so these accounts have it, showed sympathy for reform. Routinely, Justices Brewer, Stephen J. Field, Rufus W. Peckham, and the chief justice himself are singled out as enemies of all measures for improving the economic and social condition of the American masses.[2]

Fortunately, recent scholarship has demonstrated that during the late nineteenth and early twentieth centuries the Supreme Court—and the American judiciary generally—was far more receptive to reform than usually supposed. Jurists labored throughout this period to fit the Constitution and the law to the new realities created by the rapid, often traumatic transformation of the United States from a distended rural society to a centralized industrial nation. More often than not they sanctioned legislation designed to remedy the ills of the new system.[3]

Contrary to the usual assessments, Brewer accepted most of his generation's reform goals. In fact, he actively championed many forms of social legislation and regulation of business. As a public figure, he spoke out for the rights of women, decent treatment of minorities (most notably the Chinese in America), charities, and world peace.

How then did he get a reputation as an exponent of social Darwinism and laissez-faire ideology? First of all, those terms have been used carelessly by historians and others. Such misuse has served as a poor substitute for real analysis. Second, a small body of his opinions and public statements (or excerpts from them) has sufficed as evidence of his "conservatism." Also, it has been all too easy to assume that the controversial decisions of Brewer and his contemporaries were based solely on their own ideological predilections and that precedent and settled legal principles played no role.

It is true that Brewer supported property rights. But in his time and earlier, property rights were important elements of—and not necessarily antagonistic to—civil rights; protecting property was protecting the individual. Also, judicial protection of property rights did not in all instances mean shielding powerful business interests. In conflicts between large and small property owners, Brewer and many other jurists of his generation tended to side with the latter.

Certainly too he admired honest entrepreneurial activity. But on and off the bench he denounced the evils of big business. Brewer consistently opposed the concentration of power in any form: large corporations, labor unions, and government. He did so because he favored the individual, whether the individual be the initiator of a great economic enterprise or a farmer struggling to extend agriculture into the western plains. Brewer's concern for individuals stemmed not so much from any economic theory as from his religious convictions. Indeed, his responses to the public questions of the day were to a great extent shaped by the Christian beliefs of this son of a missionary.

In much of the recent writing on judicial history and biography, the trend has been to examine all of the opinions of a particular jurist or all of the decisions of an era of a court's history. This is a decided improvement over an earlier tendency to generalize from a handful of well-known opinions. The older approach was too often used to condemn or praise on the basis of a jurist's supposed conservatism or liberalism. Rather than a more complete understanding of the subject, the result was usually mere approval or disapproval, based upon limited evidence and the historian's subjective, presentist viewpoints.

This writer hopes that he has avoided that pitfall. But he cannot claim to have avoided the biographer's usual inclination to become fond of his subject. David J. Brewer proved to be too warm, genial, witty, and wise for that.

DAVID J. BREWER

I

THE PATH TO THE BENCH
From Smyrna to Kansas, 1837–1862

By AMERICAN STANDARDS David Josiah Brewer's family was New England "old stock."[1] An ancestor, John Brewer, emigrated from Great Britain to North America in 1690. David Brewer's grandfather Eliab (1770–1804) appears to have started the family's traditions of training at Yale and professing the law. Little is known of him other than that he supposedly practiced his calling with distinction at Lenox, Massachusetts. Careers at the pulpit and the bar were the common pattern among the early generations of the Brewer family in America.

David's father, Josiah Brewer, was born in South Tyringham (now Monterey), Berkshire County, Massachusetts, in 1796. He attended Phillips Academy and Yale, where he graduated in 1821 as valedictorian. Remaining at Yale for two years as a tutor, he studied at Andover Theological Seminary and entered the Congregational ministry. The dedicated young clergyman, supported by the Boston Female Society for the Promotion of Christianity among the Jews, sailed from Boston to the Mediterranean in 1826. Missionary work over the next two years took him to Gibraltar, Syria, Smyrna, Constantinople, Malta, and the Greek islands. Throughout his travels he attempted to spread the Gospel to the Jews as well as to propagate Protestantism among the Greeks. Political turmoil in the area and polite hints from British officials encouraged him to abandon his enterprise temporarily. Soon after his return to America, he married Emilia A. Field at Stockbridge, Massachusetts.[2]

The union with Miss Field was fortunate, not only because Josiah found an able and devoted helpmate but also because the children of the marriage would be favored with an association with the remarkable Field family. Emilia's brothers were David Dudley Field, an illustrious attorney, the codifier of the laws of New York, and an advocate of international arbitration; Stephen J. Field, later an associate justice of the United States Supreme Court; Cyrus W. Field, the developer of the trans-Atlantic cable; and Henry M. Field, a noted clergyman.

Two months after the marriage Josiah and Emilia were sent to the Mediterranean by the New Haven Ladies Greek Association so that he might establish a school for girls in Greece. Accompanying the missionary couple was thirteen-year-old Stephen Field. Stephen's elder brother, David, had decided that the experience would help prepare the boy for a career as a professor of Oriental languages.[3]

Rather than settle in Greece, Josiah Brewer decided to do his work in Smyrna, Asia Minor, which had a large Greek population. In addition to operating the girls' school, he published a religious newspaper in the Greek language. The Brewers remained there until 1835 when they returned briefly to the United States. In the following year, under the auspices of the Western Foreign Missionary Society at Pittsburgh, they sailed again to Asia Minor. This time local antimissionary attitudes made Josiah Brewer's task more difficult, yet he continued his work in the Near East until 1838.[4]

In the meantime the Brewer family increased. The child destined for the greatest fame, David Josiah (the couple's fourth), was born at Smyrna on June 20, 1837. Thus David Brewer, a New England Yankee by inheritance and a midwesterner during most of his adult career (thereby identified with the sections of the United States commonly thought to be the most "American"), was distinctly an exotic by birth.

Much has been made of his genetic makeup to explain his rise in later life. Did not the "sturdy New England stock" on his father's side and the "brilliant strain" of the Field family combine to produce an offspring whose success was inevitable? Perhaps—but it must be borne in mind that the attainments of his brothers and sisters were much more modest and that "good" lineage does not infallibly determine success. Nevertheless, the circumstances of his birth had much influence on the course of his life. He was to choose the profession of his uncles David and Stephen, admire the enterprise of men such as his uncle Cyrus, develop a firm belief in the uplifting value of education, and retain a lifelong commitment to Christianity and its propagation in distant lands.[5] Possibly the fact that women had helped to launch his father's career inclined him to revere the feminine half of humanity and to champion its rights.[6]

The Brewers returned to America with infant David in September of 1839. For the next several years Josiah Brewer taught at a female academy in New Haven, edited church newspapers, and held a variety of pastorates throughout Massachusetts and Connecticut. In 1844, a time of economic depression, he found himself temporarily out of work and sought, unsuccessfully, another missionary assignment.[7]

Boyhood was apparently a happy time for David and the other Brewer children. He looked forward eagerly to the time when he could enroll in school, and when he began his education, he found the experience as rewarding as he had anticipated. In 1846 he wrote from New Haven to his cousin Heman Field that he was studying Latin, arithmetic, geography, algebra, and spelling, as well as raising two rabbits. During the time when his father held the pulpit at Middletown, Connecticut, little David collected mineral specimens.[8]

Sometime during David's childhood the elder Brewer served as chaplain of the state penitentiary at Wethersfield, Connecticut. Because he was "not old enough to pick a lock or enter into any schemes to relieve an inmate," the boy had the run of the place and became friendly with many of the prisoners. One of them, a trusty, was especially devoted to him and was, Brewer recalled, "the first man who thought I would ever amount to anything." The child admired this "wonderful man" in return. Although David Brewer was to become a particularly stern and unbending judge in criminal cases, his youthful penitentiary experiences gave him an abiding concern for the well-being of prison inmates. In later life he regularly gave Fourth of July speeches at the state penitentiary in Kansas "in the endeavor to bring sunshine to the faces and smiles to the lips of those unfortunate ones whom the state has noticed to punish."[9]

Another early influence was his father's stand against slavery. Josiah Brewer edited antislavery periodicals and aligned himself with the free-soil wing of the Democratic party. In 1848 he supported the presidential candidacy of John P. Hale of the Liberty party. By 1856 he had switched his political loyalty to the new Republican party.[10]

At the age of fourteen David matriculated at Wesleyan College. There he joined a literary society, the Peithologian, and was initiated into "The Mystical Seven," a group that met for "essays and discussion." After two years he transferred to Yale, the "family college," where his elder brother Fisk was a tutor.[11] As with his other youthful experiences, Brewer remembered his Yale years fondly. The school closely adhered to the "classical" curriculum, emphasizing Greek, Latin, theology, and mathematics. In his junior year he won second prize in the mathematics competition and tied for second in Latin.

His classmates included Henry Billings Brown (later Brewer's colleague on the Supreme Court) and Chauncey M. Depew. Depew remembered that their class of ninety-seven students was considered large at the time and that upon graduation most of the members of the class entered law, medicine, or the ministry. According to Depew the faculty, headed by President Theodore D. Woolsey, was outstanding. The "learning, common sense, magnetism and all-around good-fellowship" of Timothy Dwight, then a young tutor, made him a special favorite of Brewer, Depew, and other students of the 1850s.[12]

To relieve the rigidity of the curriculum there were the literary and debating societies, such as the Linonia and the Brothers of Unity.[13] Young Brewer enjoyed those activities and, according to classmate Benjamin Magruder, had a reputation for "jumping up on the slightest provocation to make a speech, especially on political lines." Other Yale contemporaries remembered him as being more reserved.[14]

Brewer completed the requirements for a degree in 1856, finishing fourth in his class and winning first prize in the practical astronomy competition. He delivered his graduation essay at commencement, entitled "The Estimate of Life: A Criterion of the State of Civilization." The budding orator stated his belief that the measure of the greatness of any society depended upon the value it placed on personal character and the individual, not material attainments.[15] Judged by these standards, as Brewer saw it, Christianity and the United States came off well. The sentiments expressed were not merely the platitudinous mouthings of a youth seeking to please his instructors, family, and classmates. He was giving early voice to themes that he was to emphasize for the remainder of his days.

Brewer had few doubts as to a career. Even before college he was told by those closest to him that he was destined for the legal profession.[16] Accordingly, he moved to Albany, New York, and spent about a year reading law in the office of his noted uncle, David Dudley Field, after which time he enrolled in the Albany Law School.

The school had advantages. Because it was located at the state's capital city, the students had unlimited opportunities for observing the sessions of a variety of courts. It had only Yale and Harvard law schools as competitors in the northeastern United States. The solid faculty, consisting of Ira Harris, Amos Dean, and Amasa J. Parker, imparted a practical, up-to-date knowledge of the law through lectures delivered in a room of the south wing of the Medical College building. Although the instruction was competent, the school often granted diplomas after only six months of course work.[17]

As Brewer was finishing his studies, he debated whether to go West and join his uncle Stephen, who had been elected to the supreme court of California. On another point he was more certain. In a letter to his sister Henrietta, in December of 1857, he expressed determination to resist the blandishments of "crinoline & hoops" and remain "devoted to a life of bachelor independence & happiness" because a bachelor "is always necessary in a family to carry round sugar plums to nephews & nieces [and] to leave large fortunes to those who cultivate his good will."[18]

During his career as a law student his political sentiments were those of his father. In a letter to the *Middlesex Republican* (Massachusetts), he gave his unqualified condemnation of the outgoing administration of Franklin Pierce. Brewer singled out the Kansas-Nebraska Act and its turbulent aftermath in Kansas as evidence that the departure of Pierce from the White House was good riddance. The blood of the free-state men and "the crackling flames which rose from burning Lawrence and the pillar of fire and cloud of smoke that have rested on the plains of that lovely Territory [must] be the everlasting witness" to the "failure and curse" of Pierce's administration. A loyal Democrat, replying through the pages of the same paper, objected to Brewer's "tirade of abuse and misrepresentation" and predicted that the time would come when Pierce's name would be sacred and Brewer's forgotten.[19]

The antislavery scholar of law soon found another target for his outpourings: the Dred Scott decision.[20] In another letter to the *Republican*, he denounced Chief Justice Roger B. Taney's assertions that blacks were not citizens and that Congress had no power to exclude slavery from the territories.[21] The infamy of the Taney opinion also inspired what seems to have been Brewer's first published poetic effort, entitled "Dred Scott," which the *Republican* printed.[22] Among its thirteen verses were the following:

I once was free—I once was free,
  But no kind friend then told me;
And when I knew that weak and few
  Were bonds of law to hold me;

That with no right save that of might,
  They held us Slavery's drudges,
My rights I sought—in vain I sought
  For white men were my judges.

Brewer's scrapbooks for this period contain other of his poems and literary sketches, both published and unpublished.[23] Still, the study of law remained his chief concern. He received his diploma on February 18, 1858, which entitled him to practice in the state of New York without taking a bar examination.[24] After graduation he faced two tempting choices: to stay in Albany with Uncle David (in whose law office he worked briefly after graduation) or follow Uncle Stephen to California. Either alternative was bound to provide invaluable political and professional opportunities. He chose neither, announcing that "I don't want to grow up to be my uncle's nephew."[25] A quotation from John Greenleaf Whittier on the first page of his diary reflected the same determination to make his own way: "There's life alone in duty done / and rest alone in striving."[26]

He decided to try his fortunes in a frontier setting rawer even than California. According to his own account, he left for Kansas City, Missouri, shortly after graduation. He arrived there with his father's gifts of an umbrella and a pair of rubber shoes, losing the shoes while crossing "one of the quagmires that they called streets."[27]

A few months' residence in Kansas City, during which time he practiced law in partnership with W. H. Russell, did not cure his wanderlust.[28] He joined a band of other young men who had caught "gold fever" from hearing news of the rush to Pike's Peak. They traveled through Kansas Territory via the Arkansas River in a wagon drawn by "half-broken" steers. Years later Brewer joked that although he and his foolhardy companions were not killed by Indians, they should have been. Just before arriving at Pike's Peak they met discouraged gold-seekers returning east. Yet they persisted, and Brewer stayed until June of 1859. Finding no riches, he finally turned back and deserted the West temporarily. He was still restless, however, and had not given up on the West as a good prospect. After a short stay with his parents at Stockbridge, he set out for Leavenworth, Kansas Territory, arriving there on September 13, 1859.[29]

Although his motives for deciding on Leavenworth are not clear, it was a likely place for a young man to begin a legal career in earnest. Located just south of Fort Leavenworth (established in 1827), the town began in 1854, the year that the Territory of Kansas had been created. By the time of Brewer's arrival, it had attained a population of around ten thousand. It was favorably situated in the "elbow region" of the Missouri River. The energetic community had survived two devastating fires to become a center for overland freighting and staging as well as for river commerce. Residents believed that a western railroad with Leavenworth as the terminus was all that was needed to make their city the new gateway to the West.

In time Leavenworth and other towns in Kansas and Missouri along the river lost out to Kansas City in their attempts to become the hub of a western transportation system. Also, Leavenworth failed to become the capital of Kansas.[30] Nevertheless, it was the trading center of the territory. It was also the home of many of the brightest lights of the legal profession of Kansas.

Brewer landed there without friends or money. According to legend he had only sixty-five cents and an insurance policy, which generously permitted the holder to reside in Kansas and still be covered.[31] Recalling his struggle to launch a career, Brewer later described his first years in Leavenworth as "mighty hard." "But," he added, "the country was young and there were chances." Looking back, he believed that an attorney beginning his professional life in the mid-nineteenth century had opportunities not available to later generations of lawyers because American society and the economy were then decentralized and the legal business had not yet become concentrated in the cities.[32]

Brewer's first break came shortly after his arrival in Leavenworth when two of the town's most illustrious lawyers, Samuel Stinson ("the Rufus Choate of the Kansas bar") and his partner Eugene F. Havens, permitted him to occupy a desk in their offices.[33] By November he had formed a partnership with another young lawyer, P. P. Hathaway. The firm of Brewer and Hathaway maintained an office at 40 Delaware Street. Brewer roomed at the boardinghouse of Elizabeth Piper at 24 Delaware Street.[34]

The most dangerous phase of the "bleeding Kansas" territorial days had passed by 1859, and a severe economic depression had replaced the struggle between antislavery and proslavery settlers as the most pressing problem facing the people of Kansas. The depression, which lasted into 1860, aggravated another difficulty for Brewer: the intense competition for business among the lawyers of Leavenworth. Not only were there dozens of young unknowns like Brewer floating in—and out—of the city, but there were several established, politically powerful attorneys who had the best chances for a first crack at the more profitable cases: James H. Lane, soon to become the first and most controversial Kansas senator; Samuel D. Lecompte, the notorious proslavery chief justice of the territorial supreme court; Mark Delahay, a distant kinsman of Abraham Lincoln and federal district judge for Kansas during the Civil War; Marcus J. Parrott and J. W. Whitfield, territorial delegates to Congress; and Thomas Ewing, Jr., the first chief justice of the state supreme court. Other worthies of the local bar included H. Miles Moore, Benjamin Stringfellow, Franklin G. Adams, Isaac S. Kalloch, Robert Crozier, John A. Halderman, and James F. Legate.

Sometime during 1860 a young woman from Burlington, Vermont, stepped into Brewer's life to offer a pleasant respite from his often cheerless pursuit of success. Louise ("Lulu") R. Landon had come to visit her sister, the wife of a Leavenworth merchant. Brewer developed an interest in the charming woman soon after making Lulu's acquaintance. In response to her twitting him for cigar-smoking, the young attorney wrote a piece of doggerel, "To My Anti-Tobacco Friend, Lulu Landon," dated 10:00 P.M., December 31, 1860,[35] which slyly conveyed his feelings toward her:

The hours are flying, the year is dying,
  And nought can stay or bar
The smoke is whirling, in circles curling
  From off my last cigar.

Farewell to treasures, farewell to pleasures
  Which low & grovelling are!
And beaming brightly, the ashes lightly
  Drop from my last cigar.

Now backward sadly & forward gladly
  Thought wheels her rapid car;

Obeying duty & heeding beauty
  I smoke my last cigar.

Now hope is staying & fancy playing
  In brighter scenes afar
And love is blessing with such caressing
  As burns my last cigar.

On October 3, 1861, the happy New Englanders-turned-westerners were married. Brewer later claimed that his marriage ended the prospect of a life wasted in the fun-seeking ways of bachelorhood. Later in the month he was allowed to practice before the federal district court for Kansas.[36]

During the same year his hard work began to pay off. He received an appointment as a commissioner of the federal circuit court, which brought him a few more dollars in fees for preparing warrants and other routine paperwork.[37]

At the time of his marriage his partnership with Hathaway had ended. For a short time Brewer practiced alone in an office at 48 Delaware Street.[38] By 1862, however, Brewer had once again entered a law partnership, this time with C. B. Pierce. The office was located in the upstairs portion of Norton's Building, on the south side of Delaware Street between Main and Second streets. His home was situated on the south side of Oak Street, between Seventh and Broadway.[39]

He was also taking an active part in community affairs, being one of the "live, leading men" who organized the Leavenworth Mercantile Library Association on December 12, 1861. He served as the association's first secretary and later in the decade as its president.[40] Just as close to his heart was his association with the First Congregational Church, an institution that he helped to establish and to which he was to devote considerable time as Bible class teacher and Sunday school superintendent.[41]

Another self-imposed duty came with the outbreak of the Civil War. As a judge, he was not expected to serve in the Union armies. Nevertheless, Brewer felt obliged to become an active militiaman and was commissioned a second lieutenant in the "Lane Rifles," one of the companies of the local Home Guard.[42] In choosing not to become a full-time soldier for the Union cause, Brewer was not removing himself from the dangers of the conflict. Leavenworth was just across the border from Missouri, the home of Confederate guerilla bands, such as that of William C. Quantrill. Also, a large number of Missourians had rallied behind the Confederacy's General Sterling Price. Quantrill, Price, and others raided into Kansas, and although Leavenworth was relatively untouched by actual warfare, there was a constant threat of an attack. Part-time military service in his own community meant that he was in a better position to protect his wife and their first child, Harriet Emelia ("Pettie"), born in 1862, should an attack come.

Politically, he threw in his lot with the faction of Kansas Republicanism opposed to James H. Lane. Elected to the United States Senate just after Kansas achieved statehood in early 1861, Jim Lane—erratic, coarse, domineering—was the exact opposite of the steady, genial, scholarly young man from New England.

In 1862 Brewer had his sights set on a seat in the legislature and was later quoted as saying: "I want to be a legislator; I care nothing about a judicial career."[43] Working assiduously for the nomination, he contacted delegates to Leavenworth County's Republican convention and thought he had secured promises of support from a majority of them. "So I went to the convention with great spirits and large expectations, but when the results of the ballot was announced I found I had received but one vote."

His first experience with western political ways left him unhappy and bewildered. "Somehow or other there must have been on the part of the delegates a strange misrecollection of the assurances they had given me, or else on my part an equally strange misunderstanding of the scope of those assurances."[44] To salve a collective guilty conscience or to offer a consolation prize, the convention tendered the political tyro the nomination for judge of the county probate court. He declined at first but was soon persuaded to accept. In the November elections Brewer and other anti-Lane candidates were successful in Leavenworth County. He won over his opponent, one Diefendorf, by a slender majority of nineteen votes.[45] Thus began an unusually long and ultimately distinguished life on the bench.

2

JUDGE AND CITIZEN
Leavenworth, 1863–1870

THE POST of probate judge gave Brewer the modest yet steady income he needed. Brewer himself stated that elevation to the post ended three years of privation and ushered in a lifetime of "clear sailing."[1] The probate judgeship was not as lowly as it might appear because in March of 1862 the Kansas legislature had created the Criminal Court of Leavenworth County and designated the probate judge as the ex officio judge of the new tribunal.[2] And there was plenty of crime in the vicinity. As a river town, a trail town, and a town situated near a military reservation and state and federal penitentiaries, Leavenworth attracted citizens markedly different from well-bred, God-fearing young professional men such as David Brewer.

By 1863 he had changed his residence to Elm Street but kept his law office in Norton's Building. He held probate court sessions beginning on the first Mondays of January, April, July, and October, but his criminal court duties were usually more pressing than those of the probate court.[3]

Throughout his judicial career he remained rigid to the point of harshness on matters of lawbreaking. Crime offended him not just because of his Puritan background but also because he viewed lawlessness as detrimental to the progress of the new state of Kansas and to the preservation of the Union. In a charge to a grand jury, he told the members that vigorous enforcement of the law would serve the Union cause and attract population and capital to Kansas.[4]

The few cases appealed from Brewer's court to the state supreme court indicate the nature of his judicial work. In a murder case he sentenced one Bailey Smith to be executed. The supreme court reversed the judgment because two of the three justices believed Brewer had erred in not granting a change of venue. On another occasion the high court ruled that his charge to the grand jury in the case of John Millar, accused of shooting a man with the intent to kill, had been correct.[5] After Brewer had ordered that all of the gambling equipment of John T. Rice be destroyed by the sheriff, the supreme court agreed with Rice that not all of the devices were illegal, and modified Brewer's ruling accordingly. Rice also appealed his conviction for running a faro game, but Chief Justice Crozier's decision affirmed the lower court's verdict and paid the Leavenworth judge a handsome compliment: Brewer's charge to the jury was "full, clear, comprehensive, well worded and in excellent judicial taste; and we do not recollect in our reading a better specimen of judicial literature."[6]

During the spring and summer of 1864, Lulu, along with two-year-old Harriet, went east to visit her parents and the Brewer and Field families. She enjoyed meeting his relatives and became especially fond of Uncle Henry Field. Yet her letters to her husband show that she missed him terribly: "Oh! Dave I am so lonely to night. What would I give to be with you." To make matters worse, there were "the awful yarns they tell us about bushwhackers in Kansas." Most frightening of all were rumors that "Quantrell [*sic*] and his *crew* are again in Kansas. Is it so? and are you fearing an attack? How many troops have you at the Fort, and are you well protected in the City? I hope *you* will not have to stand on *guard*." Lulu seemed equally concerned about his supply of clean, warm clothing.[7]

Even though she was safe from the perils of war, Brewer worried about his wife because she was again pregnant with what David and Lulu called "him."[8] "He" was born December 2, 1864, probably after Lulu's return from Leavenworth, and turned out to be a girl, Henrietta Louise ("Etta"). The other children born later were also girls: Frances Adele ("Fannie"; born August 26, 1870) and Jeanie Elizabeth ("Bessie"; born February 16, 1875). The Civil War and the postwar years brought sorrow to Brewer and his family. A younger brother, Lieutenant Marshall B. Brewer, died in 1861 of a fever contracted in the service. His mother passed away during the same year; Josiah Brewer, who remarried a few years later, died in 1872. David's brothers Jonathan and Matthew died in 1868 and 1870.[9]

Many people in Leavenworth County had been skeptical about electing a man of only twenty-five years of age to the probate judgeship. Fears of his youth and inexperience evaporated when they saw how well their young jurist acquitted himself. As his term drew to a close in 1864, several members of the bar urged him to seek the office of judge of the first judicial district of Kansas, which embraced Leavenworth and Wyandotte counties. To the request Brewer announced that he would "accede cheerfully."[10]

At the Leavenworth County convention of the Republican (Union) party in October, Daniel R. Anthony, editor of the *Leavenworth Conservative*, and other pro-Lane delegates gave A. M. Sawyer twenty-five votes, while the anti-Lane forces mustered only fourteen for Brewer. The Brewer supporters protested that Wyandotte County also had a voice in the matter. Perhaps this argument helped put Brewer over in subsequent balloting; the Union party of Wyandotte backed Brewer. A letter to the *Leavenworth Times* from a Wyandotte man predicted that Brewer would be overwhelmingly successful with the voters of his county and that it was useless for anyone of the Lane persuasion "to come 'poking' around in this county; for a man who is corrupt enough to support the Lane fraud is too corrupt to get any votes in this county, except from horse-thieves and pimps." Another letter to the *Times* denounced Sawyer's candidacy as a joke and claimed that Sawyer was a chronic office seeker who had no standing with the local bar.

On the eve of the election Brewer joined other rising young Republicans of the state—John J. Ingalls, James F. Legate, Solon O. Thacher, Marcus J. Parrott, and Daniel W. Wilder—in addressing a "Grand Union Mass Meeting" on November 7.[11] In the election Brewer trounced Sawyer, 2,363 to 1,627. A month later the judge-elect submitted his resignation as commissioner of the federal court.[12]

The Civil War came to a close soon after Brewer assumed his new duties, but one of his earliest cases as district judge involved some prominent military figures. Soldiers from Fort Leavenworth, in the summer of 1865, seized some horses that they believed had been obtained by civilians through illegal trading with Indians. The alleged owner complained to Judge Brewer, who ordered General Stalbrand, commander of the Northern District of Kansas, to return the horses. The general refused, and Brewer cited him for contempt. General John Pope, commander of the Military Department of the Missouri, fired off a letter to Brewer, bluntly stating that the horses were contraband and that the state courts had no power to interfere.

Although recognizing that he was powerless to enforce his rulings, Brewer wrote forceful letters to Pope and his superior, William T. Sherman: "[T]he military must obey and sustain the civil Courts, (and that does not mean obeying what writs they please and resisting what they please, but obedience to all writs)."[13] Although his protests were unavailing, the episode demonstrated that Brewer, despite a smiling, easy-going manner off the bench, was capable of courage and tenacity in his official capacity, especially when the power and prestige of the courts were at stake. The event perhaps also contributed to his aversion, more pronounced in later life, to things military.

The status of blacks posed problems for Brewer and other Kansas jurists. The state's constitution allowed only white males to vote, but a decision by Brewer modified this restriction to a great extent. When a man who was one-fourth black sued for the right of the franchise, Brewer ruled that he was entitled to it since he was predominantly white and awarded him one cent in nominal damages.[14]

In Wyandotte County, Brewer had to hold court in a store on Nebraska Avenue in Kansas City, Kansas, because there was no regular courthouse. An outside stairway to the second floor "was utilized on more than one occasion as an impromptu gallows."[15]

Proceedings in his court, despite his best efforts, were not always as dignified and serious as he wished. In a trial before a jury of farmers, Brewer announced in the evening that he would return in the morning to receive the verdict. Arriving there the next day, he found a deserted jury room. He quickly rounded up the foreman who replied to the anxious judge's demand for an explanation: "Well, it looked so much like rain that we decided we had better go home and look after things."[16]

By his own later admission, Brewer was ambitious in those years, and this caused him to worry over his work late into the night. Realizing that he was endangering his health, he consulted a physician who advised him not to work at all in the evenings. The judge took the advice and found that after his evening meal he was able to ignore his work and enjoy himself by playing cards with his wife or taking her to parties and the theater. Since he now slept soundly, he developed the habit of going to bed at ten in the evening and waking up at four in the morning, at which time he spent two or three hours on his judicial labors before breakfast. He adhered to this schedule for the rest of his life.[17]

In addition to his work as an official of the Mercantile Library (which had two thousand volumes by 1866) and teaching Sunday school, Brewer assumed still other civic responsibilities that, taken together, must have consumed about as much time as his judgeship. In 1866 he became one of the directors of the newly incorporated Leavenworth Law Library, a cooperative undertaking designed to serve the city's fifty-five attorneys. In the same year he was elected secretary of the Mount Muncie Cemetery Association and was one of the incorporators of a Leavenworth group that erected a monument commemorating the Kansas volunteers killed in the war.[18]

Of greater importance were his activities in behalf of education in his community, county, and state. Brewer inherited from his father the belief that, next to Christianity, universal education was the chief agent of progress and civilization. In 1863 he was elected to the city's school board, representing the first ward (he then resided on the south side of Pottawatomie Street, between Second and Third streets). He became vice president of the board in May of 1864 and president in November. In August of 1865, while settling into the work of district judge, he became superintendent of Leavenworth's school system with a salary of $450 a year. At the same time he continued to sit as a member and clerk of the school board as well as a member of the Board of Examiners, a group responsible for certifying teachers.[19]

At the end of his first year as superintendent, Brewer published his report (an "admirably prepared document," according to one reader[20]) in which he detailed the progress of the city's educational efforts and gave suggestions for overcoming several problems. Foremost of the difficulties he faced was overcrowding in the seventeen schools of Leavenworth. Crowded conditions, he wrote, caused headaches for the teachers, a breakdown in discipline, absenteeism, and tardiness; lack of space discouraged many children from enrolling and cheated those who did attend. The situation was particularly grievous in one of the city's two schools for black children, held in the "colored Baptist Church." There Brewer had seen children jammed into all the benches and the stairs leading to the pulpit, "and even the pulpit itself was the abode of as much original sin as seven juvenile Ethiopians could embody."[21]

He warned that the problem would grow worse as the city's population increased and urged the people to vote more bonds and taxes for the building of schools. Generosity in this regard, he argued, was economical in the long run: "Every dollar invested in that way is the saving of many dollars to the next generation in the expenses of the alms houses, houses of correction, criminal courts, jails and penitentiaries."[22]

In presenting the statistical portions of the report, Brewer explained that while most of the teachers had given him accurate figures, a few had only guessed at them: "[I]f there is any guessing to be done, I, as a Yankee, can do it as well as the teacher, and prefer no report to an incorrect one.[23] He also took to task those teachers who relied on rote memorization, which produced only "weariness and listlessness [in] the school room." He approved the continuation of instruction in music "though I cannot be charged with any partiality for music." The year had also witnessed another experiment, the establishment of a high school that, although in an embryonic state and with a "crude and ill defined" course of instruction, had "prospered beyond our expectations."[24]

Toward the end of the report Brewer suggested that the building of a town clock would provide a uniform time for all the city and help eliminate tardiness. "May we not hope that our city fathers will take this matter in hand and let us know when nine o'clock comes?"[25] In closing his remarks the superintendent expressed his thanks for having been presented, along with many compliments, with a "handsome silver tea service" upon which was engraved "David J. Brewer, from the teachers and pupils of the Leavenworth Schools."

In his report for the following year, the superintendent again criticized teachers for having the students give verbatim recitations from textbooks. He stressed that the teachers instead "should, by a variety of questions, by suggestions and explanations, be satisfied that each scholar have a clear and correct understanding of the subject and its relations." Without such understanding "the ideas which fill [the student's] mind, instead of standing out clear and distinct as the stars, appear like the milky way, a mass of confused and mingling light." But he insisted that any improvements of instruction were impossible if overcrowding (which he likened to the Black Hole of Calcutta and Herod's slaughtering of the innocents) continued to work an injustice on pupils and teachers. New buildings were needed also to help the recently implemented system of graded classes and to instill a sense of beauty in the minds of the students.[26]

Another problem treated in his report was that of inadequate space for playgrounds. Without them the students turned to the streets for unsupervised recreation. "Street preaching is very good, but street teaching or the lessons learned in the streets can not be recommended." Although it was too late for Leavenworth to benefit from the proposal, Brewer suggested that the states and territories of the West require each new town site to set aside a block or an acre which, after the town grew and property values rose, could be sold and the profits used to finance local schools.[27]

Another of his general observations concerned compulsory education. He conceded that governments must avoid restricting liberty but pointed out that some restraints—jailing criminals, confining mental defectives, military conscription, sanitary regulations, and appropriating private property for public use—were necessary and beneficial. Compulsory education, he argued, brought even more benefits because it would lessen the need for jails and other restrictions of freedom. Another of his arguments for mandatory schooling was the inevitability of the franchise for blacks and women. "It is the duty of the State to educate all to whom it grants the ballot. Universal education is the only thing which will make universal suffrage safe."[28]

Since most graduates of the high school did not go on to higher studies, Brewer left Greek and Latin out of the curriculum in the belief that time was better spent on more practical disciplines, including modern languages. He favored an hour, in addition to the daily sessions, that was to be used for voluntary lessons in music and drawing; those not wanting to stay would be free to help their parents at home. Although the night school had poor facilities and little attention paid to it, Brewer supported its continuation because it was a blessing to the poor white youths "prevented by the necessities of life, from attending the day schools. . . . A like arrangement for the colored children would be productive of great benefit." Brewer also showed concern for the poor by opposing frequent changing of textbooks.[29]

His dedication to spreading the gospel of learning in the community was fittingly acknowledged ninety years after his term as superintendent. In August of 1957 a new primary school for Leavenworth was named for David J. Brewer.

Brewer's crusade for education extended beyond the bounds of his own city. In June of 1865 he took a three-day journey by stagecoach to Emporia where he delivered the address for the state normal school's first graduation exercises. Forty-five years later the institution's first president wrote that it was the finest commencement address ever delivered there.[30] Brewer's main point was that teaching had joined law, medicine, and divinity as one of the professions and was "infinitely" of more value to mankind than the first two. He noted that teachers were then receiving better pay than before and that they should receive even higher salaries so that they might become the economic and social equals of lawyers and physicians. He lauded the blessings of good instruction: "I do not believe that Humboldt with all his learning was as good a teacher as the young lady who taught me to read."

Another theme of the speech was that the opening up of the new profession to women meant that they now had the opportunity to become something other than "wives, kitchen girls, seamstresses or harlots." He stated flatly that the female made the best teacher because, among other attributes, "she has a facile and quick tongue—no doubt about that."

Brewer's final thought was that secession and the Civil War had occurred largely because the southern states had inadequate public school systems. He closed by insisting that the North bring education to the South to heal the wounds of war, eliminate the possibility of future disloyalty, and elevate the freedmen. In 1867 Brewer was elected to a three-year term on the board of trustees of Washburn College, a Congregational institution in Topeka. He did not, however, attend meetings with any regularity, possibly because of the press of other commitments.[31] Among the latter were his activities with the Kansas State Teachers' Association. He chaired the association's executive and legislative committees in 1866 and 1867. Brewer was the president of the organization in 1868 and 1869.[32]

During these years he contributed to the association's periodical. In two articles he urged that politics be taught in the schools. By "politics" he did not refer to "demagogism" and "low clap-trap" or "manipulating primary meetings and conventions by drafts on saloons, brothels and that great Falstaffian army for which no better name has yet been devised than *loaders*." Rather, he meant that teachers should inform students about matters such as the Constitution, the forms of government, and the relations of the states to the federal government. To those who said that a teacher might misinform the pupils, Brewer answered that such a teacher should be replaced. In reply to those who felt that children were unable to grasp political problems that perplexed even adults, he wrote that teaching the Bible posed the same difficulty.

To the charge that education in politics was useless for girls, Brewer responded: "She may yet be a voter. She will be a citizen. Good government benefits; bad government injures her. She can exert great influence on political questions whether voting or not." He suggested that it would "work no injury to dispense with a little piano and take a little politics. The girl that smatters French and knows nothing of impeachment is not half educated."[33]

Extending his thinking to an equally controversial realm, Brewer said that teachers must not be discouraged from active participation in politics: "Teachers of Kansas, fear not to speak your mind and bear your part in the political contests of the day. Engaging in politics is a high and holy mission."[34]

During his tenure as president, he favored the association's journal with a retelling, in blank verse, of the story of "The Woman of Samaria," which closed with:

O! thirsty pilgrim, quenching thirst at wells
Which thine own hands have sunk and ribbed with stone,
Beside thy weary way flows a living stream;
Drink of its flow, and thou shalt never thirst.[35]

Brewer's involvement with the growth of Kansas education took much time from his chosen careers as lawyer and judge. Yet his contributions to education no doubt helped his political prospects. As his judicial term drew to a close in 1868, either he decided not to seek reelection or the managers of the local Republican organization made the choice for him. In any case he was nominated for county attorney at the September 26 convention. In booming his candidacy, the Republicans claimed that his elevation to a successful term on the bench in 1864 had been supported by Democrats as well as Republicans and reminded the voters of his leadership in promoting schools, libraries, and other areas of civic improvement. Brewer himself took an active part in the campaign. He was chosen to preside over an October 1 rally; at the conclusion of his "very happy speech," the crowd gave "three hearty cheers" for "Judge Brewer, the next County Attorney." He received a boost from an October 15 resolution of the Wyandotte County bar, which praised him for "his uniform courtesy, kind disposition, his ability in the discharge of his various arduous duties as judge." Sometime in the middle of the month Brewer presided over a district judicial convention that nominated a candidate to succeed him as judge.[36]

The Republican newspapers extolled him as a man of "fine legal attainments," "highest personal character," and an "old citizen" (Leavenworth was then fifteen years old and Brewer thirty-one). The Republican press branded his Democratic opponent Cole Foster as "a sort of Copperheaded Carpet-Bagger" who lacked experience, competence, and the full support of his own party. In the November election Brewer won handily, 2,611 to 2,346.[37]

For the next two years he prosecuted the perpetrators of murder, robbery, and other crimes. When official duties permitted, he pursued a private civil practice in partnership with John L. Pendery in an office at 61 Delaware Street. The Brewer residence changed in these year to Fifth Avenue, between Marshall and Congress streets.[38]

He and Pendery handled a divorce and child maintenance suit that proved both embarrassing and humorous for Brewer. He had heard the case earlier as district judge and had ruled in favor of the wife. After he left the judgeship, Brewer and his partner were hired by the husband to appeal the decision to the state supreme court. Chief Justice Samuel A. Kingman later recalled with merriment the ludicrous state of affairs when Brewer presented his brief. He "seemed to feel that the situation was somewhat awkward, and in half apology . . . said he could not see why he should not complain of his own decision, as everybody else had done so." The court, said Kingman, "agreed in opinion with the advocate and over-ruled that of the Judge."[39] In a bastardy case Brewer was again successful before Kingman's court.[40]

The completion of his term as county attorney in 1870 also marked the end of a decade of remarkable accomplishment for Brewer— remarkable in that he had not only survived but actually advanced himself in a milieu fraught with professional and political pitfalls. He had established himself as a leading attorney in a community filled with legal talent. And he had won three elections in a particularly turbulent era of Kansas politics. Political life in Leavenworth was especially vicious, and Leavenworth had a larger number of Demo-crats than most other Kansas towns. As a judge and prosecutor, Brewer always stood in danger of making a host of enemies.

His success can be partly explained in that he played the political game carefully. Beyond that, there were more positive elements con-tributing to his rise: Brewer had gained the reputation of a solid, hardworking family man, devoted to his profession and his communi-ty's betterment. His admirers commented frequently on his impartial-ity and uprightness as a judge. His family connections and educational background probably impressed many. Leavenworth had the image of a boisterous place; yet a large number of its supposedly depraved population appreciated Brewer's virtues and achievements. By 1870 the people of his city and his state were ready to raise him to a higher position.

3

"A COTERIE OF ABLE MEN"
Brewer and the Kansas Supreme Court on Corporations, the Public Interest, Politics, and Crime, 1871–1884

THE AUGUST 31, 1870, issue of the *Topeka Commonwealth* noted that D. J. Brewer of Leavenworth was a Republican candidate for associate justice of the Kansas Supreme Court. Although he was not actively seeking to wrest the nomination from incumbent Jacob Safford, the *Commonwealth* stated, Brewer "will take the nomination if thrust upon him." To the surprise of many, the young Leavenworth man captured the prize at the party's September convention in Topeka, easily defeating Safford and four other aspirants.[1]

In the November election, the loyally Republican voters of the state gave him a whopping majority, 41,717 to 19,280, over his Democratic opponent, R. M. Ruggles.[2] Equally effortless and successful were his subsequent bids for renomination and reelection for the court's six-year terms. In 1876 he had no significant opposition for renomination; in 1882 the state convention chose him by acclamation. In the general elections he had no difficulty besting Democratic and third party rivals.[3]

With Brewer's accession to the court in January of 1871, the state's highest tribunal reached maturity. During the stormy territorial period the justices bore the stigma of proslavery partisanship. The quality and reputation of the court scarcely improved after statehood. Too often members had been inexperienced nonentities, while frequent turnover in membership had discouraged unity. Improvement came in 1867 when the respected Samuel A. Kingman became chief justice. Associate Justice Daniel M. Valentine, whom Brewer described as "one of the most painstaking and thoughtful judges I know," joined the court in 1869.[4] Two years later Brewer's elevation meant that the court now consisted of three talented jurists who worked well together. This was fortunate for Kansas since the population of the state had increased threefold between 1860 and 1870; in the second decade of statehood the population again trebled. Yet even such able men as Kingman, Valentine, and Brewer had difficulty keeping up with a mounting docket. The aging Kingman's inability to share an equal work load with his younger colleagues aggravated the problem.[5] By the end of 1876 Brewer and Valentine had written over four hundred decisions each, which taken together accounted for two-thirds of the total number of supreme court decisions since statehood.[6] That year, in an effort to lessen the burden, the court began experimenting with brief *per curiam* decisions in minor cases. Also, the beloved but now ineffective Kingman resigned. In his place was appointed Albert H. Horton, a jurist with a "clear, forceful and logical mind and untiring industry."[7]

Brewer and the other justices performed their labors in an atmosphere of mutual respect, friendship, and good humor. The bench, bar, and public appreciated the heightened stature of the court and respected the members personally. A young lawyer taking his first case before the court long remembered his encounter with the affable trio in their chambers. Each was working at a separate desk in a small room on the north side of the corridor on the first floor of the east wing of the statehouse—the only part of the building then completed. Valentine helpfully inquired about the details of the case; Brewer jokingly asked him what he was trying to do to his opponent; and Kingman twitted him about coming to Topeka while the legislature was in session. Years later the young attorney, William A. Johnston, who himself became an associate justice in 1884, expressed the opinion that the three men made up "a great court—a coterie of able men who, in simple surroundings, were laying the foundation of our jurisprudence."[8]

Brewer's early rising habits suited his busy judicial schedule. For the first week of each month, except August, the justices heard the arguments of the litigants and spent the remaining time writing opinions.[9] The cases heard ranged widely in character and significance—from momentous questions such as railroad regulation to such petty matters as the replevin of a watch.[10]

The newness of the state's system of laws and courts presented difficulties in the early 1870s. In some matters the supreme court lacked precedents upon which to base its rulings. Yet when a lawyer called upon the court to establish a precedent, Brewer replied that it was "the duty of courts to stand by ancient landmarks, to walk 'super antiquas vias' [along ancient roads]."[11] Brewer and the other justices, however, recognized that the rapid changes being wrought by industrialization and the unique conditions of the West meant they must not be hidebound. Brewer emphasized that "the law must take things as it finds them, and adjust its rules to the facts of every day life" and to "the actual experiences and necessities of life."[12]

Another problem brought about by the brief existence of the supreme court was that individual justices frequently were obliged not to participate in many decisions because they had been a party to, or counsel in, or a district judge hearing the case originally. For example, an appeal in 1871 involved a conviction for murder obtained by Brewer as county attorney before the Leavenworth County Criminal Court. He had to recuse himself as Kingman and Valentine reversed the jury's verdict.[13] A similar circumstance in the next year brought about a more favorable result for him. Shortly after taking his place on the bench, he sued the commissioners of Leavenworth County for payment for legal services rendered in his capacity as county attorney. The district court had found in his favor, and his colleagues affirmed the ruling on appeal.[14]

Nineteenth-century judges have been accused of favoritism to railroads and other powerful economic interests. Brewer in particular has been singled out as an example of judicial hostility toward the regulation of corporations. The charge was heard in his own time, and since, that he opposed the regulation of railroads. Actually, Brewer, as a member of the Kansas Supreme Court, showed a general tendency to agree with the public's insistence that the railroads and other large business enterprises be required to serve the public's best interests. So too did his colleagues on the Kansas supreme bench, and so did most jurists in other states at that time.

In one of his earliest decisions, Brewer, speaking for a unanimous court, held that the Kansas Pacific Railway had to provide safe and sufficient facilities for the shipment of cattle because all railroads "perform a public duty, are engaged in a public employment, and subserve a public use." He stressed that since railroads had received subsidies from the local, state, and federal governments, they were especially bound to serve the public and that it was "with ill-grace, then, that they seek to avoid the responsibility. . . . Receiving funds of the public to aid in construction and then claiming to be simply private carriers in transportation for that public presents an unseemly contradiction."[15]

In one of his last decisions for the Kansas court, he repeated the same viewpoints in a suit involving the Santa Fe railroad, yet added that in the case at hand the railroad was not obliged to provide for transportation of goods on other railroad lines; the Santa Fe's "entire common-law duty is limited to its own line; it owes nothing to the public beyond that."[16] In yet another decision, which required a railroad company to establish adequate depot facilities for the traveling and shipping public, he wrote that railroads were "*quasi* public agencies" and took the occasion to declare that "in [the railroads'] management they come far short of accommodating the public, or supplying its necessities, no one will question."[17]

Although Kansas did not begin the practice of regulating railroad rates until the time Brewer left the state bench, the legislature used the police power (that is, the power to regulate the public's health, safety, morals, and welfare) to regulate railroads in other ways. For example, it enacted a law in 1874 that made railroads liable for damages for killing livestock along the unfenced portions of their tracks. When the Kansas Pacific challenged the constitutionality of the law, Brewer's opinion upheld the statute, including a section of it that entitled the plaintiffs to recover attorneys' fees in addition to damages. The decision reveals Brewer's concern for the rights of owners of all types of property, not just those of large corporations. The state, he wrote, was acting within its authority in using the police power "to prescribe the manner of using one's property, and pursuing one's occupation, so as not to trespass on the property or rights of others." The "increasing complexities of our civilization, and the increasing diversities in the industries and modes of life" made the police power all the more necessary. "Probably no single agency has made so large a demand for the exercise of this power as the agency of steam in locomotion."[18]

Enlarging upon the principle in a subsequent decision, Brewer stated that the right to operate a railroad was a franchise granted by the state and that the state had the right to change the requirements for holding the franchise: "No one is compelled to accept such a franchise, and no one may complain of the conditions upon which it alone may be taken and held. . . . [T]he imposition of a new police regulation is equivalent to an original condition of the franchise."[19] In a third decision involving the same subject, he wrote that the fencing of railroad tracks was necessary not only to protect cattle but also the passengers and employees of the railroad. Although he observed that the state could just as well require the owners of livestock to construct the fences rather than the railroads, Brewer believed that there was "especial justice in casting this duty" upon the railroads because they received the greatest benefits and profits from the use of the tracks.[20]

A decision delivered by Brewer made even those railroads in federal receivership liable under the fencing law.[21] Yet he recognized that there were limits to the scope of the statute. For example, he handed down a decision reversing a lower court's ruling in a case in which stock had been killed because the railroad had not been allowed to erect a fence along a part of its line. Also, in a case in which neither the owner of the stock nor the railroad had complied with the provisions of the law of 1874, Brewer, for the court, held that the stock owner had no right to recover damages.[22]

The problem of fencing appeared before the court in other forms. In response to complaints by farmers that herds driven up from Texas strayed from the trails and ruined crops, the legislature in 1868 passed a "herd law," making the drovers liable. A second herd law, enacted in 1870, exempted certain counties from the earlier statute. A decision delivered by Brewer declared the second act unconstitutional because laws "of a general nature" were required by the Kansas constitution to be applied uniformly throughout the state.[23]

In their search for adequate fencing materials, the farmers of Kansas experimented with Osage orange hedges; a law of 1879 authorized the counties to pay bounties for the growing of the hedges. When challenged, Valentine's majority opinion upheld the law's constitutionality. A separate opinion by Brewer expressed the view that "it can be sustained only so far as respects fences along the highway, in the improvement of which the public as a whole is interested."[24]

Brewer not only accepted the regulation of "quasi public agencies" but was adamantly opposed to a particular form of public subsidization of railroads. Kansas, in common with other states, had passed legislation allowing counties and localities to purchase stock in railroad companies, paying for the stock by local bond issues. In turn the railroads were expected to build their lines through the communities voting the bonds. In short, many towns and counties, in the West particularly, were, with legislative sanction, bribing the railroads to serve them. In their eagerness to have rail service, citizens voted the bonds without anticipating other results—such as reneging by the railroads.

When the constitutionality of the laws authorizing the practice was first contested in the Kansas Supreme Court in 1871, Brewer had not yet taken his seat. The other justices upheld the laws in question.[25] When the issue again came before the court later in the year in State ex rel. *St. Joseph & Denver City R. Co.* v. *Commissioners of Nemaha County*,[26] Brewer was able to participate. Valentine, with Kingman agreeing, restated the belief that the laws were in accord with the state constitution. Brewer dissented emphatically and at length. He began his opinion by remarking that although the nation's highest courts had generally sustained such legislation, a large minority of the judges throughout the country had disagreed. Also, he noted that the public's excitement over the question showed that it was far from being settled in Kansas. Brewer urged his brethren not to accept the view that "Whatever is, is right": "Because *so many* legislatures, *so many* executives, and *so many* courts have recognized this species of legislation" did not necessarily mean that such laws were valid or wise.[27] Similarly, the "habit of regarding the legislature as *inherently omnipotent* . . . is dangerous, and tends to error." He announced his intention to examine the matter "unembarrassed by prior adjudication, here or elsewhere."[28]

First, Brewer objected to the local subsidization of railroads because it compelled citizens to become stockholders in the corporations. Although he granted that railroads were for the benefit and use of the public, he insisted that they were private companies and "it seems wondrous hard to call [a railroad] a public highway."[29] The constitution prohibited the state from being "a party in carrying on any works of internal improvement," and Brewer contended that the state could not skirt the prohibition by allowing local governments to subsidize such improvements. Again denying that a railroad was a public highway, he wrote: "It does not follow, because a state may do a certain work as a public improvement, and for public use, that it can give of the public funds to a private individual to enable him to do a like work as a private speculation and for personal gain."[30] In apparent contradiction to these remarks, later opinions by Brewer would liken railroads to public highways. He went on to blast the argument that taxation to pay for railroad bonds was akin to a railroad's power of eminent domain: "It is less grievous to compel a man to sell than to give to a railroad."[31] He closed by stating his belief that legislative action "authorizing municipalities to extend aid to private corporations cannot be sustained."[32]

In the course of his remarks, Brewer complimented "my brother Valentine" for his able exposition of the opposing view.[33] Many Kansas lawyers concluded that the opinions of Valentine and Brewer presented the issue definitively. Brewer's dissent, written in his first term on the court, "attracted the attention of the bar of the state and of the writers for law journals and textbooks of the whole country."[34]

Six years later Brewer wrote the majority opinion in a similar case in which he recognized that Valentine's railroad bond decision was the law, despite his own misgivings. In grudgingly acknowledging that Valentine's view was now conclusive, Brewer could not resist paraphrasing Solomon: "Look not thou upon the voting of railroad bonds when it is new, for at the last it biteth like a serpent, and stingeth like an adder."[35]

In three other bond decisions written for the court, Brewer took the opportunity to weaken the practice of public subsidizing of railroads. The first held that a county, even though it had voted bonds for a railroad, was not obligated to carry through with the transaction if the railroad for which the bonds had been subscribed subsequently consolidated with another line.[36] Another county was released from its obligation in the second decision on the grounds that the bond election had not been valid.[37] In the third case the ruling was that the city of Parsons need not hand over its bonds because the railroad had not complied with the stipulations to which it had agreed.[38] Both of his colleagues supported his views in all three cases.

Using public monies for private purposes always disturbed Brewer. One of his decisions voided bond issues by Blue Rapids Township (Marshall County) and Neosho Falls because the bonds had been voted to build mills for private manufacturers. Similarly, the court, speaking through Brewer, ruled that a public schoolhouse could not be used for a meeting of a private organization.[39]

Another case involving public funds touched upon a more sensitive

issue—relief for those left destitute by the grasshopper invasion of
1874. The legislature enacted a law authorizing townships to borrow
money that in turn was to be lent to farmers who had lost crops
to the grasshoppers. Almost immediately the law was challenged.
Brewer's opinion for a unanimous court invalidating the law shows
much agonizing on his part. He expressed his private wish that the
court could sustain the measure because of the suffering of a large
number of Kansans. Yet he insisted that there was a distinction
between utter helplessness and temporary destitution. The public,
he conceded, had a duty to aid those unable to help themselves
but not the duty or power to benefit a particular class of citizens
"temporarily embarrassed." Another objectionable feature of the law
was that it put the townships lending the money in the position of
speculating their funds on future crops. He concluded by reiterating
the temptation to uphold the act. "But ours is an unmixed duty to
declare the law as it is, and not as we might wish it to be."[40]

Although Brewer, as a judge, found it impossible to sanction
public aid for relieving victims of the calamity, as a citizen, he served
on the Kansas Central Relief Committee, a state agency that distrib-
uted money, provisions, and clothing donated by the people of the
East for those affected by the grasshopper plague.[41]

Another of his decisions gave him the chance to make further
distinctions between public and private interests. The constitutionality of a state law establishing a road to be paid for by the two counties
through which it ran was challenged by one of the counties. The
decision upheld the law on the grounds that a "public highway is a
matter solely of public interest" and that the counties should be
required to pay for them. "It is not," he added pointedly, "like
compelling a county to take stock in a railroad corporation, or to
invest its public moneys in any enterprise in which there is something
of private interest."[42]

Another reason for Brewer's skeptical attitude toward county bond
issues was that they frequently involved fraud. Bond cases arising
out of corrupt circumstances brought forth his judicial wrath. A
suit concerning the school bonds of almost uninhabited Comanche
County led him to the conclusion that this was "one of those swin-
dling transactions and bogus organizations with which some of our
western counties have been afflicted."[43]

Cases involving county bonds for railroads *and* fraud especially rankled him, such as one arising out of a fraudulent bond election in Grasshopper Falls, where one-fourth of the votes were cast by nonresidents, boys, and blacks (the latter then still ineligible to vote in Kansas). To Brewer the affair was particularly disgraceful because the election took place "not in one of the crowded wards of a populous city, where we must expect outrages on the purity of the ballot-box but in a quiet country community. The fact alone carries its own comment, and speaks its own shame."[44]

In one of these cases Brewer gave a further clue as to his hostility to fraudulent bond issues. In 1877 his colleagues on the court handed down a decision (Brewer not participating) requiring the vendors of forged school bonds to reimburse the purchasers. As one of the vendors, although presumably an innocent one, the ruling cost Brewer five hundred dollars.[45]

Speaking through Brewer, the court ruled in favor of the traveling public in two cases involving the ejection of passengers from railroads. In one case the passenger had bought a ticket to ride in a freight car, only to be told by the conductor, who threw him off in midpassage, that the company no longer honored such tickets.[46] The second concerned the expulsion of a man who refused the conductor's demand that he pay him more than the regular fare. In the latter decision, Brewer denounced the "robbing and oppressing" of the public.[47] In a third case of forceful ejection, he and his brethren reversed a lower court's award of damages because the jury had been overly prejudiced against the railroad. Yet he took the occasion to chastise the railroads generally for the "rudeness and inattention" of their employees and the "many annoyances" and "much actual outrage and abuse" suffered by passengers.[48]

Travelers of the common carriers, on other occasions, found a friend in Brewer. Decisions delivered by him upheld awards of damages for injuries caused by the faulty construction of a railroad and by the negligence of a drunken driver of a stagecoach.[49] In some opinions, however, he objected to the too-generous awards decreed by local juries because he believed that a railroad "doing an injury should not be mulcted in any greater sum than an individual doing like injury." Just because a corporation was a "soulless organization" whose operations "frequently develop an irritation and dislike," juries must not let their biases be expressed in "enormous verdicts."[50] In one case he and his colleagues agreed that ten thousand dollars for the loss of a hand by a railroad worker was excessive; in another he believed that the same sum was too much to be paid by a railroad for the death of a man because the deceased ("lacking in either capacity, desire, or need for work") had earned little money in his lifetime. Therefore, there was no indication that his loss worked an economic hardship upon his survivors. "The law runs little along the lines of sympathy and affection, but rather along the lines of the actual and the probable."[51] In yet another case he dissented when Horton and Valentine sustained a verdict granting what Brewer thought was an outrageous sum for the loss of a young man's hand.[52]

The last decision written by Kingman upheld an award to a man who had lent three horses to another party. Brewer dissented, arguing that the recovery of three times the value of the horses for sixteen months' use was preposterous. A member of the Kansas bar later suggested that the majority opinion in that case was one of the reasons why Brewer left the Kansas bench to take a position in the federal court system.[53]

In other matters concerning railroads and corporations generally, Brewer's responses were mixed. When the Missouri Pacific contended that a law permitting Atchison's street railway to cross its track violated the state constitution's prohibition against granting "special privileges and immunities," Brewer disagreed, stating that the privileges and immunities referred to were political, not economic.[54] Although a decision handed down by him ruled against those seeking to preempt or homestead within the Santa Fe's land grant, another of his decisions confirmed the title of a homesteader who had settled on lands that were later included in the Kansas Pacific's grant.[55] When the Santa Fe argued that it must have the right to expand its operations by exercising the right of eminent domain (in this case, the right to condemn lands owned by another railroad), Brewer agreed.[56]

The taxation of railroads and their lands—a favorite and obvious means of raising revenue in the state—brought forth complaints by the corporations. The Santa Fe challenged the validity of a Kansas law of 1876 that authorized the state treasurer to collect taxes on railroad properties in the unorganized counties. The court had reservations about the law, but since the issues were not entirely clear, its opinion, written by Brewer, gave the statute the benefit of the doubt. In his remarks he expressed belief in the justice of casting the

burden of taxation upon the railroads rather than upon the inhabitants of the sparsely settled western counties ("those who push out
beyond the limits of organized counties and commence the work of
reclaiming the desert"). The legislature, he thought, must be allowed
broad powers for setting policy for western Kansas.[57]

Various opinions by Brewer suggest that in his mind the taxing
powers of the state and local governments were virtually without
limit. *Fretwell* v. *City of Troy* validated a local license tax on auctioneers
in Troy, in part because he recognized that itinerant auctioneers
undercut established merchants.[58] According to *City of Newton* v.
Atchison, it was no violation of the state constitution for Newton to
impose an occupational tax on the local merchants, since "business
is as legitimate an object of the taxing power as property"; nor did
a "tax on avocations," in addition to a property tax, constitute double
taxation; nor did the fact that Newton's occupational tax was graduated according to the amount of a merchant's stock meet with Brewer's
disfavor, because "graduation in the matter of license taxes is not
only supported by the authorities, but also eminently just." The
principle of graduation was especially proper also since the "larger
the business, the greater the protection and benefit of organized
society and government."[59] Later in his judicial life Brewer was to
develop doubts about graduated taxation. In the opinion on the
Newton license tax, he remarked that taxation was a legislative power
limited only by a few constitutional provisions. *Graham* v. *Board of
County Commissioners of Chautauqua County*, one of his last decisions
for the Kansas court, voided a law because, in providing for the
taxation of cattle driven into Kansas for grazing, the act violated "the
constitutional rule of uniformity of taxation."[60]

The politics of the 1870s in Kansas presented a multitude of issues
with which the state's supreme court had to wrestle. Litigation to
settle quarrels over the location of county seats was especially frequent, heated, and—for the court—exasperating. Although Brewer
granted that such suits had to be settled quickly lest many persons
and local interests suffer, any county seat fight was "a vexatious,
annoying, deranging question."[61] Fraudulent elections, so common
in those struggles, evoked angry denunciations from Brewer. In one
of three cases concerning the sordid contest between Fredonia and
Neodesha for the Wilson County seat, he lashed out at "this terrible
trespass on the purity of the ballot-box. May this example [of ballot-

stuffing] preach its lesson, not alone to [the voters of Fredonia], but equally to every citizen of the state."[62] The Ness County seat fight involved vote-buying, which brought forth another rebuke from Brewer. If the practice were tolerated, he wrote, "elections will be simply the measure of the candidates' purses."[63]

The use of liquor at county seat elections was also galling to him, the more so because the legislature had not provided penalties for violating the law against liquor at polling places: "Many a thoughtful man has gone away from the polls at the end of an exciting election deeply pondering whether after all free government be not yet simply an experiment with the evidences strongly pointing to failure."[64] A majority opinion by Valentine sanctioning two or more elections when the first had been tainted by fraud elicited a lengthy dissent from Brewer that showed strong feelings on the matter: "I think it is dangerous, and fraught with peril"; a multiplicity of elections only increased the opportunities for corruption.[65]

The problem of illegally cast votes reached its grossest proportions in a Harper County election in which about eight hundred voters returned 2,947 ballots in a county seat question. A furious Brewer found that "these returns are manifestly rotten and worthless, and the truth is not in them. They do not fail of absolute truth through mere mistake or error. They are an intentional and immense lie." The affair was doubly odious, Brewer lectured, because a large number of supposedly honorable citizens perpetrated this travesty against democracy.[66]

Local politics gave rise to still other issues that were taken to the court. The state brought suit against a legislator, calling for his removal because of drunkenness. The justices, speaking through Brewer, ruled that the legislature, not the court, had the power to seat and unseat its members.[67]

A situation arising out of a disputed mayoralty election in Leaven-worth was probably a more delicate matter for Brewer. The decision he wrote favored John A. Halderman against Daniel R. Anthony, leader of Leavenworth's old Lane faction. Another case concerned a contested election for state printer, and Brewer's opinion for the court acknowledged that the case involved politically sensitive questions. In a lengthy, clear statement, he confirmed the legitimacy of the legislature's selection of George W. Martin for the profitable post.[68]

Another type of political question, more important in later generations, came before the court in 1880: reapportionment. State law required that county commissioner districts be divided equally according to population. But in *Hayes* v. *Rogers* Brewer declared that it was often impossible to comply with the law because "the changes of population in some of our new and growing counties would require very radical changes of territory in order to make the districts equal in population."[69]

The criminal cases originating in the cattle towns almost confirm the legends of frontier lawlessness. Several of them came to the state's highest court. The first decision Brewer wrote for the court was a refusal to issue a writ of habeas corpus for an Abilene man accused of grand larceny.[70] The celebrated Bat Masterson of Dodge City figured in a Brewer opinion. Masterson, as sheriff of Ford County, recaptured G. U. Holcomb, a suspected cattle thief who had escaped from jail. Holcomb then sought a writ of habeas corpus from the supreme court, challenging the constitutionality of the law that had attached Foote County (where Holcomb's crime allegedly took place) to Ford County for judicial purposes. Brewer's decision refused Holcomb's petition.[71]

Another case involving a notorious cowtown character caused a split on the court. "Rowdy Joe" Lowe of Wichita had been jailed for shooting a man with intent to kill. Shortly afterwards he escaped and was captured. A bartender, Walter Beebe, was convicted for "aiding and assisting" Rowdy Joe's flight. Beebe appealed to the supreme court, contending that Lowe had not been in lawful custody at the time of his escape. Valentine, with Brewer concurring and Kingman dissenting, found in Beebe's favor.[72]

Usually those convicted of crimes found little solace from the Kansas Supreme Court. Brewer was particularly stern in criminal matters, and his sternness extended to criminals of all classes. An opinion by him turned down a banker's appeal for a reversal of his conviction for embezzlement: "[R]eading the story of the defendant's acts and conduct as told by himself, his dereliction of duty presents a crime which no smoothness of words or politeness of language can obliterate or conceal."[73] In a habeas corpus hearing at chambers, he denied the writ to an abortionist because the petition rested "upon a mere naked technicality." Yet in another hearing he did issue the writ to a poor soul convicted of maintaining a hog pen in Leaven-worth because the police court judge had denied him a jury trial.[74]

A petty larceny case came before Brewer and his colleagues on the grounds that the local newspaper had, according to the accused, influenced the verdict through biased reporting. Brewer, upon exam-ining the news stories in question, believed otherwise and concluded that they were "simply records of matters of public interest": "If they did create a prejudice, it is simply because the matters stated therein to have been done by the defendant are not popular with a community which believes in respecting the rights of property."[75]

American states throughout the nineteenth century expanded the number and scope of their criminal statutes, particularly for the purpose of giving greater protection to property.[76] Brewer was surely in sympathy with that trend. Few Americans in this period had deeper devotion to the sanctity of property than he. His commitment to property rights was to figure prominently throughout his career on the state and federal benches. Property, he was to insist, needed protection not only from the so-called dangerous classes but from the public, acting through the state. An early and clear indication of his concern in this regard would be his judicial response to Kansas prohibition.

4

THE SUBSTANCE OF RIGHT
Brewer and the Kansas Supreme Court on
Prohibition, Family Law, Women's Rights, Race
Questions, and the Legal Profession, 1871–1884

In 1880 THE VOTERS of Kansas amended their constitution to prohibit the manufacture and sale of intoxicating liquor. Almost immediately the antiprohibition forces challenged the validity of the amendment in four separate cases. Collectively known as the *Prohibitory
Amendment Cases*,[1] they reached the state supreme court in the following year. David Brewer was given the task of writing the unanimous
decision.

In his preliminary remarks he acknowledged the bitter division of
opinion among the people: to many, prohibition was "the crowning
effort of a brave and earnest people to free itself from the curse of
intoxication"; to others, it represented "a departure from the wisdom
and experience of the past, a radical change of policy, trespassing
upon personal liberty and rights of property." These considerations,
however, were matters of policy, which was not a judicial function;
"whatever may be the individual opinions of the justices of this court
as to the wisdom or folly of any law or constitutional amendment"
was, said Brewer, of no consequence.[2]

The major question before the court was whether the amendment
had been properly submitted to and adopted by the electorate. In
arriving at an affirmative answer to the question, Brewer declared
that the "central idea of Kansas law, as of Kansas history, is that
substance of right is grander and more potent than methods and
forms."[3] Therefore, he and his brethren chose to dismiss the technicalities cited by counsel for the opponents of the amendment—"mere

irregularities or informalities in the conduct of an election are impotent to thwart the express will" of the majority of the voters.[4] As for the contention that the amendment violated the guarantees of the Fourteenth Amendment, Brewer responded by citing rulings to the contrary by state and federal courts in similar cases.[5] The opinion also concluded that Kansas's tough Dram-shop Act of 1868 had not been repealed in toto by the adoption of the new amendment. Earlier, Brewer had written an opinion in which the court approved the rigid enforcement of the act.[6]

The *Prohibitory Amendment* decision was only the first step in the interpretation of Kansas prohibition. Later in 1881 the legislature passed a law designed to enforce the amendment. The result was simply more confusion; again the supreme court was called upon to settle matters. Once more Brewer received the vexatious duty of writing the court's opinion, this time for eight suits called the *Intoxicating Liquor Cases.*[7]

On all the contested points his opinion upheld the constitutionality of the statute. The decision held that restricting the right to sell certain legal alcoholic beverages (for example, for medicinal purposes) to druggists was not "class legislation." Nor was it unconstitutional to empower probate courts to issue liquor licenses to the druggists. The greatest difficulty was in defining "intoxicating liquors" since the law had been vague on that point. Brewer reasoned that whiskey, beer, gin, brandy, and other obviously intoxicating beverages came within the scope and meaning of the statute. So too did bitters, cordials, tonics, and other products that were compounds of alcohol. He exempted items containing alcohol if they were for medicinal, scientific, toilet, or culinary purposes, such as paregoric, bay rum, cologne, and essence of lemon.

Although the decision sustained the law's constitutionality, Brewer (carefully stating that he spoke only for himself) went on to express his view that the law, if strictly interpreted, came close to being unconstitutional. He believed that it was not within the legislature's power to outlaw articles not inherently dangerous to the public. "The habits, the occupation, the food, the drink, the life of the individual, are matters of his own choice and determination and can be abridged or changed by the majority speaking through the legislature only when the public safety, the public health, or the public protection requires it."[8] Here he was voicing a warning he was later to repeat frequently against infringements upon individual liberty through questionable exercises of the police power. Also, the statement might be interpreted as the grumbling of a judge who enjoyed a glass of beer now and then.

At the conclusion of the opinion, he emphasized that the court had interpreted only the more important details of the law, leaving minor questions to be settled in later cases.[9] A criminal action against a McPherson County physician coming to the court shortly thereafter concerned such further interpretation. Brewer's decision upheld the conviction of the physician for prescribing beer to a habitual drinker. To compound his crime, the healer had joined his "patient" in the taking of the "medicine," with which they had washed down oysters.[10]

Of greater consequence was *State* v. *Mugler*,[11] in which a Salina man had been charged with illegally manufacturing and selling beer. Valentine's opinion, with Horton concurring, sustained the conviction. In a separate opinion, Brewer concurred with the upholding of the conviction only insofar as it related to the selling of beer. Beyond that, however, he commented that "while I do not care to formally dissent, I must say that my judgment is not satisfied." He repeated his doubts about the legislature's "power to prescribe what a citizen shall eat or drink, or what medicines he shall take, or prevent him from growing or manufacturing that which his judgment approves for his own use as food, drink or medicine." His most serious objection to the prohibitory law was that it had, by denying the manufacturers of beer the use they had intended for their property, taken away property without due process of law, a violation of the Fourteenth Amendment. He concluded his brief opinion by asking: "Is not this taking of private property for public use, without compensation? If the public good requires the destruction of the value of this property, is not prior compensation indispensable?"[12] Using Brewer's reasoning, Mugler took his case to the United States Supreme Court and, as we shall see, lost there also.[13] But Brewer would reiterate his arguments a few years later as a circuit judge.

In one notable case in this period, Brewer's expansive views on compensation for the taking of private property prevailed. In an opinion written by him, the court enjoined the city of Emporia from taking water from a privately owned mill pond and putting it into an adjacent municipal well. The fact that the water was to be appropriated only in case of a fire did not impress Brewer; even though the water was to be taken for a public purpose, the city had to compensate the owner of the mill pond.[14]

Brewer's opinions did not always conform to his own beliefs; in many, perhaps most, of them, he was simply expounding what he thought the law to be. Also, in writing decisions for a three-man court, he and his colleagues had to shape their remarks to reflect the collective thinking of the court's membership, which left little room for wholly personal views. Yet there were some areas of the law in which Brewer felt freer to say what was in his heart. Most conspicuous in this regard were his opinions in matters of domestic relations. Here his devotion to the family and Christian values burst out of the shell of legalism.[15]

Among the bench and bar of Kansas, the best remembered of such decisions was *Chapsky* v. *Wood*.[16] Chapsky had married and fathered a girl. His wealthy father disapproved of the marriage and threw his son upon his own resources. Chapsky then led a wandering, penniless life. His wife became ill and, unable to care for the child, turned the little girl over to the custody of her sister Mrs. Wood. Some time later the unfortunate Mrs. Chapsky died, and Chapsky and his father petitioned the Kansas Supreme Court for a writ of habeas corpus to recover custody of the daughter. Mrs. Wood, who now looked upon the girl as her own beloved child, fought back.

In writing the decision, Brewer recognized the delicate legal and emotional content of the case. According to a strict interpretation of the law, the natural parents "are *prima facie* entitled to custody of their minor child." Yet a child, he insisted, was "not in any sense like a horse or other chattel." He then declared that the decision was to be governed almost solely upon the "future welfare" of the child. "I think no man can look upon the face of a bright and happy little girl, like the one before us, and come to a decision of a question which may make or mar her future life, without hesitation and feeling: certainly we are not so insensible as to be able to do it."[17]

Guided by this consideration, Brewer then explored the relative ability of the litigants as parents. On the one hand, Chapsky and his family could bestow the many advantages of wealth on the child. But in examining the personality of her father, Brewer found flaws. In Chapsky's "testimony and his manner and appearance on the stand," he detected "a coldness, a lack of energy, and a shiftlessness of disposition, which would not make his personal guardianship of the child the most likely to ripen and develop her character fully." The "warm-hearted child," he felt, "would shrink and wither under the care of such a nature."[18] More important, the girl looked upon Mrs. Wood as a mother. Sending her to the Chapsky home would be thrusting her among strangers; "and if we should see a child of ours in the same circumstances, we cannot believe that we should deem it wise or prudent to devise a change, notwithstanding the pecuniary advantages that might seem to be offered to it."[19] Accordingly, Brewer, with the other justices in agreement, ruled that the girl remain in the modest, love-filled home of the woman who had raised her.

Another child custody case, heard and decided by Brewer alone at chambers in Leavenworth, evoked an equally emotional response from him. *In re Bullen* concerned a young girl who had immigrated with her parents to the United States from England.[20] After living in Leavenworth, the family sailed back to England, where the father died. The mother, along with the daughter, returned to Leavenworth and led a life of abject poverty. "Words fail me," said Brewer, "to picture her forlorn and wretched condition." Concerned women of the community found her and placed the then desperately ill mother in a Roman Catholic hospital where the Sisters of Charity cared for her until her death shortly thereafter. Departing from "the coldness of judicial opinion," Brewer paid a feeling tribute to those who "make us thank God that we are brothers to such sisters."[21]

Before her death the mother asked that the girl be placed in a female academy operated by the nuns. Earlier, however, she had requested that the child be sent to her grandparents in England. Meanwhile the grandfather had passed away, leaving a will that granted a comfortable income to the granddaughter if she would live with her grandmother and agree never to marry a Catholic. The Sisters of Charity, confident that they were following the true wishes of the mother, had taken steps to adopt the child; the grandmother sought a writ of habeas corpus to gain custody. As in the *Chapsky* case, Brewer considered the well-being of the child; in doing so he asked, "Do I demean myself by saying I shrink from this responsibility?" The girl loved the kindly sisters, who returned the love. The grandmother had no legal obligation to care for the child and no legal right to her custody. Moreover, Brewer found the anti-Catholic content of the will offensive.[22]

He decided, however, in favor of the grandmother, primarily because an institution, no matter how good, was no replacement for a home, where the "varied graces of true womanly nature ripen more sweetly and more surely" than in an institution. Also, despite the bigoted provision of her grandfather's will, Brewer believed the bequest she would receive was not to be disregarded and "this little girl ought to have the opportunity to decide for herself, when she comes to maturity, whether she will accept or reject the property burdened with those conditions."[23] In closing the opinion, he expressed the fervent hope that the mother, "from the calm and peaceful heights of heaven . . . will look down approvingly upon the conclusion I have reached."[24] Facts and his own feelings only had guided him; he cited not one precedent to support his soul-searching decision.

In settling the child custody question in a bitter divorce proceeding, Brewer stated flatly that the parents did not "have property rights in the possession of their children." The welfare of the children, not the supposed rights of divorced parents, was "the paramount fact" for the court's consideration. His opinion concluded that the mother was entitled to custody because the "universal laws of our nature . . . compel us to place these children where they will be within the reach of a mother's love and care." The father was to have rights of visitation, and Brewer sternly required that he be "received without insult or injury."[25] In the three foregoing cases Brewer was not breaking new ground but rather furthering the "best-interest-of-the-child" doctrine that had originated in state courts earlier in the century.[26]

In the later nineteenth century, divorce became increasingly more common, more easily obtained, and less socially condemned.[27] Nevertheless, divorce suits appealed to the court troubled Brewer because of his personal and religious commitments to the sanctity of marriage. In one case he warned against the hasty granting of divorces: "Time will heal many estrangements, and bring together those whom temporary feeling has alienated. And courts, having ever in view the public good, may often wisely use their discretion to give time and opportunity for reconciliation."[28] On another occasion he pointed out a glaring deficiency in the state's divorce law, which allowed immediate remarriage after a district court had granted a divorce. Should one of the parties remarry and the other party, in the mean-time, win a reversal of the divorce decree from the supreme court, the status of the second marriage would be questionable. Brewer suggested that the law be changed so that either the ruling of the district courts would be final or that a second marriage be prohibited until an appeal to the supreme court had been heard.[29]

The women of Kansas found Brewer to be a champion of their struggle for equal rights. *Wright* v. *Noell*, a case involving the right of a woman to hold elective office, presented him with the opportunity to advance the cause.[30] The voters of Coffey County in 1874 had elected Mary P. Wright as superintendent of schools. Her male opponent contested the validity of her election on the grounds that women, since they did not have the right to vote, were barred from holding elective office. A district court ruled in his favor.

On appeal to the supreme court in 1876, Brewer's opinion for a unanimous court reversed the lower court. He agreed that a precedent existed that held that an unenfranchised person was not entitled to election to public office, but he maintained that the previous case concerned an alien. Moreover, he saw nothing in the state constitution that expressly forbade women from holding such offices. There-fore, Miss Wright—and any other females elevated to political office by the voters—was eligible to serve.

For the rest of his life he took pride in having written the decision. Many years later he stated that "[i]t may signify little, but in 1776 a new political life began on this continent, and a century after, in 1876, a change came over that political life, and woman, whose fitness for such a position is now conceded, was declared to be qualified and legally eligible to control public schools."[31]

A suit involving the property rights of women elicited from Brewer some thoughts on the progress of women: that the expansion of women's rights brought responsibilities and even hardships as well as benefits. "While we may regret such hardships, we may rejoice in the change, believing the new rule the better rule, and that society, readjusted upon the basis of absolute independence of all adult citi-zens in matters of property, will more successfully work out the greatest good for all."[32] Brewer furthered the rights of women more concretely through an 1881 ruling that held that a woman's property could not be seized for payment of her husband's debts.[33]

It has been said that the liberalization of statute and common law regarding the property rights of women in that period was designed to insure equity rather than equality for women.[34] But Brewer's remarks and conclusions in those cases, together with his utterances off the bench, indicate that he was working for true equality of the sexes, not only in the area of property rights but in other aspects of American life.

Womankind did not always fare well in Brewer's opinions. One of them sustained the granting of a divorce to an elderly man from a younger woman who had wheedled him into deeding all of his property to her, bullied and abused him, drove him out of the home, and then tried to have him committed to an insane asylum. "Is this the love and care which a wife owes her husband?" Brewer asked in tones of barely restrained rage over the wicked woman's callousness.[35]

He showed sympathy with the Indians of the West in a case relating to the rights of the Wyandottes to their property. In 1886 Congress had granted them money to rebuild a Methodist mission. Later the tribe was removed to Indian Territory, and white Methodists took over the building. The Wyandottes sued for the amount of the congressional grant. Brewer's decision upheld their claim, holding that the grant had been to the tribe and "in no sense a grant to the great Methodist church."[36] In a case regarding the tax-exempt status of Indian lands, Brewer expressed the view that Indian treaties were intended "to protect [the Indian] in the enjoyment of his property, to secure him in its undisturbed possession, notwithstanding his ignorance, and in spite of the rapacity of his more intelligent white neighbors."[37] The court, speaking through Brewer, held in *Brown* v. *Steele* that the Shawnee nation's law of descent and the rulings of its council, rather than the Kansas law of inheritance, would be followed.[38]

Whatever his sympathies for children, women, and Indians, a dissenting opinion of his with respect to blacks casts him in an unfavorable light historically. The case *Board of Education of the City of Ottawa* v. *Tinnon* reveals much about segregation in a nonsouthern state.[39] In the first years of statehood the Kansas legislature permitted all localities to establish separate schools for black children. A law of 1879 modified the practice by allowing (and not requiring) only cities of the first class to have separate schools for the two races.[40]

After the passage of the law, Ottawa, a city of the second class, attempted to draw the color line in its schools. A black youth, Leslie Tinnon, tried to enroll in a white class and was refused. His father then sued in the district court, which ruled in his favor. The school board appealed to the state's highest court, where Valentine, joined by Horton, affirmed the lower court's decision, holding that the law of 1879 restricted the power to segregate to cities of the first class only. Valentine offered his own views on the matter and made an eloquent appeal for tolerance and for allowing children of all races, sexes, and backgrounds to mingle freely and learn from each other.[41]

Brewer entered a long dissent. The thrust of his argument was not overtly racist. Rather, he emphasized the right of all school boards to "classify" pupils as they saw fit. If a school board "has the right to classify, whose judgment controls as to such classification, that of the board of education elected by the community or that of the courts? I think the former." He believed that his brethren on the court had deviated from the many precedents upholding local control of schools. Nor was school segregation, he believed, contrary to the spirit and wording of the Fourteenth Amendment.[42]

Local self-government, a cause dear to his heart, had, in the *Tinnon* case, led him to support racial discrimination. Yet a decision written by him that involved property rights, which he also cherished, put him on the side of toleration. A white man, Falloon, sought an injunction against one Schilling because, Falloon charged, Schilling had tried to buy his property and, upon being refused, erected a shanty next to Falloon's home and rented it to a family of "worthless" blacks in retaliation. Brewer's opinion held that the building was "neat, though small" and that the black family was by no means disreputable. He went on to say that "equity will not interfere simply because the occupants of such house are by race, color or habits, disagreeable or offensive. . . . The law makes no distinction on account of race or color, and recognizes no prejudice arising therefrom." Schilling, he concluded, had "used his property for his own benefit in a legitimate way."[43]

The members of the Kansas Supreme Court in this period showed no appreciable favoritism to either creditors or debtors. At least once, speaking through Brewer, they admittedly deviated from precedent and saved a debtor from losing his land. The case, said Brewer, "presented one of those harsh time contracts for the sale of land, in which a forfeiture is sought to be enforced for non-payment at the stipulated time." Although the courts for years had held such contracts to be valid, Brewer's opinion blocked forfeiture in the case at hand because enforcing the contract would have been "grossly inequitable."[44]

In 1877 Frank Doster, a budding Kansas radical, served as counsel for the holder of a note who was trying to attach the property of his debtor. The decision delivered by Brewer went against Doster's client and for the debtor.[45] In 1893, a few years before Doster's election as Populist chief justice of the state, he praised Brewer: "It is a pleasure to read some of his opinions. He was no legal parrot, but had a voice and a vocabulary of his own."[46]

On the Kansas Supreme Court and later on the federal bench, Brewer frequently injected his views on legal ethics, misuse of the courts, and the role of judges. More than once he announced his annoyance with the number of petty matters appealed to the supreme court. Frequently he displayed his impatience with attorneys who used niggling technicalities, a practice he found dishonest as well as a waste of the court's time. Equally exasperating were long-winded briefs that made it appear that the lawyers writing them were "actuated by the one desire of seeing how much paper and ink they could waste."[47]

Another evil was "the growing disposition on the part of some counsel to regard the trial courts as simply instrumentalities for the collection of evidence, and upon the evidence so collected to raise questions of law for the first time in [the supreme court]."[48] He chastised lawyers who tried to slip incomplete records of trial court proceedings into their appeals.[49] Attorneys who "seem to think it entirely immaterial how much unquestioned fiction they incorporate into their pleadings" received a severe scolding from Brewer.[50] On the other hand, he complimented attorneys who presented "direct and pointed" briefs.[51] Brewer constantly lectured to lawyers appearing before the court about their duties to society and their profession. He felt it necessary to remark in closing one of his opinions that "to attain the highest success in the profession of law good faith is of equal value with legal cunning, and that it is never to the credit of an able man that he has taken an unfair advantage of the lesser knowledge of another."[52]

When a lawyer accused an opponent of having compelled a witness to testify falsely, Brewer deplored the "irritation and suspicion on the part of counsel which is both unfortunate and unpleasant."[53] When an attorney stated that the supreme court had no authority to investigate his moral and professional conduct, Brewer "respectfully but firmly" disagreed; the court had a responsibility to the people of the state and to the bar to see to it that lawyers practicing before the court "conduct themselves as to justify the confidence of the community." All too often, he admonished, attorneys took advantage of their knowledge of the law to create injustice.[54] He urged lawyers who were unjustly accused of professional wrongdoing to answer the charges immediately for the sake of the profession, their own good name, and their families.[55]

He was never slow to speak out against those who brought the legal process into disrepute, such as drunken jurors and suspiciously "forgetful" witnesses.[56] When the constitutionality of the state's law against malicious prosecution was challenged, his opinion for the court not only upheld it but went on to blast those who "sought to prostitute the powers of the court to the injury of another."[57] Persons who knowingly and illegally served orders of attachment of property on Sunday for the purpose of causing delay and confusion were, Brewer wrote testily, "justly liable to be mulcted in exemplary damages."[58]

When a lawyer wrote a letter to a district judge condemning him in strong terms for a ruling, the judge had the lawyer arrested for contempt. Upon appealing the case to the supreme court, the lawyer found no succor in Brewer's decision. The justice described the letter as insulting and went on to remind the hapless attorney that any judge, even a justice of the peace, was "the representative of the law, as fully as the chief justice of the United States"; a lawyer, as an officer of the court, had an obligation to extend "courteous and respectful treatment" to them all.[59]

Despite his insistence upon upholding the dignity of the courts, he often emphasized that courts and judges were not beyond criticism.[60] On at least two occasions opinions written by him reversed decisions previously delivered by himself and his colleagues, and he thanked counsel for bringing to their attention the mistakes the erroneous rulings had been based upon.[61]

Brewer's years on the Kansas Supreme Court, demanding though they were, did not turn him into a drudge. His ties with his family, his sense of humor, and his involvement with the betterment of his community and state became even stronger. A few months after he took his place on the court, he commemorated his tenth wedding anniversary by writing a poem to his wife. The nine stanzas of tender sentiments concluded with:

> Ten years to night, good wife, ten years to night
>   Ten years we've lived & loved—
> Another ten years, good wife, commence to night
>   With love not pledged but proven—[62]

When daughter Etta left Leavenworth for a visit, her father wrote to tell her how much he missed playing checkers with her and to let her know that around the home chicks were hatching and the rose bush was blooming.[63]

After finishing his early morning judicial work, he would climb into his "democratic buggy" and drive to the farm he owned four miles from Leavenworth. After strolling about, he would return to town "refreshed and ready to grind away again for another stretch of hours." On one of his journeys, his horse wheeled too quickly and the buggy overturned, breaking Brewer's collar bone. At other times he found a safer form of relaxation—pruning the trees in his orchard.[64]

Brewer made off-the-bench efforts to improve the quality of Kansas jurisprudence, such as becoming a charter member of the state's bar association in 1883.[65] Earlier he published an article in a Leavenworth periodical, the *Western Homestead*, which called for the drafting of a new constitution for Kansas. The constitution adopted in 1859, was, he argued, no longer suited to the needs of the state because Kansas had grown out of its frontier phase into an entirely new social and economic condition.

His foremost concern in the proposal was for the improvement of the judiciary. He believed that the supreme court had to be enlarged by at least two more members so that speedier and more forceful justice could be assured. His other major suggestion was for granting the governor or chief justice the power to supervise the district court system so that the underworked judges of the smaller districts could be detailed to help out their busier brethren in the more populated districts.[66] Whatever the merits of his plan, it was never acted upon.

In another article for the same journal, he wrote of the ever-growing work load of the state's courts. He explained that the increase in the number of suits came in part from the simpler forms of procedure then being adopted and from the larger number of lawyers, who had become "as plenty and as busy as the fleas of California." The rise of commerce, industry, and urbanization also played a role: "Commercial centres [sic] *are* the centres. Wall Street rules more certainly than the White House. Commerce is King. And the lawyer is the prime minister."

The growth in the number of lawsuits, he believed, was not necessarily cause for pessimism; paradoxically it was "proof of the growing brotherhood of the race, and that man is ever coming nearer to man. . . . [P]overty and isolation of life furnish no litigation." Yet some limits had to be placed upon the increase of court business because all litigation disturbed society and was expensive. He proposed first that petty cases be settled, without the right of appeal, in the lower courts because the right of appeal benefited wealthy corporations rather than poor persons. Corporations "appeal to terrify claimants, prevent them from suing and compel them to accept the corporation's offer." As a second method of preventing litigation, Brewer urged the adoption of the European system of arbitration of disputes between citizens.[67]

His article on "Preferential Voting" brought attention to another European reform idea. He explained the system of preferential voting as outlined by British lawyer Thomas Hare and asked Kansans to consider its adoption. Such a system, he believed, would make constituencies "personal and not local"; there would be less need for political parties and this in turn would mean the end of corrupt bossism.[68]

Clearly Brewer was a voice for reform in the so-called Gilded Age. His most significant call for reform during that period came in 1883 when he addressed the graduates of Washburn College on the theme "The Scholar in Politics." He began by asserting that the teachings of Christ were the bases of modern republican institutions; Christianity made the individual the master and the state the servant.[69] Yet he warned that the displacement of monarchy by democracy did not automatically solve society's problems. The citizen of the American republic needed to face up to a number of difficult situations. First, there was the matter of assimilating the multitude of races and nationalities pouring into the country: "We are gathering all nations and tongues and reuniting them in the mystic clasp of the unity of the race, the brotherhood of man." Inevitably this would result in "one great, united, homogeneous nation . . . gathering in itself the fruitage of all civilization, the rarest and ripest of every work of man."[70]

The growth of America brought on another trend that, Brewer told his audience, had to be dealt with carefully: the danger to individual liberties that were inherent in the demands for regulation. He acknowledged that regulation was needed in some matters, for instance, the rise of an aristocracy based on inherited wealth, which was, he said, more dangerous than inherited monarchy and nobility. "The Astor and Vanderbilt estates are but types and forerunners of other vast and accumulated fortunes. . . . [T]he persistence of such fortunes is a danger to all free institutions, and a menace to popular governments."[71]

As remedies he proposed a stiff inheritance tax (which would lessen the need for the tariff and property taxes) and laws requiring that estates be divided equally among heirs. Property, he insisted, was sacred; yet something had to be done to promote a more equitable distribution of wealth. He suggested the creation of "laws and arbitrations which shall secure to the laborer a larger share of the joint earning of capital and labor."[72]

A related issue was the rise of corporate wealth and power. In common with most Americans of the time, he stood in awe of the accomplishments of the corporations but also feared their potential for evil. "They are the most useful servants and they may become the most dangerous foes of civilized society." He had no cures to propose; rather, he simply asked: "Who is the wise statesman who can so direct the legislation of the nation and so organize the forces of society that these mighty organizations shall be the helpful servants instead of the tyrannical masters of the future?"[73]

Concentrated economic power bothered him; so too did concentrated political power. In his view the reaction against the South's attempted secession had brought about an equally disturbing trend toward centralization of government. States' rights and local self-government had to be preserved, he maintained, because of the diverse nature of the United States. He voiced his fears over the creation of "an unwieldy and dangerous power" at Washington. Yet he recognized that certain interests, such as the national railroad and telegraph systems, were "binding the whole country into one nation, and the grandeur and power of that nation in the presence of the world, unite in demanding supreme central power in Washington."[74]

He cautioned his audience not to follow the "man on horseback" toward military despotism and the horrors of war; neither should they admire financial buccaneers like Jay Gould, whose career brought "demoralization and ruin."[75] Americans should instead pay more heed to the nation's scholars and not dismiss them as cranks and "them literary fellers." Brewer cited the example of a professor at the state university whose opposition to the high tariff had brought about demands for his dismissal. "Would you be astonished," he asked accusingly, "if . . . back of all this was heard the jingle of the manufacturer's dollar?"[76] In closing, Brewer urged the Washburn graduates to serve the public as "scholars in politics."

In 1880 he addressed the graduating students at the state normal school at Emporia. As he had done at the school's first commencement in 1865, he stressed the growing importance of woman as the "world's teacher." This time he could proudly allude to *Wright* v. *Noell* and suggest that women be entrusted with "a larger share in the general administration of school affairs." In the course of his remarks on the benefits of education, he christened Kansas as "the School State, the leader and glory of them all." Next he outlined a plan for state loans to students at the normal school, which they would not be required to repay if they taught for a specified number of years.[77]

In 1880 he spoke at Atchison's Forefather's Day, singing the praises of the "Yankee School Marm": "We glory in her because she has been one of the mightiest of the forces that have been shaping our national history."[78]

Brewer's work for the advancement of education was not limited to rhetoric. In November of 1875 he delivered a series of twelve lectures on "practical Law" at the Kansas State Agricultural College in Manhattan. The lectures, "embracing those principles and usages of Kansas law which every farmer, mechanic, and business man or woman need to understand," proved immensely popular with the students, who crowded into the classroom to hear them.[79] His success led to another series of lectures there in the following year. Upon completion of the last talk the applause "would have rattled all the plastering off the ceiling below, if there had been any plastering there."[80] In 1877 he again delivered the series, this time before the entire student body and interested townspeople.[81]

As always, Brewer's crowded schedule still permitted work for the civic betterment of Leavenworth. In 1871 he was still serving as secretary for the cemetery association; during 1874–1876 he was president of the Law Library Association.[82]

Brewer's nonjudicial activities did much to endear him to the people of Kansas. Yet it was his labors on the state's highest tribunal that brought him to the attention of lawyers, judges, and politicians throughout the Middle West. Advancement to a federal judgeship seemed almost inevitable for the hardworking, articulate, and relatively young jurist.

5

"AN EMPIRE IN ITSELF"
The Eighth Circuit, 1884–1889

A DECISION WRITTEN for the Kansas Supreme Court by Brewer in 1877 held in favor of the plaintiff in error, Preston B. Plumb. The litigation was over a land sale and in all respects a minor case. Yet Plumb was no minor figure; he had just been elected to his first term as a United States senator. Some said that the ruling caused Plumb to think of ways of rewarding the man who wrote it—such as obtaining for him a federal judgeship.[1]

When John F. Dillon resigned as judge of the Eighth Circuit in 1879, Governor John P. St. John, Valentine, Horton, and other state officials petitioned President Rutherford B. Hayes, recommending the appointment of Brewer.[2] George W. McCrory of Iowa, however, received the post. McCrory served only until 1884, and this time the Kansas men were not to be denied. Although A. L. Williams, a former attorney general of the state had strong support in some quarters, Plumb's vigorous appeals inclined President Chester A. Arthur toward Brewer. On March 25 he made the appointment.[3]

Brewer submitted his resignation from the state supreme court to Governor George W. Glick in April. After leaving Glick's chambers, he entered the supreme court office. "Well, boys," he called out to the clerks, "you can call me 'Dave,' now, for I have just resigned"—and they did![4]

On the following day, upon receiving his commission for the federal post, he wrote his effusive thanks to Arthur.[5] That day he also was sworn into the judgeship by federal district Judge Cassius G. Foster, and Brewer sent a cordial farewell message to his "Good and Valued Friends," Horton and Valentine, recalling their warm relations and expressing satisfaction in the court's keeping up with a full docket. Difficult though his circuit court responsibilities were to be and friendly though his feelings toward his former colleagues were, members of the Kansas bar thought that the burdens of the supreme court made Brewer "willingly get out of the treadmill."[6]

The Eighth Circuit at the time of Brewer's elevation to the judge-ship embraced Nebraska, Minnesota, Iowa, Missouri, Kansas, Colorado, and Arkansas. A few years later the new states of North and South Dakota and Wyoming were added. Brewer described the circuit as "an empire in itself" because of its vast and varied area.[7]

The federal circuit court system, established in 1789, was a curious, often confusing, affair. Originally it had no judges of its own; each justice of the United States Supreme Court was assigned to a circuit; the justice and the federal district judges within the circuit made up the membership of the court. Some help for the overworked justices came in 1869, when Congress provided for the appointment of a full-time judge for each circuit, yet the justices were not entirely relieved of the duty. The federal district courts were courts of original jurisdiction; so too, for the most part, were the federal circuit courts. Original jurisdiction in federal cases was divided (not always logically or consistently) between the district and circuit courts. The area of the circuit courts' appellate jurisdiction was small; few cases were to reach Brewer on appeal from the various district courts within his circuit. The creation of a system of Circuit Courts of Appeals in 1891 further confused the division of federal jurisdiction. Congress finally abolished the old circuit courts in 1911.

As a circuit judge, Brewer would handle a broad range of cases arising out of federal law: patents, trademarks, and copyrights; mineral, Indian, and railroad lands; extradition; foreign corporations; federal elections; state boundaries; and pensions. Mostly they were civil cases because criminal law was largely a state matter. Nevertheless, cases involving federal crimes—counterfeiting, mail theft, desertion from the armed forces, sending obscene material through the mails, obstruction of federal justice, mail fraud, and fraudulent use of the federal lands—were occasionally adjudicated by Brewer. Also, the federal court for the western district of Arkansas, presided over by Isaac C. Parker, embraced the lawless Indian Territory and was within the Eighth Circuit, giving it a larger number of criminal cases than other circuits. By the end of his judgeship in 1889, Brewer was so aware of the area's lawlessness that he privately chided a Kansas jurist who was seeking to become chief justice of the new Oklahoma Territory for wanting "to go out & wrestle with the Half Breeds & toughs."[8]

In addition, there were many "diversity" cases taken to the circuit courts, cases involving no federal question but in which the litigants were citizens of different states. (The Constitution extends the federal judicial power to cases in which there is diversity of citizenship.) For example, many of the cases heard by Brewer involving railroad corporations were diversity cases wherein, typically, a railroad chartered in a state would be sued by a citizen of another state.

Other than Foster and Parker, the district judges within the circuit included: O. P. Shiras, northern district of Iowa, James M. Lowe, southern district of Iowa; Rensellaer R. Nelson, Minnesota; Samuel Treat (succeeded by Amos M. Thayer in 1887), eastern district of Missouri; Arnold Krekel (succeeded by John F. Philips in 1888), western district of Missouri; Elmer S. Dundy, Nebraska; Henry C. Caldwell, eastern district of Arkansas; and Moses Hallett, Colorado. At times, when a judge was overworked or incapacitated, Brewer assigned a judge from one of the other districts to help out. Samuel F. Miller of the Supreme Court served as circuit justice, but only occasionally did he hear and decide cases personally.

Since it was largely a court of original jurisdiction, Brewer and colleagues in the circuit were often called upon to determine questions of fact as well as of law. In this sense the work was more similar to his state district court experience than to his duties on the Kansas Supreme Court. Nor did the fact that it was a federal court mean that Brewer escaped from having to decide petty cases.

The ambiguous nature of his court's jurisdiction presented Brewer with several opportunities to broaden its scope and power. But he usually resisted the temptation and remained true to his opposition to centralization. Federal courts, he wrote in an 1885 decision, "should not be covetous, but miserly, of jurisdiction"; if there were doubts concerning jurisdiction, federal courts should remand cases to the state courts.[9] He believed that state courts were in no sense inferior to federal ones: "The removal of a case from a state to a federal court means no appeal. It is simply a change of venue."[10] The Removal Act of 1875 had greatly facilitated the removal of cases, both diversity cases and those involving questions of federal law, from state to federal courts. Business interests were quick to use the act to seek relief from state regulation and unfriendly state courts.[11] Nevertheless, Brewer was capable of turning a deaf ear to pleas—including those from railroad corporations—for the removal of cases from state to federal courts on the grounds of "local prejudice."[12] Only those suits presenting a genuine federal question or involving true diversity of citizenship could be so removed.[13] He repeatedly ruled that whatever his personal belief in a matter the decisions of the highest state courts had to stand in doubtful cases. When he found himself compelled to overturn a decision by Colorado's supreme court, he expressed profound regret.[14]

Not surprisingly, railroad cases tended to dominate the docket. Here again Brewer often found against these corporations—and just as often for them. Some of the states composing his circuit had been among the first to enact so-called Granger laws, that is, legislation creating state railroad commissions whose chief responsibility was to regulate these enterprises, especially their rates, in the public interest. The Supreme Court, in *Munn* v. *Illinois*, written by Chief Justice Morrison R. Waite in 1876, had upheld the general principle of state regulation.[15] Yet federal and state courts at all levels had the task of defining the limits of a state's power over railroads and other businesses that were, in Waite's words, "clothed with a public interest."

In an 1886 decision, Brewer emphatically announced that "railroads are performing a *quasi* public service" and that contracts and legislation must be construed to "make these public servants most fully subserve the interests and welfare of the general public."[16] But the states' regulatory powers were not unlimited. In *Chicago & N. W. Ry. Co.* v. *Dey*, the railroad alleged that the rates set by Iowa's commission would make operations in the state unprofitable. Brewer issued a preliminary injunction against the rate schedule, to be in effect until the facts were more completely known.[17]

He was less tentative in a similar case coming from Minnesota because it cost the railroad "one dollar and fourteen cents per car to do the work, and the defendants [the state railroad and warehouse commissioners] propose to allow it to charge only one dollar."[18] In both cases he stated that the railroads were entitled to reasonable remuneration for their services. Nor in his view did the two suits violate the Eleventh Amendment, which prohibits suits against a state by citizens of another state, because the railroads, both foreign corporations, sued the commissioners, not the state. In the Minnesota case he reserved judgment on the railroad's argument that the commission was encroaching upon the federal government's power to regulate interstate commerce.

Just after the Iowa decision, the commissioners there issued a new rate schedule that did not substantially differ from the one Brewer had temporarily enjoined. Yet Brewer allowed the "new" rates to stand pending further developments. He also recognized that state commissions had broad authority to set rates and were obliged by law to act upon complaints filed by shippers. Furthermore, he praised the Iowa commission for its fearless impartiality.[19] To say, as did one authority on the judicial history of this period, that Brewer's *Dey* rulings constituted a "refusal to follow the *Munn* case" is at the very least misleading.[20]

In a later Iowa case, he sided completely with the state. The Chicago, Burlington and Quincy had been found guilty of extortion and was accordingly fined by a state court. Brewer turned down the railroad's attempt to remove the case to his court, concluding that a federal court had no jurisdiction in a matter concerning Iowa criminal law.[21]

Brewer's remarks in *Burlington, Cedar Rapids & Northern Ry. Co.* v. *Northwestern Fuel Co.* are fairly representative of his feelings about monopolies. The fuel company had arranged to pay the railroad $1.60 per ton for shipping coal; smaller shippers of coal had to pay $2.40. Such contracts, Brewer wrote bluntly, tended to result in monopoly. And once established, the coal monopoly "could dictate prices to the consumer, and could dictate starvation wages to the producers in the coal fields . . . and dictate transportation rates to the railroad companies" and "become master of the business." Such agreements, he warned, had brought about, "to the detriment of all," Standard's monopoly of the oil industry. Not only did he blast the fuel company, but he also took the railroad to task for being a party to the scheme.[22]

Railroad rates and monopolistic railroad practices appear historically as conspicuous objects of public concern in this period. Yet there were several other sore points relating to railroads that the courts were called upon to consider. Congress had granted generous amounts of public lands to railroad companies to subsidize the building of a rail network in the West. In time the American people, especially westerners, came to resent these vast holdings and called upon the federal government to reclaim the unsold portions of the grants. Brewer turned down the government's attempts to (1) recover some of the Union Pacific's lands in Colorado, (2) set aside part of the Missouri, Kansas and Texas ("Katy") grant, and (3) deny the Northern Pacific an "indemnity belt." But he did agree with the government that the right it had given to the Denver and Rio Grande to cut timber on public land had been intended only for aiding the road's initial construction, not for the later building of depots and other structures.[23]

Stray cattle had caused a Union Pacific train in Colorado to jump the track, killing the engineer. His heirs were not entitled to recover from the company, Brewer decided, because neither the state's statutes nor common law required the railroad to erect fences along the right-of-way. In answer to the plaintiff's assertion that the courts must step in and "blaze the way," he replied that it was the legislature, not the courts, that should do so. "The duty of the court is simply to walk *super antiquas vias*. Many a case I decide one way when [as in this one] I should decide differently if I had authority to make as well as construe the law."[24]

Nor was a twelve-year-old boy who had burned his foot while running across a pile of smoldering slack able to recover from the Union Pacific. He was, Brewer believed, old enough to know better. A Minnesota man injured while crossing a track lost his case because his actions fell short of compliance with the Supreme Court's "stop, look, and listen" rule.[25]

Questions of contributory negligence and assumption of risk were especially troublesome in cases arising out of injuries to railroad employees. In one case Brewer ruled that a worker was to recover damages because he had not sufficient time to decide if he was working under dangerous conditions; in another he applied both the doctrine of assumed risk as well as the doctrine of contributory negligence and found for the company because the employee not only knew that conditions were hazardous but had also done little to ensure his own safety.[26]

Further complicating matters was the "fellow-servant rule," a doctrine laid down by the courts in the early days of American industrialization, which held that the employer was absolved of liability if a coworker had caused the injury. In later years the courts ruled that an employee was entitled to recover if his injury had resulted from the actions of a "vice-principal" of the company, for example, a foreman. Although his uncle Stephen J. Field had played a major role in developing the new doctrine,[27] Brewer expressed reservations concerning it in two cases, in which he decided that an engineer and a master mechanic, whose negligence had caused the deaths of the employees, were not true vice-principals. One of the decisions contained his prediction that the courts and lawmakers would soon overthrow the fellow-servant rule.[28] In a later case, perhaps grudgingly, he acknowledged that a foreman's negligence made a railway company liable for an injury to a member of his crew.[29]

Many of these railroad injury cases came to his court not because federal laws were at issue, but because of diversity of citizenship. Brewer interpreted corporate "citizenship" broadly. A man allegedly injured in Kansas by the Santa Fe railroad, a Kansas corporation, got his case into Brewer's court by having the process served upon a Santa Fe agent in Missouri. The railroad protested that since it operated no lines in Missouri the service was not valid. Brewer disagreed, ruling that lines or no, the company conducted business in Missouri and that the case therefore belonged in his court.[30]

The troublesome matter of bonds issued by local governments to subsidize the building of railroads followed him to his new jurisdiction. In 1887, no doubt unhappily, he held that Kansas law authorized a city of the third class to issue such bonds. More in keeping with his old bias, two years later he declared a contract between a railroad and a Nebraska county to be "void in toto" because the contract pledged bond aid in excess of the state's constitutional limit for indebtedness.[31]

Courts had long recognized that American state and local governments had the police power, that is, the power to restrict private rights in order to promote and maintain the public's well-being. Brewer believed that it was the "*bete noir* of courts" because of the difficulty in defining the police power's nature and extent. He deplored the tendency of courts to interpret it generously and insisted that it had limits. Nevertheless, he held that a Missouri law requiring railroads to erect depots and waiting rooms to be a constitutional— albeit questionable—exercise of the police power.[32]

Jurists in the second half of the nineteenth century were busily modifying the old doctrine of vested rights, that is, "[r]ights that have so completely settled in an individual that they are not subject to defeat by an act of another person, and which government is bound to protect."[33] In particular, companies operating older forms of transportation invoked the doctrine in efforts to continue doing business in the face of competition with the newer means of transportation. As a circuit judge, Brewer contributed to the process of diluting the doctrine of vested rights. Companies operating horse railways in Kansas City and Omaha argued that their monopoly rights were being infringed by the building of rapid transit systems in those cities. Brewer turned them down, ruling that their franchises could not prevent the public from receiving the benefits of "the superior speed and comfort of the cable road"; nor were the old companies entitled to compensation from the new ones ("a burden too monstrous to be thought of").[34]

The Supreme Court's decision in *Wabash, St. Louis, and Pacific Ry. Co.* v. *Illinois* (1886) limited the power of a state to regulate the rates of railroads doing an interstate business. The Pullman Palace Car Company seized upon this and contended that Iowa could not tax its property there because of the interstate character of the company's operations. Brewer's decision emphatically rejected the argument. Even though he conceded that taxation might affect the Pullman company's interstate business, he ruled that taxation was not necessarily regulation: "[P]ersonal property, continuously used in a state, acquires a *situs* in that state for purposes of taxation." Furthermore, since the state protected the company's property, it was within the state's authority to tax what it protected. He stated also that his decision was not inconsistent with the *Wabash* ruling.[35]

The state of Missouri, upon the instigation of the Baltimore and Ohio Telegraph Company, sought from Brewer's court a writ of mandamus to compel the Bell Telephone Company to provide service to the telegraph company in St. Louis. The Bell company replied that it was operating under a license from the American Bell Telephone Company, a Massachusetts corporation that was obliged by contract to provide service to Western Union and no other telegraph company. Brewer issued the writ. In doing so, he expressed his usual belief in the sacredness of property but cited the *Munn* decision, which authorized a state to regulate property devoted to a public use. A telephone system, like a railroad, was property put into "the channels of commerce" and was "in a limited sense, and yet in a strict sense, a common carrier. It must be equal in its dealing with all." Sitting with him on the case was Judge Treat of the federal district court for eastern Missouri, who disagreed. Treat wrote that the proper remedy was to bring suit against the parent corporation in Massachusetts. Brewer respectfully replied that the final settlement of the matter would come from the Supreme Court.[36] The high court soon thereafter dismissed the appeal without issuing an opinion.[37]

Thus far Brewer can hardly be seen as a tool of corporate power. Yet he was publicly accused of being such because of his handling of the receivership of the Wabash railroad system. Heavy indebtedness, a shaky—perhaps corrupt—corporate structure, and mismanagement led to insolvency. The Wabash, not its creditors, applied to the circuit court to be placed in receivership. At the company's request, Brewer appointed Solon Humphreys and Thomas E. Tutt as receivers. This was later criticized because the two were officers and directors of the Wabash, not disinterested outside parties. Their actions as receivers included payments to favored creditors, most notably the notorious Jay Gould, while the indebtedness to the prior mortgage bondholders remained unpaid. The latter, the Central Trust Company, brought suit in the Seventh Circuit Court in Chicago. There Judge Walter Q. Gresham dismissed Humphreys and Tutt as receivers east of the Mississippi, where the Wabash did most of its business.[38]

In a later decision arising out of the receivership, Brewer defended the appointment of Humphreys and Tutt, asserting that they were experienced railroad men who were putting the Wabash system on a sound basis. He also criticized Gresham's action for its disregard of the comity usually practiced among circuit courts. But he concluded that he did not wish to review Gresham's ruling because their courts were of equal rank. Judge Treat appended an opinion that, with a hint of sarcasm, defended the Eighth Circuit Court's course in the matter.[39]

Letters from attorneys involved in the affair attempted to absolve Brewer of wrongdoing and bad judgment. One of the attorneys, Wager Swayne, stated that it was Treat, rather than Brewer, who had been "virtually responsible" for the disputed appointments. Privately, Gresham regretted that others had interpreted his decision as a reflection upon Brewer, for such had not been his intent.[40] Nevertheless, the reform and legal press were critical of the Eighth Circuit Court's actions, and the public blame fell on Brewer, not Treat.[41]

According to a biography of Gresham written by his widow, Brewer, while on the United States Supreme Court, issued a rebuke to Gresham in an opinion in another receivership case. Others believed that the rebuke, if such it was, was intended instead for Brewer's successor on the Eighth Circuit bench, Judge Caldwell.[42]

Far more damaging to Brewer's historical reputation was an accusation made concerning yet another receivership case. William Allen White made the allegation in his *Autobiography*, published in 1946. The Emporia editor claimed that in 1910 he had seen a letter from Brewer, written while he was on the United States Supreme Court, in which he complained that the two men whom he, as circuit judge, had appointed as receivers of the Katy railroad had not been making the agreed-upon monthly payments to Brewer's sister.[43]

Serious Kansas historians have long known that much of White's autobiography must be taken with a grain of salt despite its status as a classic. He and others of his generation sought to convince themselves and posterity that before their time American political life was rampantly corrupt and that they and they alone rescued the nation with the reforms of the so-called Progressive Era. This caveat does not of course mean that there can be no substance to White's accusation. But so far as is known, it is the only one that charges Brewer with corruption. There is nothing else to suggest that he enriched himself or others by illegal or shady means.

In 1888 Brewer did indeed place the Katy into receivership. He announced his reluctance to do so ("I should be glad to be free from the annoyance of a receivership") and went on to say the following regarding the appointment of a receiver: "If parties agree upon a receiver, of course I shall appoint whoever you agree upon. If not, I will hear any suggestions from any of the parties of interest, and reasons for or against any person to be named by one side or the other."[44] This is hardly the language of one who expected to profit himself or someone else with the appointment. Yet one of those appointed was wholesale grocer Ephram Gregory, who, according to a later account, was an old friend of Brewer's and had been the manager of Brewer's campaign for judge of the Leavenworth County Probate and Criminal Courts.[45] In the following year, in one of his last cases as circuit judge, he expressed satisfaction with the progress made by the Katy under receivership.[46] Strong evidence either to substantiate or dismiss White's allegation is lacking. Until such evidence appears, Brewer's reputation, perhaps unjustly, will remain damaged.

Speaking many years later, Brewer remarked that throughout his then thirty-six years as a jurist "no one, directly or indirectly, by word of mouth or letter, or in any other way, ever proposed, suggested, or intimated that any decision I might be called on to make would be for my benefit pecuniarily, politically, socially, or otherwise." To have been corrupted, he continued, it would have been necessary for him to have sought someone to tempt him.[47]

Railroad receiverships were a continuing concern for the Eighth Circuit for the rest of the century. Judge Caldwell, of the eastern district of Arkansas and Brewer's successor as circuit judge, developed an approach to them that Brewer did not approve. Caldwell would allow railroads to go into receivership only if they agreed to pay off unsecured debts for labor and materials before beginning to pay the debts secured by bonds. Later, while on the Supreme Court, Brewer criticized this practice as destructive of "the sacredness of contract obligations."[48]

Railroad receiverships gave Brewer his first judicial experience in dealing with labor questions. A number of the nation's railroads went into receivership in the 1880s by orders of the circuit courts, thereby bringing those tribunals directly into disputes between labor and management because management was in the hands of court-appointed receivers. Three such cases came before Brewer's court. All resulted in punishment of striking workers.

Strikers on the Wabash, St. Louis and Pacific Railway were accused of spiking and blocking the tracks and of threats of violence against the company's agents and nonstriking employees. Consequently, they were charged with contempt of court. Their attorney asked Brewer at the trial if he believed that the act of striking was itself illegal. Brewer replied that the right to quit work was unquestioned but interference with the operation of a railway under federal receivership and with the right of other employees to continue working constituted contempt.[49]

Before sentencing the leaders of the strike, he cited a recent, similar case in which a federal judge had sentenced the offenders to six months. Brewer felt that the offenses of the Wabash strikers, although intolerable, were of a lesser sort. He handed out sentences of sixty days and costs. His colleague Treat remarked that he had no choice but to go along with Brewer's "lenient punishment" but that left to his own devices he would have meted out stiffer sentences.[50]

Colorado was the scene of a bitter struggle between the Denver and Rio Grande line and the Knights of Labor. A case arising from this strike elicited a similar decision from Brewer. Again he acknowledged the somewhat meaningless "right" of union members to cease working and went on to reiterate his stand on the rights of employers to operate their businesses and of nonstriking workers to be free from violence and intimidation. His careful review of the testimony revealed that those on trial sought only to stop a train, not destroy property. Nevertheless, in attempting to prevent the operations of the company's trains, the four leaders of the strike were guilty of contempt because the company was in receivership.[51]

Once more he handed out what he believed to be light sentences: one was discharged "on giving his personal recognizance to keep the peace and not interfere with the management of the road by the receiver"; another, although as guilty as the others but not a "ringleader," received ten days in jail; a third man ("more of a leader" than the first two but whose words were worse than his conduct) was given a thirty-day sentence. The chief offender perhaps deserved six months, said Brewer, but he gave him only four because apparently he had not attempted to destroy property. He closed these lengthy proceedings by commending the strikers for not intending the destruction of property and with a warning that future interference with property in receivership would result in stronger punishment, such as other federal judges were ordering in similar cases. "I want to say most kindly, but most emphatically, so that nobody may misunderstand, that any parties who are engaged in [interfering with property in receivership] and who are brought before me for contempt, must expect the severest penalty which the law permits."[52]

In the foregoing ruling he also admonished dissatisfied workers to petition the court regarding grievances rather than to hinder the operations of the railroad.[53] Yet when employees of the Denver and Rio Grande submitted such a petition to him, he saw no merit in their complaints. They contended that the receivers had unjustly cut wages, required extra work without pay, dismissed some workers unnecessarily, and caused them to suffer at the hands of a "blasphemous and tyrannical" foreman.[54]

In "Dutch uncle" tones, Brewer informed the petitioners that many of their complaints were "very trivial." He emphasized the poor financial position of the company, the inherent need for efficiency in railroading, and the lack of unfairness in the company's decisions affecting individual workers. He found the foreman to be "capable and efficient and not . . . unjust" who, according to the evidence, "did not swear half as much as perhaps nine-tenths of the people right here in this court-room." He urged the road's receiver not to fire the "good" workers who presented the grievances but warned against keeping the "vicious" ones who had shown an ugly attitude toward the company. In closing, Brewer said that the Denver and Rio Grande strike and the handling of the workers' complaints had been "an embarrassing, difficult question," which he believed he had settled as fairly and objectively as possible. As for the punishment given to the strikers, "I did it reluctantly; I did it firmly."[55]

No doubt Brewer was sincere in believing that he had dispensed impartial justice. Yet obviously the workers received nothing except punishment for some of their number. Were Brewer's decisions in these cases examples of stereotypical favoritism toward capital and hostility toward labor by the federal courts in this period? Perhaps not. True, he showed his usual concern for the rights of property, but he was equally, if not more, concerned with upholding the dignity of the federal judiciary. He saw obstruction of the railroad's operations as a challenge to the court's authority. Moreover, it is plain that he took no delight in punishing the strikers and that he was more lenient toward them than some other federal judges.

In other disputes between the common man—particularly the property-owning common man—and the railroads, he often found against the latter. He ruled in favor of a settler in a land dispute with a railroad: "Nothing could be plainer than that both congress and the [Minnesota] state legislature intended to give to actual *bona fide* settlers priority to the railroad company. Such intent breathes in every statute and permeates every section."[56]

Other land cases revolved around far more momentous issues. None of the suits before his court offered more complexity and controversy than the three concerning the Maxwell land grant. Congress, in 1860, had affirmed the original Mexican grant of 1841. At first the lands were believed to cover ninety-seven thousand acres in New Mexico. Conflicting claims by the Maxwell Land Grant Company, antigrant squatters, cattlemen, mining interests, and the federal government brought the lands into frequent and bitter litigation. The land company's investors touched off still more disputes by contracting for a hasty and suspect resurvey of the grant, upon which they now claimed two million acres. In 1871 the secretary of the Interior refused to recognize anything beyond the acreage originally claimed. Later the United States land commissioner stated that the size and validity of the grant could be determined by the federal courts. Meanwhile, the Supreme Court, in *Tameling* v. *United States Freehold & Emigration Co.* (1876), upheld a similar land grant in Colorado.

In 1884 the first of the Maxwell cases came before Brewer. At issue was the extent of the grant in Colorado, but the federal government and the land company had agreed that the decision would also determine the status of the much larger New Mexico portion of the claim. Brewer decided in favor of the company by following the *Tameling* precedent, which had held that Congress's affirmation of an original grant was the same as a grant *de novo*. The second main question was the allegation of fraud in the resurvey that had enlarged the grant's boundaries. Brewer held that in the absence of convincing evidence of fraud the disputed survey was valid.[57]

The federal government brought a new suit in 1886, arguing that *Tameling* was not a similar case and therefore not a proper precedent. Brewer, at some length, reiterated his earlier stand and once again upheld the land grant company's claims. He also repeated his views that the government had not proved the charge of a fraudulent survey. A year later the Supreme Court upheld that decision.[58]

Brewer delivered his third and final circuit court decision on the Maxwell grant in 1889. Here he denied the validity of the so-called Beales grant, a sixty-million-acre *empresario* grant made by the Mexican governor of Coahuila and Texas in 1832. The grant remained unasserted until this late date, when it was claimed that the Beales grant embraced the Maxwell domains. Brewer rejected the argument on the grounds that the requirements of the original *empresario* grant, that is, colonization, had not been fulfilled.[59] Thus, in all three instances he ruled in favor of the Maxwell forces, whose claims and practices have been viewed as dubious, even corrupt.

Perhaps as vexing as suits over land titles were those involving patents. Brewer frankly confessed that he lacked any aptitude for mechanical matters and avoided patent cases whenever possible. Yet often they were unavoidable, and he decided a number of them. Despite his aversion to technical questions, he found a telephone patent case "a matter of intellectual interest" from a legal, as opposed to a technical, standpoint. The Southern Telephone Company had built a system assuming that the Supreme Court would later hold for it and not the Bell Company in a patent case. The Court, however, ruled in favor of Bell, and Brewer decided here that Southern Telephone was clearly violating Bell's patent.[60]

To settle a dispute between the Westinghouse Corporation and a rival manufacturer of an air-brake coupler, Brewer and the two Iowa federal district judges tested the device "in our own rooms" and concluded that it infringed upon Westinghouse's patent.[61] In another case ("one of the hardest I have ever had to try") Brewer held that the famous Glidden barbed wire was patentable because it was a new invention, not the product of "mere mechanical skill."[62] Less important and complex was a suit between two firms, each claiming to have designed a new washboard. "In view of the many devices which have been manufactured and patented for washboards," Brewer remarked, "it is obvious that neither party can be regarded as a pioneer in this field of invention."[63]

In spite of his reluctance to wrestle with patent questions, he denied a request for a jury trial in one such case, giving his view that the opinion of a single judge, even one as mechanically uninclined as himself, was preferable to the judgment of several men.[64] Similarly, in a mining accident case, he voiced his disapproval of judges who too readily turned matters over to juries, thereby shirking their own responsibility and inviting criticism of the jury system.[65]

While on the Kansas Supreme Court, Brewer had upheld the validity of the state's prohibitory amendment and the legislation to enforce it but, in a separate opinion in the Mugler case, had expressed the thought that manufacturers of beer were entitled to compensation for the loss of the value of their property hitherto devoted to brewing. As a federal judge, he had an opportunity, in *Kansas* v. *Walruff*, to assert the same view more emphatically. Brewer noted that Walruff's property, for brewing purposes, was worth fifty thousand dollars; without the right to make beer it was worth only five thousand dollars. Since "property" included not just the title but also the right to use, the state of Kansas had in effect, said Brewer, taken property worth forty-five thousand dollars from Walruff without compensating him for the loss. Therefore, he held the Kansas prohibitory amendment and its enforcement laws to be void insofar as they conflicted with the Fourteenth Amendment, which prohibits a state from depriving a person of property without due process of law.[66] Shortly before the *Walruff* decision, Brewer rejected another challenge to Kansas prohibition, even though the issue seems at first glance to be similar to that in *Walruff*. Atchison County authorities enjoined one Bradley from operating a saloon; Bradley claimed that this violated his rights under the Fourth, Fifth, Sixth, and Seventh Amendments as well as the Fourteenth. Brewer's decision stated that the state had the undoubted right to adopt and enforce prohibition; that the Fourth, Fifth, Sixth, and Seventh Amendments limited the federal government, not the states; and that Bradley had suffered no abridgment of Fourteenth Amendment rights because the "property" that had been "taken" from him was a clearly illegal business. Walruff's business, on the other hand, had been legal until "taken" from him.[67]

The *Walruff* ruling caused a great stir in Kansas, in prohibition circles nationally, and the legal profession.[68] Yet the Supreme Court, in an 1887 decision, upheld the Kansas Supreme Court's majority view in *Mugler*, thereby nullifying Brewer's *Walruff* decision.[69] His uncle Stephen J. Field dissented, contending that Kansas prohibition encroached upon the federal commerce power and also that it took property without due process. This prompted a wag to affirm that "Blood is thicker than water, even beer."[70] Justice Harlan's majority opinion held that state prohibition was a legitimate exercise of the police power and not in conflict with the Fourteenth Amendment.

Brewer successfully asserted a citizen's right to compensation in another case, holding that the damaging of property caused by street grading was tantamount to taking property without compensation. This ruling, however, rested on his interpretation of the Missouri constitution's bill of rights, not the Fourteenth Amendment.[71]

The commerce clause of the United States Constitution was at issue in a habeas corpus proceeding arising from a violation of Topeka's meat inspection ordinance. The ordinance limited the slaughtering of animals to an area within one mile of the city limits. After pointing out that the ordinance was obviously designed to protect local butchering interests from outside competition, Brewer decided that it hindered the interstate shipment of dressed beef. On those grounds he found the ordinance in conflict with the federal government's constitutional power to regulate interstate commerce and therefore void.[72] Other federal judges in this period were handing down similar decisions, thereby promoting national meatpacking interests at the expense of local butchers.[73]

Brewer admitted in *Walruff* and elsewhere that "due process" was difficult to define.[74] The extent of the concept was an element in what was one of the most sensational events of his circuit judgeship.[75] The newly elected reform city council of Lincoln, Nebraska, initiated an investigation of a police judge whom the councilmen believed to be corrupt. Claiming that the investigation was in essence a trial that was depriving him of liberty without due process, the judge sought and received from Brewer a preliminary injunction against the council. Believing that Brewer had issued the injunction without adequate knowledge of the facts and further believing that the circuit court's jurisdiction did not include the power to enjoin it, the council voted to defy the injunction. The councilmen were then taken before Brewer and Judge Dundy at Omaha on contempt charges.

Confidently expecting to be released, they were shocked when Brewer, before a packed courtroom, imposed heavy fines. "If the court should say that men occupying so high a position can disregard the process of the courts," said Brewer, "what may we expect from men having no such backing or position, respectability, and influence?" He compared their defiance of the law to the recent Haymarket Riot in Chicago.[76]

Lacking the money to pay their fines, the councilmen were taken to the Omaha jail. There they received many gifts and calls from sympathizers, including a visit from the governor of Nebraska, who thundered against "judicial tyranny." The councilmen were paroled pending an appeal to the Supreme Court. Meanwhile, steps were taken to request a pardon from President Cleveland should the appeal be unsuccessful.

Fortunately for them, the Supreme Court reversed Brewer. The majority opinion, written by Justice Horace Gray, held that the circuit court's equity jurisdiction did not extend to such matters. Field wrote a concurring opinion; Chief Justice Waite and Justice Harlan dissented.[77]

The case *In re Sawyer*, although ultimately a rebuke to Brewer, is yet another example of his insistence that the nation's judiciary was not to be trifled with. Another case gave him an opportunity to defend the powers of the marshals attached to the federal courts. In St. Louis the marshal appointed a number of special deputy marshals. Brewer upheld the legality of the appointments, even though he acknowledged that they were perhaps neither necessary nor wise.[78]

Brewer supported even the lowest of courts. When a justice of the peace in Minnesota was sued for false and malicious imprisonment, Brewer's opinion admitted that the justice had probably acted erroneously, even maliciously. Nevertheless, Brewer found in his favor, basing his decision on the principle of the independence of the judiciary—at all levels. Justices of the peace, as well as judges of superior courts, he wrote, had to be protected from suits for private damages.[79] In another case he pooh-poohed the charge that a judge had been biased because he was seen talking with a lawyer: "[I]t is the right of a judge, nay more, I think it is his duty, to maintain pleasant personal, social relations with members of the bar practicing before him."[80]

Protecting the judiciary also called for the policing of the actions of lawyers. Members of the bar accused of unethical behavior could usually count on punishment, a tongue-lashing, or both from Brewer. He ruled for the disbarment of attorneys accused of disloyalty to a client, perjury, misconduct, and contempt of court. In one decision Brewer underscored the importance of honest dealing with judges by lawyers, particularly judges of courts such as his that covered several states and handled so many diverse questions: "I should never feel safe, or act promptly, or enjoy my work, unless I felt that I could implicitly depend upon every statement that counsel made to me." He was happy to add that after twenty-one years on the bench, he could recall only one instance "in which I ever knew a counsel deliberately to impose upon me."[81]

Lawyers owed high professional standards not only to clients and judges but also to themselves. A lawyer tardily suing for the collection of fees drew only sarcasm from Brewer: "While, of course, as we in the profession all agree, lawyers are benefactors to the race, and entitled to special consideration at the hands of any intelligent tribunal, yet I think that the lawyer who waits a year and a half before collecting his fees is guilty of great negligence. He certainly presents no equitable claims for preference."[82] He was contemptuous also of a lawyer who presented a complaint with "too many words in it."

To demonstrate the point to this prolix attorney, Brewer polished off the decision in half a page.[83]

His judicial duties were burdensome, and Brewer probably shared the belief that his six-thousand-dollar salary and those of other federal judges were inadequate.[84] He thrived on hard work, but he also valued social and family life. Court work and the extensive travel necessary in the Eighth Circuit cut severely into both.

During his first year on the federal bench, the bar of Shawnee County held a banquet in his honor at Topeka. There he spoke feelingly on the need for more judges for both the Kansas and federal courts in order to handle the increasingly heavy case loads. He also urged that Congress pass legislation to curtail the number of cases removed from state to federal courts.[85]

Speaking at such gatherings was a pleasure that the busy circuit judge often had to forgo. He devoted one of his few public addresses in this period, delivered before the state bar association of Kansas, to the disturbing increase of libel by newspapers.[86]

The pleasures of the family circle were too seldom his in these years. When he was able to return to Leavenworth, he enjoyed euchre sessions with Lulu at their residence, which was then on the corner of Fifth Avenue and Middle Street and later at 324 Delaware Street. He maintained an office at Leavenworth's federal building, located on the corner of Fourth and Shawnee.[87]

Overwork had weakened him, and Brewer took a long trip west in 1889 to restore his health. He traveled to Colorado, Yellowstone National Park, Idaho, Oregon, and California.[88] It was perhaps this trip that provided the setting for a Brewer anecdote. According to the story, he was accompanied on the train by a number of distinguished persons, among them the witty and acerbic Kansas editor and novelist, Edgar Watson Howe. His companions were treating Brewer with the formality befitting his office. While Brewer was playing cards with them, he mentioned that once they crossed into Wyoming, which was not then part of his circuit, he would no longer be a judge. When the conductor announced the train's passing over the Wyoming border, Howe said: "Dave, it's your deal." All, including Brewer, laughed heartily.[89]

In San Francisco he sat alongside Stephen J. Field while his uncle was performing his duties as circuit justice of the Ninth Circuit.[90] Only the day before, on August 14, 1889, Field had been a central figure in the slaying of David S. Terry, a former member of the California Supreme Court. David Neagle, a deputy federal marshal, was accompanying Field as a bodyguard because Terry and his wife had made threats against the justice; the bodyguard shot and killed Terry when the latter accosted Field in a railroad dining room at Lathrop, California.

Sensational though the Neagle affair was, it may not have been the thought uppermost in Brewer's mind at the time. He was aware of a strong possibility that he would be sitting with Field on a more regular basis—as a fellow member of the United States Supreme Court.

6

A CENTENNIAL JUSTICE
Elevation to the United States Supreme Court

W HEN ASSOCIATE JUSTICE Stanley Matthews of the United States Supreme Court died on March 22, 1889, President Benjamin Harrison soon found himself inundated with suggestions for filling the vacancy. Some were of a general nature, such as the helpful admonition of two correspondents: "Under no circumstances appoint a kicker or a mugwump as the position is for life."[1] Usually the advice was more specific, and several possibilities were pressed upon the president. Among the many names to ponder over was that of Circuit Judge David J. Brewer.

Brewer's old friend Senator Preston B. Plumb had earlier asked Harrison to consider Brewer for secretary of the interior. Other Kansans started a movement supporting him for the appointment but, according to later accounts, Brewer scotched it. He also wrote to Plumb in support of John W. Noble, whom Harrison did name to the interior post.[2]

By his own later admission, Brewer had wanted a seat on the Supreme Court ever since the beginning of his professional life. Yet he felt "that the office was not to be contested for, being too high and sacred."[3] His resolve not to promote himself for an appointment to the Court proved fortunate because Harrison preferred to pick men who did not actively seek offices. Fortunate also was Plumb's early and vigorous pushing of Brewer as the man to replace Matthews.[4] Other Kansas men, such as the members of the state supreme court, wrote letters to Harrison urging Brewer's elevation to the high court. Chief Justice Horton pointed out the noteworthy fact that Brewer, without being a radical himself, had been "elected to so many judicial positions in radical Kansas."[5]

Prominent among the other names put before Harrison was that of Judge Gresham, who stood no chance because he and the president were old rivals in Republican circles in Indiana. Southerners pointed out that the Supreme Court had but one member from their region.[6] If geography were to be a consideration, Brewer's chances would have been slight because the Court already had a justice from one of the states within the Eighth Circuit, Samuel F. Miller of Iowa.

Harrison, who was to name four men to the Supreme Court during his one term, took these appointments more seriously—and slowly—than most other presidents.[7] It was not until July of 1889 that he was able to give the matter the attention it deserved. In a private letter he indicated that there were three men in whom he was particularly interested: Henry Hitchcock, president of the American Bar Association; Judge Henry Billings Brown of the United States District Court for eastern Michigan; and Brewer. "I am very anxious to get the best man," he wrote, "and shall not be very much constrained by geography." By fall the choice for Harrison seems to have narrowed down to Brown and Brewer, but he continued to delay making the final decision until the Senate was in session. Meanwhile, the newspapers reported that Justice Miller spoke of Brewer "in the warmest terms, ranking him among the ablest judges on the bench."[8]

During the lengthy process of choosing, a letter from Brewer to a mutual friend came to Harrison's attention and helped turn the tide in Brewer's favor. In it Brewer expressed the wish not to be a rival candidate for the appointment against Brown, who was an old friend and Yale classmate. Such gentlemanly sentiments impressed Harrison and, many believed, finally induced him to appoint Brewer.[9]

According to William Allen White's *Autobiography*, Brewer's most steadfast and energetic advocate almost cost him the appointment. White wrote of an incident related to him by Harrison himself. After Harrison had made his decision in favor of Brewer and had the commission on his desk, Plumb stormed into the president's office. It seems he had heard rumors that candidates other than Brewer were still under consideration. He spoke to Harrison in threatening and abusive tones, so much so that Harrison, once the senator left, felt the temptation to tear up the commission and appoint someone else. But, as he told White (or as White tells us), he overcame the urge; forever after it was a source of pride that he not only stayed with his choice of Brewer but also that he never told Plumb that he had already prepared the commission.[10]

Harrison's attorney general, William H. H. Miller, in a private letter, announced his pleasure with his chief's selection, pointing out that Brewer had "not only the courage to decide against wealth and power and corporations, but what is a much more severe test to decide in their favor when the law and justice of a case demand it." Brown wrote to the president, telling him of his disappointment over not being chosen but also of his approval of the selection of Brewer.[11]

The date of the appointment was December 4, 1889. Brewer first learned of it in Topeka from a reporter. The news surprised him because he had no assurance that he would be Harrison's choice. When attorneys and friends rushed to his office to congratulate him, he was moved. The Kansas press rejoiced, in part because "[t]he president has not oppressed Kansas, heretofore, with a heavy load of appointments."[12]

Before he could take his place on the Supreme Court, Senate confirmation was necessary. It was not to be entirely smooth sailing for Brewer. Even while Harrison was still mulling over the possibilities for filling the post, opposition to Brewer emerged. After the appointment the opposition became more public and pronounced.

The most vocal group to announce its unhappiness were the prohibitionists, who interpreted the *Walruff* decision as "conclusive proof of what we already fear—the total surrender to the liquor dealers of the country."[13] Several letters from this quarter came to Harrison's desk. Others voiced their apprehension over the Wabash receivership, despite assurances that it was really Judge Treat's doing, not Brewer's.[14] Members of the Kansas State Grange protested decisions by Brewer that they regarded as favorable to railroads and other corporations, as well as his prohibition opinions. The *New York Times* sniffed at the unseemly "booming" spirit of the westerners who demanded Brewer's appointment.[15]

Before the appointment was voted upon by the whole Senate, its judiciary committee took the first steps toward confirmation. The committee deliberated on the matter for an unusually long time, December 9–16. Brewer's friends feared a hitch, but the newspapers reported that the committee's chairman, Senator George F. Edmonds of Vermont, wanted to consider the matter with dignity, not haste.

In the course of the committee's deliberations, criticisms of Brewer's judicial record were aired.

Nevertheless, the committee reported favorably on the nomination; it went to the full Senate, which met in what the *Times* described as an "absurd" secret session. There were long speeches, mostly from the Senate's prohibition advocates; others spoke of their concern over the Wabash receivership and other supposed favoritism toward railroads. Still others, such as the senators from North and South Dakota, had petty grievances. These newly admitted states had been attached to the Eighth Circuit, and Brewer had committed the sin of appointing Kansas and Nebraska men as clerks in the Dakotas. The Arkansas senators were critical of Brewer for having convicted some of their constituents for using "harsh language to a colored man."

At first Plumb was absent from the debates and the junior senator from Kansas, John J. Ingalls, had to lead the fight for Brewer. Later Plumb appeared and pushed the matter with his customary zeal. The final vote, taken on December 18, was 52–11 favoring confirmation.[16]

On the day of the vote Harrison sent his congratulations to Brewer, who responded with a telegram: "You named me for, in my judgment, earth's highest position[,] your own great office not excepted. . . . My heart is filled with joy and gratitude, but also burdened with a solemn sense of responsibility. It is my hope and prayer that I may so discharge official duties that all good men shall approve your action."[17]

The *Times* reported that the debates had brought out "some blemish in the judicial soundness and impartiality of Judge Brewer's record" and wondered if the appointment had not all along been intended as a snub for Gresham, who was "very distinctly [Brewer's] superior." Nevertheless, the *Times* believed the new justice to be acceptable.[18]

The legal press likewise voiced qualified approval. After noting that four of the votes against confirmation were cast by senators from states within the Eighth Circuit, the *American Law Review* commented that Brewer had "delivered a great many excellent opinions while on the Supreme bench of Kansas, intermixed with some indifferent ones." This journal was critical of the fact that he had delivered many of his circuit court opinions orally, which were simply taken down by stenographers and thus "not really in proper shape to be reported." The article dismissed the opposition from "temperance fanatics" but found the Wabash receivership to be valid grounds for objecting to the appointment.[19] Perhaps helping to overcome the lukewarm reaction of the *American Law Review* was an enthusiastic piece on Brewer written by his friend Horton and published in a popular lawyer's magazine.[20]

All in all, the public and professional reaction was not as favorable as a new appointee to the Supreme Court and his supporters would want. Yet even the most serious objections to his elevation to the Court could have been (and sometimes were) mitigated by pointing out that Brewer had ruled that a state had the absolute right to enact prohibition; that the responsibility for the Wabash receivership was not his alone; and that his record did not reveal a clear bias in favor of powerful economic interests.

Whatever the doubts raised elsewhere, the great majority of his fellow Kansans were pleased. Even some influential prohibitionists endorsed the appointment. The state bar association passed a resolution declaring its unbounded joy.[21] At the Congregational Club banquet in Kansas City, Brewer responded to a congratulatory toast by warmly acknowledging his wife's role in his success.[22] During the next twenty years he would hold an exalted and demanding position in the nation's capital. Yet he was to remain ever devoted to his family and to his adopted state.

The Brewer family moved to Washington in the winter of 1889–1890. The new associate justice's official duties with the Supreme Court commenced when he was sworn in on January 6, 1890. His salary was to be ten thousand dollars a year.[23]

Soon after arriving in the capital city, he paid a visit to the White House to express his gratitude to Harrison for the appointment. "I had barely started on my words of thanks," Brewer later recalled, "when he showered cold water on me with the following assertion: 'I never did a more cold-blooded act in my life.' " Perhaps Harrison's memory of the unpleasant encounter with Plumb was still fresh. Despite the distinctly chilly beginning, the relationship between the two men became warm, particularly after Brewer "came to understand the President."[24]

His personal associations with his colleagues on the Court were amicable from the beginning. Chief Justice Melville W. Fuller gave a banquet in his honor after Brewer took his oath of office. In addition to the other members of the Court, the guests included the members of the Senate judiciary committee. Fuller was attempting—successfully it turned out—to lobby the committee on behalf of legislation to relieve the Supreme Court of some of its burden. Soon thereafter a bill to create a new set of courts, the circuit courts of appeals, cleared the committee and both houses of Congress and was signed into law by the president on March 3, 1891.[25]

The new appellate courts did indeed make life easier for the justices of the highest court. But the old circuit courts remained in existence, and Brewer and his fellow justices continued to be assigned as circuit justices. Since Samuel F. Miller was the justice for Brewer's old circuit, Brewer replaced the deceased Matthews as justice for the Sixth Circuit, which embraced the states of Kentucky, Michigan, Ohio, and Tennessee. The death of Justice Miller later in 1890 made it necessary for Fuller to assign the Eighth Circuit to Brewer. Responsibility for both circuits ended shortly when Henry Billings Brown, Brewer's friendly rival earlier, was appointed to the Supreme Court and given the Sixth Circuit. Briefly, in the winter of 1897–1898, Brewer was assigned to be justice of Field's circuit, the ninth, upon his uncle's retirement.[26]

In addition to renewing his friendship with Brown, Brewer established especially good relations with the chief justice, who preceded Brewer to the Court by only a year and a half. Brewer surprised Fuller by telling him that he was initially "rather prejudiced" against the diminutive chief, a Democrat who had been appointed by Grover Cleveland. "But," Fuller told his wife in 1891, "he became at once one of the warmest friends. . . . Brewer is a great favorite with me. He is a genuine man." Brewer and his family also became close with Mrs. Fuller.[27]

Other than Fuller, Field, and Miller, members of the Court at the time of Brewer's appointment were John Marshall Harlan, who, like Brewer, was a great raconteur, and the two men enjoyed each other's stories; Joseph P. Bradley; Horace Gray; Samuel Blatchford; and Lucius Quintus Cincinnatus Lamar. During the first decade of Brewer's service on the Court, Miller, Bradley, Lamar, Blatchford, and Field died and their places were taken respectively by Brown, George Shiras, Jr., Howell E. Jackson, Edward D. White, and Joseph McKenna. The vacancy caused by Jackson's death in 1895 was filled with the appointment of Rufus W. Peckham.

There is no hint of ill feelings between Brewer and any of the men who sat with him on the Court in the 1890s. Curiously, though, his relationship with his Uncle Stephen was less warm than could be expected. It was said that Field undertook to instruct his nephew in "proper" ways of writing opinions and that Brewer let it be known that he would do things his own way. In fact, the two men, despite the ties of blood and a similar ideology, disagreed often as justices on the Court, sometimes clashing sharply. Field's biographer reports that "some say that Field never quite forgave Brewer for some of his differences." The often seen assertion that Brewer's elevation to the Court meant another vote for Field is simply incorrect.[28]

Impressive ceremonies in February of 1890 in New York marked the centennial of the federal judiciary. Brewer and other members of the Supreme Court attended the opening exercises at the Metropolitan Opera. Grover Cleveland presided over the affair's executive committee, of which Brewer's uncle David Dudley Field was a member. His other uncle and now colleague, Stephen J. Field, gave the main address.[29] No doubt as a plea for the pending circuit courts of appeals bill, Field spoke feelingly of the Court's need for "some relief from the immense burden now cast upon it." He listed the kinds of litigation that gave the tribunal a load unforeseen by the framers of the Judiciary Act of 1789: "the great increase in the number of admiralty and maritime cases, from the enlarged commerce on the seas, and on the navigable waters of the United States, and . . . the number of patent cases, from the multitude of inventions brought forth by the genius of our people." Also contributing to the expansion of Court business were cases brought about by the rise of industry, grants of public lands, and mineral discoveries.[30]

Brewer was finding out for himself just how busy the Court was. Each year the Court (housed since 1860 in the Old Senate Chamber of the Capitol) formally began its term on the second Monday of October and continued until the last week in May, with occasional recesses for the writing of opinions. Brewer described the Court's conduct of business during a term: "Five days . . . are given each week to the hearing of arguments, the court convening promptly at twelve and adjourning promptly at four, and these hours are fully occupied by arguments of counsel." Each of the justices received a printed copy of the records and briefs. Saturdays were given over to consultation wherein the members of the Court discussed the cases.

"Each justice is expected to have made full examination of each record and the questions involved before that time, and if any one has not done so the consideration is postponed one week or until all are ready. As to the vigor and earnestness of these discussions I can only say that I have never known anything to equal them." If necessary, consideration of a particular case was continued on subsequent Saturdays.[31]

After a full discussion of a case, the justices voted and each was entitled to keep a record of how the others voted. On Saturday night the chief justice would assign the writing of the majority opinion, that is, the decision of the Court, notifying the individual justices which opinions they were responsible for writing. "The duty of assigning cases," said Brewer, "is a most delicate one and could if unwisely discharged provoke no little irritation. To the great credit of the present Chief Justice be it said that no one could be more fair and wise than he in such distribution."[32]

The justice to whom the opinion had been assigned would then write it. Next it went to the printer, who provided copies for each of the justices. After that the members of the Court met to discuss the opinion, offering suggestions and criticisms regarding substance and style. The opinion was then altered to make it acceptable to a majority on the Court and ready to be announced as the Court's decision on the following Monday. Still later the majority opinion would be published in the official *Reports* of the Supreme Court.[33]

In writing opinions for the majority, a justice would sometimes seem to contradict his own views as expressed in other opinions. Such inconsistency is usually more apparent than real, because the shaping of an opinion for a majority often involves compromising the viewpoints of the individual members of that majority, including the writer of its opinion.[34] This helps to explain the occasional lack of consistency, to be noted later, in some opinions written by Brewer.

Those justices disagreeing with the majority would dissent, sometimes with a formal dissenting opinion, sometimes not. In either case, the *Reports* recorded the dissents and contained the dissenting opinions. Of course, dissenting opinions allow a far greater freedom for unfettered personal expression of convictions and feelings than do majority opinions. A third type, the concurring opinion, also appears in these volumes. A concurring opinion is the view of a justice who announces his agreement with the results of the case as determined by the majority opinion but which indicates disagreement with some points contained therein. Two opinions by Field, in which he disagreed with decisions delivered by his nephew, illustrate the two kinds of separate opinions. He began his dissent in *Iron Silver Mining Co.* v. *Mike and Starr Gold and Silver Mining Co.* with "I am unable to agree with my associates in the disposal of this case."[35] He went on for over twenty pages to communicate his views. The first sentence of his opinion concurring with Brewer's majority opinion in yet another Iron Silver Mining Company case is "I concur in the judgment of the affirmance in this case, but as I do not agree with all the views expressed in the opinion of the court I have concluded to state my own separately."[36] Of all the members of the Court during the Fuller era, Harlan entered the most dissents, 283. Brewer was second with 219.[37]

Of course, Brewer had written majority, concurring, and dissenting opinions during his Kansas Supreme Court years. But there disagreement between three justices of the same state and party was minimized. On the federal supreme bench, the possibilities for differences were much greater. There sat nine men representing a variety of legal philosophies and sectional and party biases. Also contributing to the relative lack of agreement was the fact that many of the cases heard by the United States Supreme Court were of great national consequence, thereby provoking more soul-searching and emotion in the individual justices than would cases before a state court.

"The real hard work," said Brewer, "is in shaping up the opinion as it is to be written. When that is done the rest is easy. I dictate my opinions to my secretary, who takes them down in shorthand." After the secretary had prepared a manuscript of the opinion, Brewer would go over it and pencil in anything omitted in dictation.[38]

Brewer was the only member of the Fuller Court who consistently had proof copies of his opinions prepared for the newspapers. Unlike the other justices, he believed it to be a waste of the Court's time to deliver opinions by reading them in full; he read only his conclusions and gave the press his proofs.[39]

The great majority of cases brought before the Supreme Court came there on appeal from lower federal courts. The usual form for getting a case before it was, in those days, a writ of error. For a case to get into the system of federal courts in the first place, it had to involve a federal question (that is, the interpretation of the Constitution, a federal law, a treaty, or a federal administrative action) or diversity of citizenship.

Although some of the cases embraced important constitutional questions or matters of national concern, most were routine affairs, of significance only insofar as they might provide precedents for deciding later cases. Before the creation of the circuit courts of appeals in 1891, the busy justices had several hundred cases on the docket by the end of a term, and litigants often had to wait four or five years before receiving a determination by the Court. The new appeals courts brought welcome relief but no great reduction in the amount of work performed by the justices of the Supreme Court.[40]

The seating arrangements for the justices during the sessions depended upon seniority; the chief justice sat in the middle, with the senior associate justice (by date of commission) on his right, the second most senior member on his left, and so on. At one point during the 1890s this method of arranging the justices, Brewer observed, presented "curious facts": "On the right [of the chief justice] each justice had but a single syllable to his name, Field, Gray, Brown, White. On the left each had two syllables, Harlan, Brewer, Shiras, Peckham." The colors Gray, Brown, and White appeared on the right, whereas the left was "colorless."[41] When the joke was circulating through Washington that the president appointed a Brewer to make the Court "full," Brewer quipped that "no matter how full any one of them might become the Chief is always Fuller."[42]

Brewer presented one of the more striking personal appearances among the members of the Fuller Court. Journalist Arthur Brisbane wrote that he "looks something like an actor. His face is thin and he looks lean. . . . It is a very long face—much longer than any of his associates' faces—and his nose is the longest on the bench." He had a "severe, almost sour look," said Brisbane, but "he really is not sour. He looks something like Dante." He reminded another journalist of a medieval archbishop.[43]

Helping him to keep up with his share of the work load was the retention of what Washingtonians saw as Brewer's "western habits" of early rising and working on his opinions in his study before dawn.[44] But he rid himself—for reasons he said were a secret—of another of his regional attributes: about a year after taking his place on the Court, he had his glistening black hair severely shorn and he shaved off what the eastern press called his "wild western beard" and untrimmed mustache. When he first came before his colleagues with his new appearance, the reaction was mixed. Bradley and Harlan, both clean-shaven, smiled approvingly; the bearded Field frowned; Fuller and Gray "exchanged comical glances." It took several minutes before Lamar noticed, and he at first thought that a new justice had joined the Court. When told that it was Brewer, he "gave a prolonged stare and then sank back and smiled." A New York newspaper commented: "Gone was the wild prairie beard; gone were the untrimmed locks; gone was the look of Western dash and energy; the breezy air of vigor and promptness which Justice Brewer brought from Kansas." Now he looked "like a professor in a Jesuit college" and "all about him is neat and trim and even sanctimonious. His silk gown hangs more decorously than was its wont a year ago."[45]

The new associate justice told his daughter Etta of the first consultation of the Court's October 1890 term, "at which we decided eleven cases; and am waiting for the Chief to distribute the loaves and fishes." By the end of that term, he was proud to inform Etta that the Court had disposed of "over six hundred cases—four hundred seventy-one being the largest number ever reached before."[46]

Fuller began assigning opinions to Brewer almost immediately. The first two he wrote covered what was for him familiar ground and provoked no dissents; the first, *United States* v. *Hancock*, upheld a Mexican land grant in California, which had its validity challenged by the federal government; the second, *Comanche County* v. *Lewis*, concerned fraudulent bridge and courthouse bonds in western Kansas.[47]

He delivered his first dissenting opinion in *Iron Silver Mining Co.* v. *Campbell*. Joined by Fuller, he took issue with Miller's majority view on a conflict between lode and placer patents in Colorado. The chief justice's biographer has noted that Brewer's "advent ended the nondissenting era of Fuller's first year."[48] In later years he described a family reaction to his disagreements with his colleagues after his first year in Washington. He arrived home still disturbed by one of the disagreements and told his wife and a daughter "I have been fighting all day to make my associates accept some elemental propositions of law and I could not budge one of them. They are the most obstinate men I ever saw." To which the daughter replied: "Well, father, if obstinacy is one of the qualifications of a justice of the

Supreme Court, don't you think you are tolerably well equipped?" Brewer informed her that he was "only reasonably firm."[49]

Unfortunately, there is little in Brewer's extant correspondence and other personal papers that reveals the inner workings of the Court. But in several newspaper interviews and his own published works he often informed the public of the tribunal's conduct of its business. After a few years service on the Court, he told a reporter, "We justices are very much like the members of a big family. We are all obstinate, just as obstinate as we can be, and we usually have very decided opinions of our own, nor do we fail to express them when we feel like doing so." And, with a mischievous twinkle, he added: "You know we don't have to appeal to higher courts to uphold our opinions."[50]

7

THE COURT AND THE ECONOMIC REALM
Regulation, Public Finance, Trusts, Patents, and Land, 1890–1900

Historically, the Fuller Court (1888–1910) has the reputation of being friendly to corporations and hostile to efforts to regulate them. Brewer especially has often been singled out as a probusiness member of the Court. Recent scholarship has done much to correct those facile generalizations. Nevertheless, support for the older view remains strong because there are too many examples of the Court's supposed conservatism during this period to dismiss altogether the charges of favoritism to corporations.

Contributing much to the support of the established interpretation is the Fuller Court's response to state and federal attempts to regulate railroads. Earlier, in 1876, the Waite Court had handed down the *Munn* decision, which stated that it was within the power of a state to regulate railroads and other businesses that were "clothed with a public interest." This encouraged the spread of state legislation creating railroad commissions with powers to set rates.

Later in the Waite era, however, the Supreme Court placed limits on such regulation. In *Santa Clara County* v. *Southern Pacific Railroad* the Court recognized corporations as persons within the meaning of the Fourteenth Amendment, the first section of which prohibits a state from depriving "any person of life, liberty, or property, without due process of law."[1] In this and later decisions the Court was saying that unfair or excessive taxation and regulation of railroads and other corporations was "taking property" without due process of law. That interpretation is called substantive due process, as distinguished from the procedural due process. The latter usually refers to common law rights (for example, trial by jury) in criminal proceedings. The former usually involves interpreting the Fourteenth Amendment's due process clauses to prevent "unreasonable legislative interference with private property."[2] Brewer had made early contributions to the newer doctrine of substantive due process in his *Mugler*, *Walruff*, and *Dey* opinions.

More directly damaging to the power of states to regulate railroads was another 1886 decision, *Wabash, St. Louis and Pacific Railway Co. v. Illinois*, in which the Waite Court held that a state had no power to regulate rates in such a way as to interfere with a railroad's interstate rate structure. That, said Justice Miller, encroached upon the power granted by the Constitution to the Congress to regulate commerce between the states.[3] Up to that time Congress had exercised the commerce power sparingly. The *Wabash* decision, along with the awareness that the question of railroad rates was a national, not just a state, issue, helped induce Congress to pass the Interstate Commerce Act of 1887.

The act created the Interstate Commerce Commission (ICC), whose main duty was to protect the public from unreasonable railroad charges. Further, the act outlawed or limited certain railroad practices to which the public had long objected: rebates, pools, discriminatory rate agreements, and long haul–short haul discrimination.

In spite of the Interstate Commerce Act and the limits placed upon state regulation by the courts, state regulation remained constitutionally valid in principle and vigorous in practice for the remainder of the nineteenth century.[4] Certainly Brewer found himself much involved with the question from his earliest days on the Court.

It is often stated that Brewer never accepted the basic premise of the *Munn* doctrine, leaving the impression that he believed all regulation of business to be wrong. His record on the Kansas Supreme Court clearly shows that this impression is erroneous. Yet his concern for the rights of all property owners, large and small, caused him to be particularly wary of legislative attempts to diminish those rights.

In an 1892 opinion written by him upholding a Michigan law that set passenger rates, Brewer put his views concisely: "The legislature has the power to fix rates, and the extent of judicial interference is protection against unreasonable rates." He went on to suggest that the high operating expenses of some railroads consisted in part of exorbitant salaries for their officials.[5]

Shortly thereafter, Blatchford's majority opinion in *Budd* v. *New York* found a state law that set maximum rates for "elevating, receiving, weighing, and discharging grain" to be a legitimate exercise of the state's police power and cited *Munn* as precedent. Brewer's dissent (concurred in by Field and Brown) voiced his objections to the latter doctrine. He made a distinction between public *use* of property and public *interest* in its use. A railroad, he reasoned, was a highway; the building of highways was a public duty; and if a state chose to allow private parties to build such a highway, the state retained the right to set rates for its use by the public. But a business such as a grain elevator (at issue in both the *Munn* and *Budd* cases) was strictly private property, not a quasi-public utility; merely doing business with the public did not subject a business to state interference as long as the owner of the property did not injure the public.[6]

The majority in *Budd* had justified its decision partly on the grounds that the businesses regulated by the New York statute were monopolies. To this Brewer replied that there were monopolies of law and monopolies of fact; another law could break the former and "any one" could break the latter by establishing a rival business. If there was a monopoly in elevator operations in New York, it was because no one had undertaken to compete with the existing companies. Therefore, those companies should not be punished by regulation. Especially repugnant to Brewer was the provision in the New York law that compelled the elevator companies to provide certain services at cost, that is, without real compensation.[7]

In the course of his remarks, he made the statement that has ever since linked his name to opposition to reform: "The paternal theory of government is to me odious." The remainder of the paragraph makes it clear that he sought to protect all forms of property from what was to him unwarranted governmental encroachments: "If [government] may regulate the price of one service, which is not a public service, or the compensation for one kind of property which is not devoted to a public use, why may it not with equal reason regulate the price of all service, and the compensation to be paid for the use of all property?" If so, he warned, the paternalistic society portrayed in Edward Bellamy's recently published novel *Looking Backward* "is nearer than a dream."[8]

Briefly stated, Brewer was saying that a railroad was subject to public regulation because it was devoted to a public use and that most other forms of property, including most other businesses, were not subject to regulation as long as they did no harm to the public. His thinking in these matters was virtually identical—and probably largely based upon—the position that Justice Field had been developing since the 1860s.[9]

A writer in a leading law journal scored Brewer's *Budd* dissent, accusing him of "laboring under the hallucination that he is a legislator instead of being merely a judge." As for the justice's statement that paternalism was odious to him, the writer asked: "What if it is? He was not put [on the bench] to decide constitutional questions according to what was or was not odious to him personally."[10]

Following *Budd*, the Court next upheld a state law regulating grain warehouses and elevators in *Brass* v. *North Dakota*. Brewer, joined by Field, Jackson, and White, dissented, reiterating his objections to the *Budd* ruling.[11] He further pointed out that the North Dakota statute, which specifically declared grain warehouses there to be public warehouses, compelled their owners "to engage in a business which [they] never intended to engage in, to wit, the business of maintaining a public elevator." He observed that the businesses affected were not monopolies (the respondent, Brass, operated one of three elevators in a village) and that the law required the owners of the elevators to pay the cost of insuring the grain they were now compelled to store. If courts continued to sanction such laws, he concluded, "it seems to me that the country is rapidly travelling the road which leads to that point where all freedom of contract and conduct will be lost."[12]

His dissent in *Northern Pacific Railroad Co.* v. *Washington Territory* amply demonstrates that Brewer believed that railroads had a duty to the public and that the courts had the power to compel them to perform it. The Northern Pacific had built a depot at a "paper town" of its own creation rather than at the Yakima County seat, Yakima City. The Supreme Court, speaking through Gray, declined to issue a writ of mandamus ordering the railroad to erect a depot at Yakima City. Brewer, speaking also for Field and Harlan, wrote a blistering dissent. He found "no reason of a public nature" why the Northern Pacific did not have a stopping place at "the largest and most prosperous town in the county." Perhaps, he suggested darkly, the real reason was that Yakima City had not paid a "bonus" to the railroad's managers; or maybe it was because the managers were seeking "a real estate speculation" in favoring North Yakima. In closing, he chastised the majority for holding that courts could not prevent the corporation from putting its private interests before its public duty.[13]

Brewer and his colleagues announced in case after case that a state's right to regulate railroad rates was unquestionable. Yet Brewer always insisted that the rates set by a state had to allow the railroad a reasonable compensation; imposing unreasonably low rates violated Fourteenth Amendment rights because they took away property without due process of law. As a circuit judge, he had pioneered in that interpretation of due process when he enjoined Iowa's rate schedule in the *Dey* case. He was to do more of that as a member of the Supreme Court.

Quite soon after coming on the Court he voted with the majority in *Chicago, Milwaukee & St. Paul Railway Co.* v. *Minnesota*, which voided a Minnesota statute because it did not allow rates set by the state railroad and warehouse commission to be appealed to the courts. Blatchford's majority opinion emphasized that the reasonableness of a rate schedule was "eminently a question for judicial investigation, requiring due process of law for its determination."[14]

From this it was an easy step for Brewer to write the unanimous decision striking down a Texas rate law in *Reagan* v. *Farmers' Loan and Trust Co.* With customary attention to economic details, he found the rates unreasonable, particularly in light of the poor financial condition of the railroads affected by the law. The decision held that a court could not itself set rates; it could only pass on their reasonableness. He further stated that this suit was filed against a state official, not the state itself, and was therefore not in violation of the Eleventh Amendment.[15]

His most important statement in this regard came in his decision in *Ames* v. *Union Pacific Railway Co.*, which he heard and decided in his capacity as justice for the Eighth Circuit in 1894.[16] Although circuit duty was becoming nominal and the writing of circuit court decisions by Supreme Court justices was by then uncommon, perhaps the importance and difficulty of this case impelled Brewer to involve himself in it at the circuit court level. At issue in *Ames* was the reasonableness of the rates set by a 1893 law enacted by the Populist majority of the Nebraska legislature. His upholding of the act's constitutionality was a hollow victory for the Nebraska reformers because he went on to pronounce the rates too low for a fair return on the capital invested and therefore tantamount to taking property without due process. His long, careful opinion restated his view that a government had the perfect right to own and operate a railroad, but that since governments in the United States had authorized private corporations to carry out these enterprises, the railroad companies were entitled to just compensation: "The value of the property cannot be destroyed by legislation depriving the owner of adequate compensation. The power which the legislature has is only to prescribe reasonable rates."[17] Alluding to the somewhat shady past of this railroad and others, Brewer commented that it mattered not how a railroad came into being, how it was built, or how it was managed; the fact that a railroad was property meant that it had rights to be protected.[18]

After an exhaustive examination of the rates set by the law, the costs of operating the railroad, the depressed state of the railroad industry, and other pertinent financial data, Brewer's computations led him to decide that the rates were unreasonable and therefore invalid. He closed the opinion by stating that he came reluctantly to this conclusion and that the court was open to "a reinvestigation of the question of the reasonableness of these rates."[19]

Socialist historian Gustavus Myers roundly condemned the *Ames* decision as an "undisguised justification of every species of fraud and theft."[20] Populists in Nebraska and elsewhere were of course appalled by the ruling, but the Populist attorney general of Kansas pointed out that Brewer had in effect endorsed the party's insistence that the transportation of persons and goods could, like the postal system, be conducted by the government.[21] A few years later this case, now called *Smyth* v. *Ames*, came to the Supreme Court. Harlan's opinion for a unanimous court upheld Brewer's ruling.[22]

Brewer's last decision concerning state regulation of rates in this period was one in which the Court, speaking through him, reversed a federal district judge's dismissal of a railroad's complaint that South Dakota's maximum rates were unfair. The decision sent the case back to the lower court with instructions to appoint a master to examine the railroad's expenses, not just its receipts, and to render a decision based upon this larger body of facts.[23]

Smyth v. *Ames* was a major blow to state regulation of railroads. By the end of the 1890s, the best hope for regulation was the Interstate

Commerce Act and the federal regulatory commission created by it. Perhaps Brewer's decision in *Gulf, Colorado and Santa Fe Railway Co.* v. *Hefley* helped to keep the hope of effective federal regulation alive. It struck down a Texas regulatory statute on the grounds that it conflicted with the Interstate Commerce Act: the Texas legislation made it unlawful for a common carrier to charge more than the amount specified on the bill of lading; the Interstate Commerce Act made it unlawful to charge more than the published rates. Said Brewer: "The national law is unquestionably one within the competency of Congress to enact under the power given to regulate commerce between the States. The state statute must, therefore, give way."[24]

Throughout the decade, however, the Supreme Court had severely limited the Interstate Commerce Act and the Interstate Commerce Commission. Brewer wrote one of the most important decisions doing so, *Interstate Commerce Commission* v. *Cincinnati, New Orleans & Texas Pacific Railway Co.* (Harlan dissenting).[25] A year earlier, an opinion written by Shiras stated that it was "not necessarily so" that the ICC could set rates.[26] Brewer's opinion put it more emphatically: the Interstate Commerce Act granted to the commission the power to disallow unreasonable rates but not the power to set new ones because that was a legislative power that was not to be exercised by an administrative body unless specifically authorized by law to do so. Thus, the ICC had only a negative power of rate-making. A later critic, in speaking of this case, charged that the Fuller Court was "really now the Brewer-Peckham Court." Myers damned the ruling for "reasserting and even amplifying some of [the Court's] previous anti-interstate commerce decisions."[27]

Later in 1897 Brewer was part of the majority in the *Alabama Midland* decision, which held that the circuit courts, when hearing appeals from ICC rulings, were not restricted to the evidence presented by the commission but were free to consider additional facts. This not only reduced the importance of the ICC as a fact-finding body, it also broadened the power of the courts to review ICC decisions.[28]

More evidence of the Court's supposed hostility to the federal regulation of interstate commerce was Brewer's opinion for a unanimous court in *Parsons* v. *Chicago & Northwestern Railway Co.* Narrowly interpreting the Interstate Commerce Act, he wrote that a shipper could not recover damages from a railroad that had allegedly charged a discriminatory rate because the plaintiff had not clearly demonstrated that the rate injured him or that it was unreasonable.[29]

One opinion written by Brewer in the 1890s represented at least a small victory for the Interstate Commerce Act. It sustained a lower court's ruling that the Baltimore and Ohio Railroad had violated the act's prohibition of rebates.[30]

Otherwise, Brewer was almost always among those members of the Court arrayed against the act and the ICC. When the majority stated that courts could cite persons for contempt if they refused to testify before the ICC, Brewer, joined by Fuller and Jackson, dissented. Such a power, he wrote, broke down the barriers between the executive and judicial branches and made the courts "mere agents to assist an administrative body in the prosecution of its inquiries."[31]

Most of the foregoing cases concerned the police power of the states and the commerce power of the federal government. Brewer and his colleagues consistently upheld both as valid exercises of governmental authority. But Brewer, perhaps more than the other members of the Court, was loath to give a broad interpretation of either, mostly because these powers tended to impair the rights of property owners, large and small.

Also, the police and commerce powers were often in conflict with each other. A prominent example of this conflict in the Fuller era was *Leisy* v. *Hardin*. This majority opinion, written by the chief justice, voided that part of an Iowa law that prohibited the sale of alcoholic beverages shipped into the state. Fuller and the majority believed that as long as the product was sold "in the original packages or kegs, unbroken and unopened" it was an article of interstate commerce and subject only to federal regulation. Brewer and Harlan joined the dissent written by Gray, which argued that the Iowa legislation was a proper exercise of the police power.[32]

A few years later the Court appeared to reverse the *Leisy* decision in *Plumley* v. *Massachusetts*, in which Harlan's majority opinion upheld the constitutionality of a law prohibiting the shipment of colored margarine into the state. Fuller dissented because he again felt that the product was a "recognized article of commerce." This time Brewer, along with Field, agreed with him.[33]

The original package doctrine was at issue again in *Austin* v. *Tennessee*. After hearing the arguments in the case, which concerned the constitutionality of a Tennessee act outlawing the shipment of cigarettes into the state, all members of the Court agreed that cigarettes were a legitimate article of commerce.[34] But they divided over whether the cigarettes that the tobacco companies were attempting to ship into Tennessee (in baskets containing packages of ten cigarettes each) were in the original package or not. Four believed they were, another four thought not, and White wavered in the middle.

Brewer began writing the opinion for those who said that the cigarettes were in their original packages and therefore protected under the commerce clause, not knowing if the opinion would be the decision of the Court or a dissent. He privately wrote to Fuller, giving the chief some further thoughts on the matter that he hoped would bring White into their camp or, failing that, that would produce a stronger dissent.[35]

White eventually concurred with those favoring the law. But Brewer's opinion, now a dissenting one, was an able exposition of the controversial doctrine and was praised by Fuller's biographer as "one of [Brewer's] best opinions and shows long and laborious effort."[36] It was widely and favorably cited in the legal journals. In it Brewer chastised the majority for letting the size of the cigarette packages determine whether they came within the scope of the original package doctrine or not.[37]

In another dissenting opinion he again argued for the supremacy of the federal commerce power over a state's police power. An opinion written by Harlan upheld a Kansas law making railroads liable for damages resulting from the importation of diseased Texas cattle. Brewer agreed that legislation of this sort was necessary but contended that it could only come from Congress; the fact that Congress had "only partially" legislated in this area (the Animal Industry Act of 1884) could not justify the Kansas statute.[38]

He concurred with Brown's opinion that an Illinois law requiring trains to stop "a sufficient length of time at county seats to receive and let off passengers with safety" was an unconstitutional encroachment upon the commerce power.[39] Yet soon thereafter he wrote the Court's opinion validating a state law that authorized cities to regulate the speed of trains. "Such act is, even as to interstate trains, one only indirectly affecting interstate commerce, and is within the power of the State until at least Congress shall take action in the matter."[40]

The broad yet nebulous commerce power came into conflict with state and local powers other than the police power. A Titusville, Pennsylvania, ordinance requiring agents soliciting orders for a manufacturer to pay a fee for a license was, according to the decision handed down for the Court by Brewer, an exercise of the taxing power, not the police power. As such, he wrote, it was imposing a tax upon interstate commerce and therefore void.[41] Similarly, he dissented from a decision that held that a Mississippi tax on a telegraph corporation was not a regulation of interstate commerce; Brewer (joined by Harlan) thought it was.[42]

Later, however, another Brewer opinion upheld the right of a state to tax the intangible property (that is, "privileges, corporate franchises, contracts [and] obligations") of a firm doing an interstate business: "Does substance of right require that [a corporation] shall pay taxes only upon the thousands of dollars of tangible property it possesses? Accumulated wealth will laugh at the crudity of taxing laws which reach only to one and ignore the other." Here, unlike the two foregoing opinions, he was saying that the tax was not for the privilege of conducting an interstate business.[43] When railroad companies protested that an Indiana law that permitted the state to take into consideration a railroad's assets and earnings outside the state in determining the tax to be paid to the state, Brewer, speaking for the majority, disagreed with the contention that this was interference with interstate commerce and upheld the act. Harlan and Brown dissented, arguing that the tax did indeed place "illegal burdens upon interstate commerce under the guise of a valuation for purposes of taxation of property within the State."[44] A unanimous decision written by Brewer ruled that an Illinois statute that exempted the lands of the Illinois Central Railroad from taxation did not make the corporation's lands immune from a municipal assessment for the grading and paving of a street.[45]

The Court, speaking through Brewer, further sustained the power of a municipality to tax a corporation. St. Louis imposed a tax of five dollars on each of the telegraph poles along its streets. The Western Union company protested that its federal franchise, granted in 1866, exempted it from such payments. Not so, said Brewer for the majority: just as the public could not take private property without compensation, a corporation could not use public property without compensation. Brown dissented on the grounds that the tax was excessive and was upon the franchise, not for the use of the property.

Following a second hearing, Brewer wrote that the Court saw no reason to change its position.[46] In yet another taxation case it was argued that a territory (in this instance Montana) did not have the same power as a state to tax a national bank. Brewer, speaking for all of his colleagues, said that it did.[47]

Brewer and the other members of the Fuller Court were inclined to give much latitude to state and local governments in the taxing of corporations. Somewhat ironically, this Court's best-known response to questions of taxation contributed much to its reputation for favoritism toward corporate and other forms of wealth: its decision in *Pollock* v. *Farmers' Loan and Trust Co.*, the income tax case.[48]

During the Civil War the Congress imposed a graduated tax on incomes. The tax was discontinued after the war, but in 1881 the Supreme Court was called upon to pass on its constitutionality and the justices upheld it. The Constitution originally required that all direct federal taxes be apportioned among the states according to population. It was generally understood that by "direct" taxes the Framers meant land and capitation taxes. Congress had long avoided the necessity of such apportionment by relying upon tariffs and excises, which were considered to be "indirect" taxes. The 1881 decision, *Springer* v. *United States*, held that the Civil War income tax had not been a direct tax.[49]

In the 1880s and 1890s, reformers, especially from the South and West, demanded a permanent federal income tax. They argued that this form of taxation would force corporations and the wealthy to pay something like their fair share for the upkeep of a government that was benefiting the interests of wealth. Also, many believed that an income tax would narrow the gap between rich and poor and redistribute wealth more equitably.

In response to this cry, Congress included a provision in the Wilson-Gorman Tariff Act of 1894 that placed a flat 4 percent levy on incomes, including income from rents, dividends, interest, profits, and salaries. Those who would be paying the tax of course insisted that it was unfair because it fell on only a small fraction of the population, most of which group lived in one section of the country, the Northeast. They said further that it was unconstitutional, charging that at least parts of the tax were direct and that they had not been apportioned in accordance with the constitutional requirement.

In March of 1895 the first *Pollock* case came before the Court—a collusive-appearing suit brought for the purpose of getting a decision on the constitutionality of the income tax.[50] After hearing arguments from the able teams of lawyers on both sides, Fuller wrote an opinion for the majority, in which it held that parts of the 1894 measure were void. It was decided that the tax on the income from land was a direct tax and therefore unconstitutional because it had not been apportioned among the states according to population and that the tax on income from state and municipal bonds was also void because it amounted to federal taxation of states and their instrumentalities.

Only Harlan and White dissented on the first question, contending that the tax was constitutional in its entirety; all of the justices agreed on the second. The Court, however, was unable to reach a conclusion on two crucial points: whether the voiding of two parts of the tax meant that the entire tax must be declared void and whether the tax violated the Constitution's requirement that all federal taxes had to be uniform throughout the United States. On these questions the Court divided four to four. Illness had prevented the ninth member, Jackson, from participating. To break the deadlock, the Court heard *Pollock* a second time some weeks later, after Jackson had returned to the bench. A five-to-four decision declared all of the income tax provisions of the Wilson-Gorman Act void. This time Fuller based his opinion on broader grounds, that taxes on income from all forms of property were void. Further, he and the other members of the majority (Field, Gray, Shiras, and Brewer) held that since so many parts of the tax had been found to be in conflict with the Constitution, all of it had to be declared void.

The public then and critics later saw the killing of the income tax as yet more evidence of the Fuller Court's protecting of the affluent and powerful. Adding to the unhappiness over the final decision was that, apparently, one of the justices had changed his mind between the first and second hearings. In the first opinion Fuller named neither the four justices who voted to declare the entire tax unconstitutional nor the four who voted otherwise. After the second hearing Jackson voted with the dissenters—Harlan, White, and Brown—meaning that one of the four justices voting not to void the measure after the first hearing had switched sides.

Obviously it had not been Fuller, and until recently Field has been ruled out because of his vehement denunciation of the tax, which he delivered in a concurring opinion at the first hearing. But the foremost authority on the Fuller Court has argued that Field might have voted with the protax justices in the first hearing because he believed the tax should have been voided for its failure to meet the Constitution's requirement that federal taxation be uniform throughout the nation, and hoped that a decision based on those grounds would result from a second hearing. Lately, there has been a tendency to eliminate Shiras as the "Vacillating Judge." So was it Field, Gray, or Brewer? No one knows, but there is no lack of educated guesses.[51] Brewer's off-the-bench defense of the majority opinion, to be noted later, would suggest that he was not the man in question.

Views presented by Brewer in two later tax cases deserve attention. He agreed with McKenna's majority opinion upholding an Illinois inheritance tax but dissented in part because he believed that the graduated rates imposed upon one form of legacies were "purely arbitrary" and therefore invalid.[52] Likewise, he concurred with White's opinion sustaining a federal estate tax except for "so much of the opinion as holds that a progressive rate of tax can be validly imposed."[53]

The narrowly decided *Pollock* case is not a clear instance of coddling the rich. The slender majority that decided it had grave doubts about the fairness of the tax. More than that, the justices showed understandable confusion in the efforts to determine whether or not this form of taxation conformed to the Framers' intent with regard to direct taxation. And they never ruled that an income tax per se was unconstitutional. Nevertheless, the decision obviously departed from the *Springer* precedent.

The Fuller Court's response to another area of reform legislation, antitrust laws, has also contributed to its conservative image. The federal antitrust law, the Sherman Act of 1890, ran into serious difficulty with the Court in *United States v. E. C. Knight Co.*[54] In the *Knight* case the Justice Department had attempted to break up the American Sugar Refining Company, which controlled over ninety percent of the manufacturing of sugar in the nation. In a curious and highly unpopular opinion written by Fuller, the Court (with only Harlan dissenting) declared that while the Sherman Act was a valid exercise of the commerce power, the sugar company could not be dissolved under the terms of the act because it was engaged in manufacturing, not commerce.

The decision threatened to make the Sherman Act a dead letter.

Yet over the remaining years of the nineteenth century the Court demonstrated a tendency toward a broader interpretation of the antitrust act and away from the odd distinction between manufacturing and commerce. Brewer voted with the majority in *United States* v. *Trans-Missouri Freight Association* in which Peckham's opinion held that a group of western railroads had violated the Sherman Act by fixing rates. White, Field, Gray, and Shiras dissented.[55] A unanimous Court in 1899 ruled that a combination of pipe manufacturers were in violation of the act because they divided markets among themselves and fixed prices.[56]

The Fuller Court's interpretation of the Fourteenth Amendment's relationship to business is usually discussed in connection with rate-making and taxation cases. Yet the Court interpreted the amendment in other kinds of decisions in the 1890s—sometimes broadly, sometimes narrowly; at times for the benefit of business, at times to its detriment. As in the rate and tax cases, those rulings frequently provoked division within the Court.

A Texas law of 1889 provided that persons winning suits against railroads would have their attorneys' fees paid by the railroad. When its constitutionality was challenged, Brewer wrote the Court's opinion. After emphasizing that it was "well settled that corporations are persons within the provisions of the Fourteenth Amendment," he went on to find the statute unconstitutional. He and the majority saw it as denying the amendment's guarantee of equal protection of the laws. Gray, Fuller, and White disagreed, especially regretting that only the railroads' side had been adequately presented, because the original plaintiff's arguments had not been placed before the Court.[57]

Two years later, with apparent inconsistency, a Brewer opinion upheld a Kansas statute that made railroads liable for attorneys' fees as well as for damages if a plaintiff suffered a loss because of fires caused by a railroad. This time Brewer found the statute to be a legitimate exercise of the police power and not in conflict with the Fourteenth Amendment. In dissent, Harlan, Brown, Peckham, and McKenna cited Brewer's opinion in the Texas case and argued that the Kansas statute likewise constituted a denial of equal protection.[58]

Brewer made distinctions also in cases involving compensation for the taking of property. In 1897 he dissented from a decision that held that a city need not pay full compensation to a railroad when the city acquired, through condemnation proceedings, a crossing belonging to a railroad. Harlan's opinion for the majority noted that the railroad was still allowed to use the crossing. Brewer insisted that property was property regardless of use and that the Fourteenth Amendment mandated compensation. "The claim that leaving the present use of his property to the owner destroys the right of compensation is a proposition which to my mind is simply monstrous."[59]

Soon thereafter he delivered the unanimous opinion of the Court in another compensation case. The City of Brooklyn had obtained by condemnation a water company and paid compensation. But the company protested that this violated its previous contract with the city. Brewer clearly stated that Brooklyn had satisfied the constitutional requirement. "Whenever public uses require, the government may appropriate any private property on the payment of just compensation."[60]

Just as the Fourteenth Amendment constrained states and municipalities from taking property without compensation, the Fifth Amendment similarly constrained the federal government. When the latter condemned a company's lock and dam on the Monongahela River, Brewer, speaking for the Court, announced that although it was within the government's commerce power to remove obstructions to navigation, the commerce power was limited by the Fifth Amendment; therefore, the federal government had to pay the company for the loss of its property.[61]

There were also cases involving conflicts between taxation and due process. Brewer wrote the opinion of the Court in three of them. In *Bellingham Bay & British Columbia Railway Co.* v. *New Whatcom* he did not accept the railroad company's argument that it had been denied due process because it had not received sufficient notice of a reassessment of taxes on its property.[62] In a Minnesota case his opinion held that the state, in depriving a railroad's lands of their tax-exempt status, had violated neither the Fourteenth Amendment's guarantee of due process nor the Constitution's contract clause.[63]

The contract clause, which prohibits states from "impairing the obligation of contracts," had earlier been used by the Court to protect business enterprise from state interference. By the 1890s it had declined in importance, having been replaced for that purpose by the Court's interpretation of the Fourteenth Amendment. But Brewer's majority opinion in *Stearns* v. *Minnesota* used it to strike down an 1896 Minnesota statute. An earlier law had taxed railroad property on the basis of gross receipts; the act of 1896 changed the basis to the actual cash value of the property. Brewer said that the earlier law was a contract and therefore the later one was void. Brown concurred in a separate opinion. White, speaking also for Harlan, Gray, and McKenna, concurred in the result but believed the second law was unconstitutional because it denied due process and equal protection.[64]

A novel question concerning the Fourteenth Amendment resulted in an ingenious opinion by Brewer. A New Orleans ordinance had set the boundaries of the city's red-light district; residents of the district who were not engaged in the business of prostitution alleged that the ordinance had caused their property to decline in value and that this amounted to depriving them of property. Brewer thought not, pointing out that no prostitutes had complained that the ordinance had deprived them of rights; those owning property outside the district had not complained that the ordinance had deprived them of possible tenants; and the ordinance did not require anyone in the district to engage in prostitution or otherwise misbehave.[65]

But Brewer did call for a broader interpretation of the amendment in *Taylor* v. *Beckham*, a case arising out of a disputed election in Kentucky. Fuller's majority opinion stated that the Court had no jurisdiction in the matter. Brewer and Harlan, in separate dissents, said that it did, because in their view the disputed offices were property within the meaning of the Fourteenth Amendment and that the case thus presented a legitimate federal question for the Court to consider.[66]

Of the several patent cases heard by the Fuller Court, none was of greater consequence than that which involved the federal government's attempt to cancel the "Berliner patent." The patent was for a telephone transmitter and was held by the American Bell Telephone Company. The government argued that the company had delayed in pressing for the final approval of the patent in order to extend its rights to the device and that the patent was actually a reissue of an earlier one. Brewer wrote an opinion for the Court that embodied his characteristic concern for property. He could not accept what he saw as the government's assertion that an inventor was "a quasi trustee for the public" who was therefore "under a sort of moral obligation to see that the public acquires the right to the free use of that invention as soon as is conveniently possible." The government, he wrote, had no property interest in the invention, and he suggested that the suit had been initiated for the benefit of another private party rather than for the protection of the public from a monopoly.[67]

Of far less national significance, but revealing Brewer's penchant for going beyond legal points and looking at facts, was his opinion in another patent controversy. At issue was "a means for strengthening the crotch in the fly of pantaloons." Brewer saw no new invention here. All boys tore their pantaloons, and their mothers, "not content with sewing the torn ends together," also reinforced the torn area with another piece of cloth. The idea was "as old as pantaloons themselves" and therefore not patentable.[68]

Land questions, in a variety of forms, took up much of the Supreme Court's calendar in the nineteenth century, even in its last decade. Particularly vexing were those arising from Mexican grants. Brewer wrote decisions in several of them. In one he emphasized the difficulties they presented because there was "so much indefiniteness and lack of precision" in the wording of the grants and also because it was questionable whether persons with the proper authority had made them in the first place.[69]

The most famous of them was of course the Maxwell grant. Perhaps because of his experience on the circuit court in handling cases concerning the Maxwell Land Grant Company, he was chosen to write the Court's opinion in two Maxwell cases in the 1890s. Both upheld the company against the claims of other parties. One of the decisions reaffirmed the validity of the disputed survey of the grant.[70] Another opinion written for the Court by Brewer held for a private claimant of a Mexican grant and against the federal government. Gustavus Myers blasted the decision, charging that it benefited certain mining and railroad corporations, including the Southern Pacific.[71]

Myers also castigated "another characteristic decision written by Brewer," *United States* v. *Des Moines Navigation and Railway Co.*, because it validated "an enormous land grant" that had been obtained by "proven briberies."[72] Adding credibility to the charge that Brewer favored corporate interests in land disputes is his dissent in *Barden* v. *Northern Pacific Railroad Co.* Joined by Gray and Shiras, he took issue with Field's opinion for the majority, which held that the federal land grant to the railroad corporation did not include the mineral lands within the grant. Brewer accused his uncle and the others of ignoring precedent and assuming that the large size of the grant implied that Congress had reserved the mineral lands for the United States. "If ever there was a case in which the rule of *stare decisis* should prevail," he fumed, "this is one."[73]

Taking into consideration only the foregoing opinions and Myers's interpretation of some of them, there would be no escaping the conclusion that Brewer was bending over backwards to serve the interests of rapacious capital. But other opinions by Brewer modify that view considerably. Speaking for the majority, he twice denied the Southern Pacific's claim that it had acquired title to the forfeited lands of the Atlantic and Pacific Railroad Company. Both times Field (with Gray) dissented.[74] Three times in this decade decisions delivered by Brewer favored persons who had allegedly settled on railroad lands.[75] In other opinions in this period he let it be known emphatically that the law favored actual settlers rather than those who sought land for speculative purposes.[76] He was noticeably unsympathetic to a claimant to Texas lands who had not pressed his claim until the growth of the state's population had made the lands valuable.[77]

Just as western lands were increasing in value with settlement, so too was water. Along the Rio Grande there developed a clash of interests between a private irrigation scheme and federal efforts to stabilize the river's flow. An important result of the controversy was the case *United States* v. *Rio Grande Dam & Irrigation Co.*, for which Brewer wrote the Court's opinion in 1899. By the end of the nineteenth century, it was well understood that Congress, through the commerce power, had the power to control navigable waterways. This decision marked an important step toward even greater federal control because Brewer concluded that the government's authority over a navigable stream extended to *any* waters that affect a stream's navigability. The ruling was of much significance for the embryonic federal reclamation program, as well as for its contribution to the growing tendency toward a greater federal presence in American life.[78]

Membership on the Supreme Court gave him opportunities to strike at an economic practice he had denounced since his days on the Kansas Supreme Court: the issuing of bonds by local governments to aid railroads. Brewer considered these bonds as bribes solicited by railroad officials, in return for which it was expected that the railroads would build their lines through the localities issuing the bonds.

Moreover, Brewer and others (including Justice Field) were appalled at the corruption and burdensome indebtedness inherent in this form of local aid to railroads.[79]

In keeping with his long-standing opposition, he was no doubt happy to write two majority opinions in bond cases that were decided against the railroads. In one, on the grounds that it was contrary to the state's constitution, the decision struck down an 1880 Ohio law authorizing townships to issue such bonds: "This provision was inserted in the constitution . . . in view of the fact then and since well known in the history of all States, particularly in the West, that municipal bonds to aid railroads were freely voted in expectation of large resulting benefits—an expectation frequently disappointed."[80] Anger over unrealized expectations may well have prompted his dissent, without opinion, from a decision holding that the Texas and Pacific railway was not permanently obliged to keep shops and its eastern terminus in Marshall, Texas. The company, in return for land and county bonds, had earlier agreed to do so. The citizens of Marshall, and perhaps Brewer too, believed that the company should have kept its part of the bargain.[81]

In one of his rare decisions delivered in his capacity as a circuit justice, Brewer gave the land-grant railroads and other major corporations cause for unhappiness. Here again was the issue of the keeping of corporate promises. The congressional legislation that provided land and loan subsidies for building the transcontinental rail system stipulated that the corporations were each to operate telegraph lines and provide nondiscriminatory telegraphic service. The railroads interpreted it to mean that they could delegate the obligation to telegraph companies. In 1889 the Justice Department initiated suits in the circuit courts to compel the railroad companies to abide by the wording and intent of the law and provide telegraphic facilities themselves.[82]

The suit to sever the connection between the Union Pacific and Western Union came before the court for the Eighth Circuit in 1892. Upon learning that Brewer would personally hear and decide the case, Union Pacific officials became apprehensive because Brewer, as circuit justice, had recently decided against the corporation in a suit brought against it by the Rock Island line.[83]

The fears proved justified. Brewer held that the connection between the railroad and telegraph companies must end and that Union

Pacific had to maintain its own telegraph franchise. The Circuit Court of Appeals reversed his decision, but a unanimous Supreme Court, speaking through Harlan, soon ruled otherwise, thus vindicating both Brewer and the Justice Department. Brewer of course participated in neither the hearing nor the deciding of the case at this level.[84]

Critics of the Fuller Court have been essentially correct in their belief that Fuller himself, Brewer, Field, and others were determined to protect property rights. Yet the concern for property did not always mean that the Court in the 1890s was solely or even primarily determined to protect the interests of large corporations and the private fortunes they created. In a number of well-publicized and well-remembered decisions, Brewer and his colleagues showed skepticism and occasional hostility toward attempts to regulate, tax, or break up large economic enterprises. But in the main they sustained the police power of the states, the commerce power of the federal government, and the taxing powers of all levels of government when those powers were used in attempts to challenge the might and influence of the immense wealth produced in the early decades of American industrialization. It is true that the states and federal government failed to curb corporate power in this period, but explanations for the failure need to go beyond blanket condemnations of the United States Supreme Court.

8

THE COURT AND HUMANITY
Minorities, Labor, Crime, and
Legal Ethics, 1890–1900

THE PRIMARY INTENT of the Fourteenth Amendment, adopted in 1868 during the Reconstruction era, had been to prevent states from denying due process and equal protection of the laws to the newly freed blacks of the South. Throughout the remainder of the century, and especially during the Fuller era, the Supreme Court expanded the amendment's coverage to corporations—a process in which Brewer played a conspicuous part.

But how did blacks, the original objects of Fourteenth Amendment concern, fare in the hands of the Fuller Court? Not well, as the most famous civil rights case of the period attests. In *Plessy* v. *Ferguson*, Brown's majority opinion held that the Louisiana law requiring separate railroad cars for blacks and whites was not a denial of equal protection of the laws.[1] The decision laid down the "separate but equal" doctrine that served as the judicial underpinning of segregation until overturned in the mid-twentieth century.

Because of another commitment to be discussed later, Brewer did not participate in the case. Harlan, a Kentuckian from a slave-owning family, alone dissented. Given Brewer's earlier Kansas opinions in cases involving blacks, we can assume that he would have been with the majority and not in agreement with Harlan's eloquent dissent. Brewer did, however, praise Harlan publicly for his courageous dissent in the *Civil Rights Cases* (1883).[2]

On the other hand (and probably more accurately reflecting Brewer's personal views), he wrote an 1890 opinion upholding a Mississippi statute requiring separate railroad cars for blacks and whites. With Harlan and Bradley in dissent, Brewer's majority view stated that the act, which embraced only intrastate transportation, was no burden to interstate commerce and therefore did not conflict with the federal commerce power. The leading authority on the Court during this period believes that the case, *Louisville, New Orleans & Texas Railway Co. v. Mississippi*, was more important in the establishment of legalized segregation than was the later, more notorious *Plessy* decision.[3]

Another narrow reading of the Fourteenth Amendment came with the unanimous *In re Lockwood* decision of 1894. Although Brewer was usually supportive of women's rights, he joined the rest of the Court in rejecting Belva A. Lockwood's contention that Virginia had denied the noted suffragist and attorney any Fourteenth Amendment rights when the state refused to admit her to the bar.[4]

The Chinese and other orientals, like the blacks, were a besieged minority in late nineteenth-century America. In marked contrast to his position on the rights of blacks, Brewer quickly emerged as the Court's foremost champion of orientals. His opinions in cases involving their rights are among his most eloquent and forceful.

Responding to demands for limiting or prohibiting Chinese immigration, Congress passed exclusionary legislation in 1888, which the Supreme Court upheld the next year.[5] Brewer had not then taken his seat on the Court, but soon after doing so, he had an opportunity to show his sympathies for the Chinese living in the United States as resident aliens. An opinion written by Field in 1891 denied one Quock Ting the right to reenter the country because his testimony and that of other Chinese that he had been born in America was likely to be perjured. Brewer, in dissent, took issue with his uncle's reasoning: "The government evidently rested on the assumption that, because the witnesses were Chinese persons, they were not to be believed. I do not agree with this."[6]

The case of Fong Yue Ting presented a more important issue and provoked a stinging dissent from Brewer. The majority upheld the act of 1892, which authorized the executive branch of the federal government to expel resident Chinese aliens without trial or other elements of due process. The Court, speaking through Gray, held that this power was inherent with any sovereign government.[7] In separate dissents, Brewer, Field, and Fuller argued that the Chinese living in the United States had rights under treaties and that the Fifth Amendment's guarantee of due process extended to all *persons* in America, not just citizens.

Brewer further believed that the act was contrary to the Fourth, Sixth, and Eighth Amendments. He pointed out that the Chinese were entitled to an especially secure status because they had been invited to the United States, whereas other aliens had "simply drifted here because there is no provision to keep [them] out." Always wary of the extension of central power, he could not accept Gray's "indefinite and dangerous" notions of the powers inherent in sovereignty. "The governments of other nations," he continued, "have elastic powers—ours is fixed and bounded by a written constitution. The expulsion of a race may be within the inherent powers of a despotism," but not within the powers of America's constitutional government. He acknowledged the power of the United States to prohibit the entry of aliens ("to build, as it were, a Chinese wall around our borders") but not the power to banish resident aliens without due process. He concluded with a pointed question: "In view of this enactment of the highest legislative body of the foremost Christian nation, may not the thoughtful Chinese disciple of Confucius fairly ask, Why do they send missionaries here?"[8]

Probably for the same reasons, he dissented, without opinion, in two other oriental exclusion cases. One was from another of Gray's opinions denying a writ of habeas corpus to a Japanese woman being detained on the basis of an act of 1891 that excluded immigrants likely to be a public charge; the other was a response to Harlan's opinion denying reentry to a Chinese having a "commercial domicil" (*sic*) in the United States who had temporarily left the country.[9]

In one notable case in the decade, *United States* v. *Wong Kim Ark*, the Chinese won a victory. After several months of internal wrangling, the Court, speaking through Gray, held that Chinese born in the United States were citizens, as defined by the Fourteenth Amendment.[10] Brewer, of course, sided with the majority rather than the dissenters Fuller and Harlan. He celebrated the outcome of the divisive, time-consuming case with some lighthearted doggerel:

U S
vs
Wong Kim Ark

Argued Mar 1897—Decided Mar 1898
  Defendant discharged from custody
At last the end of Wong!
We've studied[,] written long,

and may be wholly wrong—
Yet join the happy song
Goodby, goodby, to Wong—

No more, no more of Kim!
We've had enough of him.
And close his case with vim—
So raise the gladsome hymn
Goodby, goodby to Kim—

The last, the last of Ark!
His prospects had been dark
If Gray had missed his mark;
But now he's on a lark
Goodby[,] Goodby to Ark[.]¹¹

Americans of later generations might well ask why Brewer could appear so unsympathetic to blacks and yet so strongly pro-Chinese. In the first place, he was not hostile to blacks. But he did not believe that an expansive view of the Constitution, including the Fourteenth Amendment, was a proper way to insure justice for them. Unlike many other nineteenth-century Republicans, Brewer generally opposed the growth of federal power at the expense of the states. He believed that the states, subject only to the most clearly defined constitutional limitations, were largely free to determine the status of their citizens. By the 1890s most white Americans, including Republicans and northerners, had come to believe that the whites of the southern states (where most American blacks resided) knew best about race relations; no doubt Brewer shared the prevailing view.

But the Chinese, for Brewer, were a different matter. Since most were immigrant aliens, he saw their status as a proper concern of the federal government and the protection of their rights as a federal responsibility. But beyond these cold, legalistic considerations, Brewer obviously had an emotional commitment to the Chinese equal to that of Harlan to the blacks. Perhaps the fact that he was himself an "oriental" by birth helps to explain his sympathies. A more plausible explanation (hinted at in his *Fong Yue Ting* dissent) is his lifelong support of the movement to bring Christianity to all the peoples of the world: decent treatment of the Chinese in America would promote the missionary movement, both here and in the Orient. American blacks, in theory at least, already had the blessings of Christianity, western civilization, and American citizenship; the Chinese as yet did not, and so perhaps Brewer thought they deserved special consideration.

Of course, some might suspect that Brewer, as the supposed friend of business interests, would want to encourage the influx of cheap oriental labor. But there can be little doubt that his concern for the Chinese was genuine and heartfelt. The depth of that concern will be further evident in later opinions as well as in some of his off-the-bench remarks.

Even if his position in the Chinese cases was not intended to be detrimental to native-born labor, there is much in Brewer's judicial record to show that he was not friendly to organized labor and that he was unconcerned with the woes of individual workingmen. The best known of his opinions in labor matters during the 1890s is *In re Debs*.

In his *Ames* opinion of 1894, he mentioned the "fearful strikes" of that summer, an allusion to the Pullman Boycott.[12] In support of striking workers at the Pullman Palace Car Company, the American Railway Union, led by Eugene V. Debs, refused to handle Pullman cars in the operation of trains. As was usual in those days, the strike and boycott were accompanied by riots and other forms of property-destroying violence. President Cleveland ordered federal troops to the center of the strife, the Chicago area. Also, the attorney general of the United States took the unusual step of directing a federal district attorney to seek an injunction against the union, to enjoin it from obstructing the mails and trains engaged in interstate commerce. The federal circuit court for the district of northern Illinois issued the injunction. Debs and other union officials ignored it. They were tried and convicted of contempt of court. The circuit court based its decision in part upon the union's purported violation of the Sherman Act, the leaders of the union having been accused of entering into a "conspiracy in restraint of trade." The case then went to the Supreme Court as *In re Debs*, in which Debs and the others sought their release through a writ of habeas corpus.[13]

Brewer spoke for a unanimous Court. The decision not only denied the writ but upheld the use of injunctions in labor disputes. His opinion recognized the novelty involved: ordinarily, courts issued injunctions at the request of private persons seeking the abatement of a private nuisance; here, however, the government was seeking to abate a "public nuisance."[14]

Virtually ignoring the lower court's use of the Sherman Act, Brewer's opinion rested largely upon the right of a sovereign nation to carry out its constitutional function of protecting commerce and carrying the mails. Throughout his remarks there is ample evidence of his abhorrence of violence and his concern for the protection of property. In his sweeping language we find little of Brewer's characteristic reluctance to grant power to the federal government. Equally uncharacteristic was his sanctioning of military force. Nevertheless, he congratulated both the government and the union officials for their ultimate reliance upon the courts rather than force to settle the matter.[15]

From the standpoint of constitutional history, the decision expanded the hitherto limited equity jurisdiction of the federal courts. More noticeable was the decision's impact on organized labor: it ushered in the era of the labor injunction, which lasted until the 1930s. During that time unions regularly found their operations thwarted by court orders, obtained by government or management, prohibiting many activities relating to strikes and boycotts.

The *Debs* ruling, and the fact that it came on the heels of the *Pollock* and *Knight* decisions, has given the impression ever since that the members of the Court in the 1890s—Brewer especially—were the friends of capital and the enemies of working people.[16] Even if that impression is not wholly accurate, other opinions by Brewer in the decade reinforce it. In a second case arising out of the Pullman Boycott, his opinion for the Court upheld the conviction of union leaders for conspiracy to obstruct commerce and the carrying of mail. It also sustained a law that provided greater punishment for conspiracy to do a criminal act than for committing the act itself.[17]

Almost without exception his opinions in workmen's injury cases during the nineties went against the workers. One was a dissent from an opinion by Gray, in which the majority decided that a federal court could not force the plaintiff to submit to a medical examination prior to the trial; Brewer, joined by Brown, believed that the courts had this power.[18]

Justice Field and his nephew came into sharp disagreement over the fellow servant rule. In *Chicago, Milwaukee & St. Paul Railway*

Co. v. *Ross* (1884), Field had ushered in the vice-principal doctrine, which held that if an employee were injured by the actions of another employee acting in a supervisory capacity, that is, a vice-principal, the employer was liable for damages. As a circuit judge, Brewer had opposed the new rule and continued to oppose it as a Supreme Court justice. A majority in *Baltimore & Ohio Railroad Co.* v. *Baugh*, speaking through Brewer, held that Baugh, a fireman, had been injured by the actions of a fellow servant, a locomotive engineer, and therefore could not recover from the railroad. Field, usually portrayed as the Court's most reactionary member, wrote a powerful dissent, objecting in no uncertain terms to the fellow servant rule. Since Brewer's opinion rested in part on the controversial notion that the federal courts, and not just the state courts, could develop their own body of common law, Field found the *Baugh* decision repugnant on those grounds also because he had long been hostile to the concept of a federal common law.[19]

In numerous other opinions in this decade Brewer almost always concluded that injuries to the workers resulted from the negligence of a fellow worker or the worker himself.[20]

State efforts to protect workers by means of maximum workday legislation at first met with a favorable response from the Court. Utah's law imposing an eight-hour day for miners was, in *Holden* v. *Hardy*, accepted as a permissible police power measure.[21] Brewer and Peckham dissented without opinion. Although Brewer did not state his objections, it is reasonable to assume that they stemmed from his usual skepticism concerning a broad application of the police power and agreement with the mine owners' contention that the law interfered with liberty of contract.

What began as a labor case, *Church of the Holy Trinity* v. *United States*, became, in Brewer's hands, a decision affirming the religious nature of the American people.[22] In 1885 Congress had passed an act that prohibited the contracting of laborers from abroad. The intent was to diminish the flow of cheap foreign labor into the country. A church in New York secured the services of a British pastor, thereby apparently violating the law. The church lost the case in the circuit court and appealed it to the Supreme Court. The matter was ticklish because although Congress clearly had not intended to have this legislation apply to clergymen, the act did not list them among those exempted from its terms.

Brewer, with some ingenuity, fashioned the opinion of a unanimous Court. He stated that even though ministers of the Gospel were not specifically exempted, the aim of the law was to limit the entry of unskilled foreign workers; to enforce it against clergymen would tend to defeat its original purpose. Therefore, he believed, justice dictated that the law must not be used against churches and ministers.

This reasoning may well have been sufficient to dispose of the case. But Brewer went on with an elaborate argument, mostly from history, to demonstrate that since the colonial era the Americans were a religious people and that the United States was a Christian nation.[23] Since that time religious zealots have seized upon the decision as proof that the Supreme Court had proclaimed the United States to be a Christian nation. Advocates of the separation of church and state are probably on better grounds arguing otherwise.[24] Brewer's "Christian nation" remarks have every appearance of *obiter dicta*. And the single headnote preceding the published opinion mentions only the points necessary for holding that the contract labor law applied solely to manual laborers.

In the *Holy Trinity* opinion Brewer was obviously anxious to allow the church to escape the charge of law-breaking. He was noticeably less sympathetic to other defendants in criminal cases for which he wrote opinions, most notably in cases coming from the court of Fort Smith's notorious "hanging judge." Among the letters written to President Harrison recommending the appointment of Brewer to the High Bench was one by Isaac C. Parker, judge of the federal court for the western district of Arkansas.[25] Brewer's elevation to the Court was to give Parker a highly placed ally. For years there was no right of appeal from his verdicts in Indian Territory cases, and the number of hangings he ordered is legendary. But in 1889 Congress permitted appeals from the lower federal courts to the Supreme Court in capital cases. From 1890 until 1896 (when Congress stripped Parker's court of its Indian Territory jurisdiction) the Supreme Court reviewed forty-four of his death sentences and reversed thirty-one of them.[26] Even at a time when appellate courts were not known for sensitivity to defendants' rights, the Court would not countenance the high-handed procedures of the notorious judge sitting at Fort Smith.

Brewer proved to be Parker's only consistent friend on the Supreme Court. In case after case he voted to uphold the "hanging judge's" verdicts and usually found himself dissenting from the reversals ordered by his brethren. Often he dissented without opinion, but occasionally, as in his dissent in *Brown* v. *United States*, he forthrightly showed his support of Parker's hard line: "[T]he testimony in this case discloses an outrageous crime [that is, the killing of two law officers]. . . . Justice and the protection of society unite in saying that it is high time that such a crime be punished."[27] Of the decisions upholding Parker, Brewer wrote the Court's opinion in four. In one of them even he felt compelled to criticize "the careless way which prevails in the Western District of Arkansas."[28]

Other than the appeals from Parker's court, Brewer and his colleagues seldom had to deal with criminal matters, thanks largely to the establishment of the circuit courts of appeal. But one of the first in which he participated was *In re Neagle*, the famous case involving the 1889 attack by David Terry upon Justice Field. The Court ruled that in killing Terry, Deputy United States Marshal Neagle was carrying out his lawful responsibilities as a federal officer. Brewer joined the majority, whose opinion was written by Miller; Field, of course, disqualified himself. Lamar and Fuller dissented.[29] For years the decision was denounced for its broad implications for the expansion of federal power.

Three cases concerning the Constitution's prohibition of state *ex post facto* laws further illustrate Brewer's antipathy toward those accused of crimes. When the Court, speaking through Miller, declared a Colorado murder statute to be an *ex post facto* law, Brewer, joined by Bradley, voiced his sharp disagreement. He believed that the grounds upon which the majority had voided the law were "trifling," and he fretted that the decision allowed "a convicted murderer to escape the death he deserves and to be turned loose on society."[30]

A provision in the constitution of the new state of Utah permitted eight-man jury trials of persons accused of committing felonies while Utah was still a territory. Brewer, without opinion, dissented from his brethren's ruling that this was an *ex post facto* law.[31] His views did, however, prevail in *Hawker* v. *New York*, wherein the Court (except for Harlan, Peckham, and McKenna) agreed with him that a statute prohibiting persons convicted of a felony from practicing medicine was not an *ex post facto* measure.[32]

Another example of Brewer's less-than-lenient approach to defendants' rights is his dissent in *Bram* v. *United States*. The majority ruled that a sailor's confession to murder had not been "freely and voluntarily made." Brewer, joined by Fuller and Brown, felt that "the fact that the defendant was in custody and in irons does not destroy the competency of a confession."[33]

In a rare instance of favoring a defendant, *Bassett* v. *United States*, Brewer's opinion for the majority found that the wife of a man accused of polygamy could not testify against him. The law, he explained, permitted a wife's testimony if the husband was accused of committing a crime against her person; in this case, however, the crime was not against her but rather against "the marital relation."[34]

The century closed with the brief war between the United States and Spain. Brewer would later have much to say about America's acquisition of former Spanish colonies. But at the close of the conflict he and his brethren were more immediately faced with several cases concerning vessels captured in the course of the war. In determining whether they had been lawfully condemned as prizes of war, the Court was usually divided. Brewer showed no tendency to vote consistently either for or against condemnation.[35] He was of the majority in a five-to-three decision that denied Admiral George Dewey's claim for prize money in addition to what he had already been awarded for his victory at Manila Bay.[36]

As he had done in his other judicial positions, Brewer, in writing opinions for the nation's highest tribunal, frequently made known his views on the proper functioning of the bench and the bar. In one case he deplored a brief presented to the Court in which counsel cast "aspersions on the conduct of opposing counsel." He firmly reprimanded the offending attorney, reminding him that "language used in briefs, as well as that employed in oral argument, must be respectful."[37]

The United States Court of Claims denied the widow of a federal court commissioner payment for her late husband's services because he had used his office for partisan purposes, that is, striking the names of several persons from a roll of voters in Louisiana. In upholding the Court of Claims' decision, Brewer made known the Court's indignation over the deceased's misuse of judicial power: "The very thought of a judicial office is that its functions are not partisan or political, and that he who occupies such office stands indifferent to all questions of party success." The commissioner's abuses were "abhorrent to the true and reasonable understanding of the conditions of judicial action."[38]

Justice was served, he believed, when judges could admit their own mistakes, as he himself did in an opinion concurring with a decision delivered by his uncle: "I had supposed the law to be otherwise. . . . I am glad to know that I was mistaken, and that the law is as it is now adjudged to be."[39]

On at least two occasions it is apparent that he was not to be swayed by either the fame of someone arguing before the Court or the relationship of an attorney to one of the justices. He wrote the majority opinion in a case in which the former president, Grover Cleveland, appeared as counsel—and lost. And when Aaron P. Jetmore, the husband of his daughter Harriet, argued a case before the Supreme Court, he too lost, not even receiving the vote of his father-in-law.[40]

As with other Supreme Court justices before and since, Brewer often used his dissenting opinions to chastise his colleagues for failures to follow the law's most fundamental precepts. For example, in disagreeing with the majority view in a tariff case, he stated that "a change in the personnel of a court should not mean a shift in the law. *Stare decisis* is the rule, and not the exception."[41]

His concern for more efficiency in government was not confined to the federal judiciary, as is seen in an opinion that contributed to a more businesslike operation of the federal legislative branch. Before Thomas B. Reed became Speaker of the House of Representatives in 1889, members of Congress used the lower house's antiquated and confusing rules to delay or kill proposed legislation. A favorite tactic was for members of the House not to answer their names when the roll was called, thereby preventing a quorum. Reed successfully forced changes in procedure by refusing to entertain "dilatory motions" and by counting all members present for determining a quorum. Objections to the "Reed rules" were an important element of a case before the Supreme Court in 1890, in which it was argued that the tariff act of 1890 had not been legally passed. Brewer's opinion for the majority upheld the Reed rule for determining quorums.[42] It is somewhat ironic that Brewer would sanction a change that streamlined the work of Congress and thus facilitate the growth of centralization.

In the last year of the nineteenth century, Brewer summed up to a reporter the work of the Court since his arrival ten and a half years earlier. When he took his seat in 1889, the Court had 1,500 cases on the docket, "an overwhelming amount of work." He gave credit to the new circuit courts of appeals for helping to reduce the number to 304 by 1899 and pointed out that only 27 of those had been filed before the beginning of that year. Brewer was pleased to note that the Supreme Court was now "only a year behind in its business."

When the reporter asked the justice if he liked the work, Brewer unhesitatingly replied "Immensely." "It's a student's life," he explained. "There are neither witnesses nor jurors to worry the justices. Everything submitted to the court is printed. The justices study the papers and pass opinions on them, without worry and without haste. That is why I say it is a student's life."[43]

9

ROSTRUM AND FIRESIDE
Off-the-Bench Activity, 1890–1900

Brewer's description of Supreme Court work as "a student's life" must not give the impression that he was a cloistered scholar in the years from 1889 to 1900. His off-the-bench activities, both social and professional, were numerous and varied. In fact, he was the most visible and widely known member of the Fuller Court.

The public's acquaintance with Brewer resulted as much from his platform appearances as from his judicial work. He had been an accomplished orator before taking his place on the Supreme Court. As a youth in New England, he had been mightily impressed with the magnetic temperance lecturer, John B. Gough. He began developing his own speaking skills early in his career. Soon after arriving in Washington, a city filled with forensic talent, he gained a reputation "as one of the most interesting and eloquent speakers."[1]

His appreciation of oratory led also to his editorship of a ten-volume set of *The World's Best Orations*, published in 1899. The selections ranged from Demosthenes to William Jennings Bryan. He told an interviewer that the project "entailed a great deal of labor." As for his own tastes, he found Edmund Burke "ornate and diffuse"; the Earl of Chatham was "perhaps the greatest of English orators." Brewer observed that oratory was declining in American courts, which, in the appellate courts, he said, was just as well.[2] Another ten-volume set, *The World's Best Essays*, also edited by him, appeared in 1900.[3]

Brewer became well known to the public also through his willingness to grant interviews to newspapers and to write for periodicals. He spoke and wrote not only because he enjoyed it but also because these activities sometimes yielded fees—welcome supplements to his salary. Unlike some of his fellow justices, he had not been born to a wealthy family, had not married into one, and, as a career judge, had never had a lucrative private practice. He needed more than his annual salary of ten thousand dollars to live well in Washington. Also contributing to his need for extra income were the hard times of the 1890s; in 1896 he learned that the Kansas Land Investment and Improvement Company, a concern into which he had put fifteen hundred dollars, had failed.[4]

Some of his colleagues were unhappy that he sought to add to his income by speaking and writing. They were even more displeased by his willingness to comment publicly on controversial questions of the day, including some of those dealt with by the Court.

Of his many public utterances in the 1890s, four are especially remembered today. They have since been frequently quoted or anthologized, usually to support the charge that the Fuller Court, and Brewer in particular, opposed reform.

The first of these major addresses was given to the graduating class of Yale's law school in 1891. His theme was "Protection to Private Property from Public Attack."[5] Government, he said, had the responsibility to protect all property, large and small. The "public attacks" on property to which he referred were mainly in the form of taxation, eminent domain, and the police power. Brewer acknowledged that all three were legitimate governmental powers but subject to abuse. He took particular aim at the police power, which was "undefined and perhaps indefinable." It was the duty of jurists, he insisted, to see to it that the power was not misused or extended into the wrong areas, as had been the case in the *Munn* decision. "[The police power] is the refuge of timid judges to escape the obligations of denouncing a wrong, in a case in which some supposed general and public good is the object of legislation."[6]

In the course of his remarks, he made the surprising statement that the proposal that all property be forfeited to the state at death, by means of a prohibition of inheritances, was an idea "worthy of most serious consideration." Under such a system (which Andrew Carnegie also advocated) "personal toil and accumulation" would be the basis of American aristocracy, not "accident of birth." He concluded by predicting the coming of "great social changes," including "a more equal distribution of the wealth of the world, and the elimination of the pauper from our midst."[7]

The tone and content of his address before the New York State Bar Association in 1893 were similar to those of the Yale address.[8] In it Brewer denounced what he called "The Movement of Coercion." Once again the emphasis was on threats to property. He began by noting that wealth was always concentrated "in the hands of a few, while the many subsist upon the proceeds of their daily toil. But security is the chief end of government; and other things being equal, the government is best which protects to the fullest extent each individual, rich or poor, high or low, in the possession of his property and the pursuit of his business."[9]

Threats to property, he said, violated the Eighth and Tenth Commandments, which forbid stealing and the coveting of property. His first example of a major threat was "the improper use of labor organizations to destroy the freedom of the laborer and control uses of capital." Strikes usually meant not only quitting work but also limiting the employer's use of his own property and perhaps preventing him from discharging a duty to the public, for example, the operation of a railroad. Striking workers, moreover, used violence and intimidation to prevent those who wanted to work from doing so. Small wonder, he said, "that deeds of violence and cruelty attend such demonstrations as these."[10]

Brewer's other example of a major threat to property-owning Americans was rampant overregulation. Here too he criticized the *Munn* doctrine, which subjected to regulation all property in which the public had an interest: "[I]f there be any property in the use of which the public or some portion of it has no interest, I can hardly know what it is or where to find it." Also pernicious to him was the practice of "reducing charges for the use of property, which in fact is subject to a public use [for example, railroads], that no compensation or income is received by those who have so invested their property."[11] Here he was echoing his *Budd* dissent and his *Ames* decision.

He made it clear that he considered neither labor unions nor business regulation to be bad in themselves. "Indeed the great danger is in the fact that there is so much of good in them." Labor unions "are the needed and proper complement of capital organizations," for they checked "the unscrupulous rapacity which dominates much of capital" and gave working people the strength needed to contend with their employers, which as individual laborers they did not have.

Also legitimate and "commendable" was state regulation of businesses that were truly devoted to a public use.[12]

Much of the remainder of his remarks was on the need for an independent and fearless judiciary to protect property from unwarranted assaults. He saw the forces who attacked property as the same forces who attacked the judiciary. Courts, he argued, could not only protect property but were also as capable of dealing with labor disputes and railroad rates as any arbitrators, commissions, or other supposed experts: "[T]he the great body of judges are as well versed in affairs as any." Judges, moreover, "unlike commissions and boards of arbitration, are concerned primarily with justice, not the profit or welfare of one party or the public. This is the way it should be."[13]

A few months later, in a letter unsuccessfully urging Harrison to accept the New York bar association's invitation to be the next year's speaker, Brewer spoke glowingly of his own experience: "I met many of the leading lawyers of the state, had a brilliant audience . . . & look back upon it as a red-letter day."[14]

In the year following this speech came the Pullman troubles and the *Debs* decision. In an address before the Marquette Club of Chicago in 1898, Brewer stoutly responded to those who were denouncing "government by injunction."[15] "I am as much opposed to government by judges as any man. . . . But the writ of injunction is not an act of legislation. . . . It only enforces rights which the constitution and law have heretofore declared sacred. . . . The great strike of which this city was the historic center attests the wisdom of judicial interference." The name of Circuit Judge William B. Woods, who issued the injunction during the Pullman Boycott, would be "revered and honored through the coming ages." Brewer admitted that the Supreme Court was not infallible ("I know it is often wrong—it frequently overrules me") but it was better "to suffer the injuries which come from its occasional mistakes than the marvelous wrong which would flow from the attempt to settle all questions of right and wrong, of power or the lack of power, by mere numbers of the accumulation of majorities."[16]

Replying to protests over yet another controversial decision was the occasion for the fourth of his major speeches of the nineties, entitled "The Income Tax Cases."[17] Although Brewer had written no opinions in either of the *Pollock* cases, he forthrightly defended the final result in this address before the law graduates of the University of Iowa in 1898. He praised Fuller's opinion as "among the great historic opinions of the court" and "majestic and immortal."[18] Unlike Field's concurring opinion in the first *Pollock* case, in which Field damned the income tax as part of an "assault upon capital," and the attorney who had argued against the tax, who had used similarly alarmist rhetoric, Brewer said he opposed the tax not only upon constitutional grounds but also because it represented the tendency toward greater centralization of power and a corresponding decline of state and local power. He suggested that the Framers had inserted into the Constitution the apportionment requirement for direct taxes in order to discourage such taxation.[19]

Brewer agreed that the rich were not bearing their "proper burden of taxation" but urged that the remedy was with the states: "If [state] laws are so illy contrived or so carelessly enforced, that the rich escape while the poor man pays, it is your privilege and your duty to readjust those laws and inspire a more zealous sense of duty in the taxing officers, so that all property within the state shall bear its equal and just share of taxation."[20] He even allowed that a *state* income tax might be an effective way of taxing wealth. As for those who still felt that a federal income tax was desirable (and he certainly indicated that he did not believe that it was), he suggested that the proper means for implementing it was by adopting an amendment to the Constitution that would give Congress the clear power to tax incomes.[21] This was done three years after Brewer's death, with the ratification of the Sixteenth Amendment.

In addition to those four widely known addresses, he gave many others during the decade. In those less widely circulated speeches he reiterated the themes of the major ones, often assailing the enemies of property as anarchists and socialists. He pointed out that legislation based upon the "apparently illimitable" police power was not always for the benefit of the public at large. For example, he told a Rhode Island church group that "oleomargarine is prohibited, not inspected, and all because some farmer wants a market for his rancid butter."[22]

Yet he announced his support for a number of genuine reform efforts. To the 1895 meeting of the Kansas State Bar Association he offered "Some Thoughts about Kansas."[23] Kansas, he allowed, was known as a land of radicals and cranks, even supplanting New England in this regard. He hastened to add that this was cause for pride, not alarm, because radicals and cranks brought benefits to humanity. He gave John Brown as an early Kansas example. More recently Kansas was advancing women's rights—a movement Brewer heartily approved—and was showing the rest of the nation the blessings of temperance.[24]

Brewer even had some kind words for the Populists, who, in a coalition with the Democrats, had been enjoying political success in Kansas. He told the Kansas lawyers that the "central thought" of Populism was "emancipation from the domination of money, the elimination from society of classes based upon wealth." Of course, he gave his usual warnings about the excesses of reformist crusades but went on to condemn the "often selfish, remorseless, and cruel" actions of corporations and the dangers that their monopolistic ways presented to the individual.[25]

At a Fourth of July celebration in 1893 at Woodstock, Connecticut, he told the audience that while combinations of capital and labor brought benefits, they also brought about a loss of liberty. In addition, he explained to his eastern listeners that Populism was a movement of ordinarily conservative farmers who were demanding radical change, not out of selfishness but from the conviction, "erroneous though it may be, that wealth is the creature of law, and that regulating all human actions by law will work such a change as to make wealth the equal inheritance of all, instead of recompense of superior toil and brain." Although he believed a few Populist leaders were dishonest, he felt most had sincere objections to present injustices. Brewer sympathized with their goal of a better distribution of material things but feared that they were ignoring the "lessons of history" and that their programs would lead to socialism.[26]

Despite his hostility to socialism, he told one group that "[t]here is nothing which more inclines me to the doctrines of the socialist than a sight of those loafing sons of wealth, who seem to live with no other object than to waste time, and to spend that money which their fathers have earned." Such drones were to him worse than "lazy tramps."[27]

At the other extreme were three minorities, the blacks, Indians, and the Chinese, whose shameful treatment by the majority elicited a scolding from Brewer: "[W]ithin our borders by virtue of an earlier right, through our compulsion, or at our solicitation, are to-day the three despised races of America—races whom to wrong is for so many a habit, whom to plunder and oppress is justified by our greed and their weakness."[28]

As we have seen, he was consistently supportive of the Chinese. Although he professed to deplore the South's successful efforts to disfranchise the blacks and to virtually nullify the Fifteenth Amendment, he argued that the resistance to the amendment demonstrated the futility of forcing changes where they were not wanted. On those grounds he warned against any attempt to impose women's suffrage nationally through a constitutional amendment.[29]

At the close of the century, he spoke of the changes that he hoped to see in the next century: the end of the "maladjustment of social conditions" and the "fearful inequality between accumulated wealth on the one side and abject poverty on the other." He looked forward to an era "when poverty shall vanish from the face of the earth" and "when wealth shall have lost its social power, and manhood be the single test of social distinction."[30]

Thus far we see that Brewer's approval of reform was either couched in general terms or, as in the case of business regulation, greatly qualified. But there was one movement gathering momentum in the 1890s in which he became a conspicuous and dedicated participant: peace.

Earlier in the nineteenth century, pacifist sects and antiwar organizations of a general nature, such as the American Peace Society, had characterized the movement in the United States. In the 1890s, by which time arbitration of international disputes had long been practiced in American diplomacy, many conservative leaders embraced this device as a favorite remedy for preventing armed conflict. The arbitration movement gained much popular support in the last years of the century. David Dudley Field, Brewer's uncle and a leading spokesman for arbitration, proudly announced in 1893 that the United States was doing more than any other nation to advance the cause of arbitration.[31]

The practice appealed strongly to Brewer's judicial temperament. As early as 1871, in a proposal for a "Woolsey Professorship of International Law" at Yale, he wrote: "An international court supported by the public opinion of the world, and arbitrating all questions between nations, is something more than a flitting vision of fanatic or madman."[32]

His attachment to the movement is more evident in the early

1890s. The press of court business prevented his acceptance of an invitation to attend the Lake Mohonk conference on arbitration in 1895, but for the next several years he regularly participated in its annual gatherings.[33]

That summer he addressed the American Bar Association in Detroit. His remarks on arbitration were especially well received. He noted the growing number of successful arbitrations and the progress being made toward the establishment of a world tribunal to adjudicate international conflicts.[34] Notions of a world federation or a "parliament of man" were, he argued, impractical dreams; a more realistic way to insure peace was adjudication by international courts. The lawyer and the judge, he told his appreciative audience, would lead the way.[35]

Soon thereafter Brewer had the opportunity to put his faith into action. The Cleveland administration, in an effort to goad Great Britain into accepting arbitration to settle the disputed boundary between Venezuela and British Guiana, persuaded Congress to establish a commission, consisting of lawyers, jurists, and scholars, to investigate the question. Congress appropriated $100,000 to finance the commission. To it Cleveland appointed: Brewer, Richard H. Alvey, chief justice of the Court of Appeals of the District of Columbia; F. R. Coudert of the New York bar; D. C. Gilman, geographer and president of Johns Hopkins University; and Andrew D. White, historian and diplomatist.

The other members unanimously elected Brewer as the commission's president. Severo Mallet-Prevost, an authority on international law, became its secretary. The commission and its staff of experts began poring over a mass of documentary evidence in their offices in the *Sun* building on Washington's F Street. When it became apparent that their findings would be detrimental to the British claims, Britain agreed to arbitration. In November, Secretary of State Richard Olney requested the commission to suspend its labors, which it did.[36]

In submitting their four-volume report, Brewer and the other commissioners pointed out that the boundary question had created "no little bitterness of feeling between the people of Great Britain and the United States" and that there had been talk of war. The commissioners took pride in the influence of their work in bringing about arbitration and in allaying fears of war. They expressed the hope that their findings would facilitate the work of the arbitral tribunal.[37]

Another source of satisfaction was, as Brewer told his daughter Etta, that "Uncle Sam will pay me a good sum for my Venezuela work."[38] While he was busy with the commission, his Supreme Court colleagues handed down the *Plessy* v. *Ferguson* decision.

Britain and Venezuela signed an arbitration treaty in February of 1897. Under its terms a five-man tribunal would convene, hear the arguments, sift the evidence, and reach a decision with which the two nations would abide. The treaty further stipulated that the Supreme Court of the United States and the government of Venezuela were each to appoint a member to the tribunal and the Judicial Committee of Britain's Privy Council would select two members; the fifth man would be chosen by the other four. The Supreme Court chose Brewer, and the president of Venezuela named Fuller. The British selected Lord Chancellor Herschell, who soon died and was replaced by Lord Chief Justice Russell of Killowen, and Sir Richard Henn Collins, Lord Justice of Appeals. Since these men were unable to agree on the fifth member, the King of Norway and Sweden, as provided for in the 1897 treaty, named the distinguished Russian diplomat and jurist, Frederic de Martens.[39]

Venezuela appointed Benjamin Harrison as its chief counsel. The former president wrote to his friend Brewer, discreetly inquiring just how much evidence there was to master.[40] To assist him in preparing the arguments for Venezuela were Mallet-Prevost and two others. Britain's legal team was headed by Sir Richard Webster.[41]

Since the tribunal was to undertake its arbitral labors in Paris, this meant that Brewer and Fuller had to take time out from a busy docket. But both men were strongly committed to the cause of arbitration and saw the Anglo-Venezuelan treaty as an important opportunity for advancing it.

Brewer, accompanied by daughter Bessie and Mallet-Prevost, sailed across the Atlantic on the *Majestic* in January of 1899. After a comfortable voyage they reached London by January 19. From there he sent Etta news of their safe arrival.[42] Brewer, other members of the tribunal, and the attorneys for both sides attended dinners and held discussions. Then they departed for Paris to attend to preliminary details. There it was agreed that the tribunal would reconvene in May. Leaving Bessie in Paris, he returned to the United States temporarily, sailing on the *Etruria*.[43]

Stormy seas marred the voyage and caused Brewer "pain and anxiety" but not seasickness. Through the ordeal he found "comfort and strength" by recalling the black group that had sung "God be with you 'till we meet again" for the African Methodist Episcopal bishop aboard the *Majestic* prior to its departure.[44]

By June Brewer and the other arbitrators had reassembled in Paris to receive the formal written and oral arguments. In addition to the mass of maps and documents collected earlier by the American commission, other historical and cartographic evidence was piled up before the tribunal. The proceedings dragged on through an unusually hot summer into the fall. To accomplish his tasks, Brewer stayed with his customary work habits, which included arising before dawn. The porter at his hotel was suspicious of his early departures because Parisians preferred to begin the working day much later in the morning.[45]

To relieve the tedious business, there were rounds of dinner parties. The American members found still other diversions: Fuller took his first automobile ride, and Brewer visited the city's impressive marketplace. The retrial of Alfred Dreyfuss, taking place also in Paris at that time, provided the world with more drama than the resolution of the Anglo-Venezuelan question.[46]

The final settlement proved a disappointment for Brewer and Venezuela. According to a posthumous statement by Mallet-Prevost, Martens desired a unanimous decision and gave in to British pressure in order to get one. Mallet-Prevost wrote that in late summer he received word from Brewer and Fuller that they wished to see him. When he arrived at their hotel, an agitated Brewer gave him the bad news: Martens had apparently struck a deal with the two British members, who would settle only for an award that gave their country virtually all of the territory in dispute. Brewer and Fuller had the choice of filing a minority report or going along. They chose to do the latter but not until they had wrung some concessions for Venezuela, namely, control of the Orinoco River. Britain came away with about ninety percent of the disputed area, including valuable gold lands.[47]

The decision was publicly announced in a terse statement on October 4, 1899, which said nothing about the reasoning behind it.

Brewer's comments to the press indicated his less than enthusiastic support of it. He said that the tribunal reached its conclusions at the last minute, after any agreement seemed all but impossible, and that it was a compromise with which none of the members were entirely satisfied: "[W]e had to adjust our different views, and finally to draw a line running between what each of us thought right."[48]

For their work Brewer and Fuller received seventy-five hundred dollars each from the government of Venezuela, plus an additional three thousand dollars each.[49] Although disappointed with the settlement, Brewer could console himself with the knowledge that war had been averted. Also, the experience strengthened his conviction that arbitration was the best means of solving quarrels between nations.

Severely impairing his optimism for a pacific world was the bellicose mood of his own countrymen in the 1890s. Numerous American politicians, journalists, intellectuals, and other public figures were preaching the desirability and necessity of war—war with anybody and for any reason. Oliver Wendell Holmes, Jr., who was to join Brewer on the Supreme Court in 1902, is a prominent example of a fin de siècle exponent of the benefits of war.[50] Brewer stoutly opposed all glorification of war. Even when addressing the cadets at West Point during the dedication of a battle monument in 1897, he reminded them that their highest duty was to be "defenders of law and the guardians of peace."[51]

He openly ridiculed patriotic and veterans' societies that were whipping up the war spirit. Such organizations "must have their local branches, and each with a roster of officials startling in number and amusing with the magnificence of their titles; presidents and president generals and honorary presidents. . . . It seems sometimes as though the dictionary had been ransacked not merely to find titles but adjectives to adorn those titles."[52]

As tensions between Spain and the United States mounted in the later 1890s, Brewer voiced the belief that war was not likely since Spain could not hope to conquer and hold any portion of American soil.[53] Such wishful thinking was no match for American demands for military action against Spain. When war did come, he damned it with faint praise. He believed it to be justified only because of Spanish atrocities and by the freeing of Cuba.[54]

After the fighting began, Brewer told his countrymen that America's strength lay "not so much in its army and navy as its public schools", and warned against "the dazzle of military glory." He spoke also of his anxiety over the talk of seizing the Philippines, Cuba, and Puerto Rico. The nation, he believed, would be far better off if it let the oceans continue to separate the new world from the old and ceased looking beyond her borders for wrongs to make right; instead, Americans should use their energy to promote domestic reform and commercial and industrial advancement. "So doing we shall make the United States the mightiest of nations, mightier than Great Britain with her navy, than Germany with her soldiers, than Russia with all her vastness of territory; mightier through the might of a great and bold example and thus more than in any way hasten the day when the tramp of the armed battalion and the boom of the destroying cannon shall no more be heard, and peace shall fill the earth with the blessed sunlight of heaven."[55]

His grudging endorsement of the war did not include acceptance of the imperial expansion resulting from the conflict. He frequently and vigorously denounced his country's venture in imperialism. Even before the peace treaty was signed, he told an interviewer that American ownership of Puerto Rico and the Philippines would be contrary to the nation's traditional opposition to government by force and would weaken the Monroe Doctrine.[56]

Once the former Spanish possessions became United States property, Brewer inveighed against American participation in European-style colonialism. In a magazine article he wrote of his difficulty understanding how the Constitution—written by men who had overthrown colonial rule—could be interpreted so as to grant power to Congress "to hold other people in like colonial subjection."[57]

His major statement on the war and the acquisition of the Spanish islands was an address before the Liberal Club on February 16, 1899, in Buffalo, entitled "The Spanish War: A Prophecy or an Exception?" In it he conceded that the war was waged mostly for humanitarian reasons, but he noted other less praiseworthy causes: threats to American commercial relations and investments; the "tempestuous utterances of those jingo orators who shouted for war but never enlisted"; and of course the desire for military glory.[58] As the title of the address suggests, Brewer hoped that the war and its imperialistic aftermath were aberrations, not portents of things to come, and that the United States would not seek other wars or more colonies to govern by force.

The main theme of the Buffalo address was anti-imperialism, but throughout his remarks he emphasized peace and opposition to militarism: "[I]s there not such a thing as overdoing this getting ready for war? I have noticed that a man who goes about with a chip on his shoulder is very apt to have many quarrels, but the gentleman who minds his own business is ordinarily let alone and goes through life without a fight." He noted the irony in the fact that at the close of the century "the head of the most arbitrary government in the civilized world, the Czar of the Russias, is inviting the nations of the world to decrease their arms, while this, the freest land, is proposing to increase its." Brewer told his audience that the acquiring of colonies brought about an enlarged military establishment.[59]

As for the argument that the United States needed overseas coaling stations, he pointed out that the nation had survived and prospered without any, that Dewey achieved his victory without one, and that if such were needed, why was it necessary to have one the size of New England (that is, Hawaii)? "I know of but one place that needs such a large coaling station and that is a place we all hope eternally to avoid."[60]

At the end of the nineteenth century Brewer predicted that the coming century would bring a better day for mankind: [P]eace, with its white wings, hovers everywhere in the air," even though "the steady arming of the world goes on and the great battalions and huge armaments increase."[61] Had he not added these qualifying words he would appear impossibly naive because the first years of the century were marked by the increase of tensions that were to culminate in the outbreak of World War I.

Brewer's religious convictions much influenced his positions on the issues of the day. And religion itself played a major role in his public and private lives. On Sunday, November 9, 1890, he united with the First Congregational Church of Washington. A week later he addressed his fellow parishioners. Recognizing that some of them might feel that it was inappropriate for a lawyer to address them from the pulpit, he announced his belief that "the law and the gospel ought always to go together."[62] Throughout his Washington years he regularly taught Sunday school at his church. His favorite topic for leading the classes was the life of Christ.[63] At the church, in 1892, he addressed the annual meeting of the American Home Missionary Society. Without mentioning the *Holy Trinity* opinion by name or himself as its author, he made the debatable statement that "[t]his is a Christian nation. Such is the declaration of your highest court."[64]

Brewer, the son of a missionary, wholeheartedly supported efforts to spread Christianity outside the United States. He was a life member of the American Bible Society, an organization dedicated to reaching non-Christians by translating the Bible into many languages and distributing it throughout the globe. In 1896 he became a corporate member of the American Board of Commissioners for Foreign Missions.[65] He even departed from his usual antimilitary, anti-imperialist stance and endorsed American military actions in China during the Boxer Rebellion because the rebels threatened American missionaries there.[66] No doubt recognizing that not all Americans abroad were model Christians, in 1896 he became a member of the Seaman's Friend Society, an organization for instilling higher morals in sailors.[67]

As one of the nation's most prominent Protestant lay figures, he accepted an invitation to speak before the students of Yale's Divinity Department on April 2, 1897. He advised the budding ministers to be businesslike in their personal dealings by paying debts promptly and to keep from becoming objects of charity. Brewer also urged them to avoid too much theology and cold abstractions when speaking to their congregations: "Do not give a lecture, but preach. . . . [L]eave your manuscript at home and talk to us."[68]

In 1899 he gave an address to three groups (two of them religious organizations), which was entitled "The Twentieth Century from Another Viewpoint." In published form it enjoyed wide circulation. In it he touched upon a number of themes, but mostly his thoughts were on religion and its future in the upcoming century. "Greater unity in Christian life," he predicted, would mark the new century. His examples of growing unity were the Young Men's Christian Association, the Christian Endeavor Society, Chautauqua assemblies, and the work of Cardinal James Gibbons and Archbishop Patrick John Ryan. Secondly, he prophesied that "the coming century will be noted for greater economy in Christian work"; as in his talk to the Yale divinity students, he advocated more businesslike practices in the administration of church affairs. He felt certain that the "marvelous" material and moral progress made in the nineteenth century would continue "with accelerating speed" in the twentieth.[69]

Brewer spoke also of "two truths": there was an "infinite being" behind the material world, and Christ was "the incarnation of the infinite . . . bearing to us the message of peace and hope and the promise of eternal life."[70] Toward the end of the address he warned against overreliance on sumptuary legislation as a means of improving society: "The Master taught a more excellent way," which was "not to fill the statutes with prohibitions, but to reach the individual and strengthen his character."[71]

Almost equaling Brewer's faith in Christianity was his faith in the American legal system. Here too, though, he made suggestions for improvement. In 1894 he published his thoughts on patent law reform. He defended the practice of patenting inventions: granting exclusive rights to the inventor for a limited time rewarded and encouraged creativity. But too many worthless patents were being issued, and as proof he pointed out that the Supreme Court seldom sustained a contested patent. To remedy this he suggested that instead of *ex parte* hearings, patent applications should be subjected to judicial hearings, with the federal government (representing the public) contesting every application approved by the Patent Office.

Brewer believed that the real troubles began *after* a patent had been issued; many an inventor had to sell his rights to a large corporation because he was too poor to pay the legal fees when a patent was contested. Often this meant that the inventor received little, while the corporation enjoyed a profitable monopoly, which in turn burdened the public. His proposed solution was to avoid costly litigation for the inventor by prohibiting testimony by experts, who were expensive and biased; patent attorneys usually had enough knowledge to present expert testimony themselves. Brewer would also require, for purposes of comparison, that models or copies of the invention be used in all litigation. Lastly, he proposed giving the inventor and his heirs a permanent, inalienable half interest in the patent in order to provide "a reasonable share in the benefit from his invention, and to prevent its being all monopolized by some wealthy purchaser." This plan would reduce "mere speculation in patents." In conclusion, he warned that the patent system had to be "radically reformed." If not, he predicted, the public, in anger over the monopolies bred by the unreformed system, would abolish patents entirely.[72]

Brewer's views on the patent system more truly show his economic biases than do his often-cited "Movement of Coercion" and "Protection to Private Property from Public Attack." His proposals for patent law reform show that his sympathies were for the innovative persons whose hard work, thoughts, and creations benefited society, and not with corporations whose sole concern was profit.

Brewer advocated changes not only in the laws but in the legal profession as well. His major statement in this regard was a paper read to the Section of Legal Education of the American Bar Association in 1895, which he entitled "A Better Education the Great Need of the Profession." He began by announcing that the lawyer, not the soldier nor the wealthy man with a "$200 silk night shirt," was the true leader in America.[73] Therefore, the lawyer and his profession, Brewer insisted, must adapt to the rapid and complex changes in American life. In addition to simpler legal procedures, less reliance on technicalities and artifice in pleading, and speedier handling of litigation, he called for limits on the right of appeal: "Terminate all review in one appellate court" and require parties seeking appeal to show that alleged errors in the trial court would make an actual difference in the result. "It may be said that this would make reversals difficult to obtain. They should be difficult." Too much reliance on appeals to higher courts, he argued, also detracted from local self-government and contributed to the dangerous drift toward centralization.

Yet he recognized that these reforms were "only mechanical."[74] As the title of the paper indicates, his main plea was for the improvement of legal education. Although he did not mention it, many lawyers even by that time had entered the profession not through training in a law school but by the informal process of "reading" the law; that is, by serving an apprenticeship with an established attorney. Brewer recognized that even formal education could be insufficient— his own, for example: "I hastened through my legal studies and was . . . declared fit to advise as to all rights and liabilities and to carry on any litigation before I was old enough to be entrusted with the right to vote. I appreciated the mistake when I attempted to practice, and I fear some of my clients became equally aware of the fact." Extending the course of study and stiffening the requirements for admission to the bar were his answers to the problem of ill-prepared lawyers. Too many lawyers were simply unfit: "It would be a blessing if some Noachian deluge would engulf half of those who have a license to practice."[75]

Brewer made a more direct contribution to legal education. By the end of the century he was teaching courses in corporation and international law at Columbian (now George Washington) University, an activity he vastly enjoyed. He found the students' questions stimulating and announced that it was "a satisfaction to . . . be able to do them some good."[76]

Outspoken though he was on public issues, Brewer, as a member of the nation's highest court, was careful about speaking out on partisan political matters. Privately, however, he occasionally let his feelings be known. Following the 1892 election, in which the Democrats were victorious and Kansas went Populist, he commented to daughter Etta that "we got badly thrashed in the election. Still it don't interfere with my work or my pay. Mrs. Fuller is of course jubilant—Uncle Stephen quite the reverse."[77] Justice Field, although a Democrat, had hated Cleveland, the victor in the 1892 presidential election, ever since they had fallen out over California patronage during Cleveland's first term.[78]

After the Republicans returned to national power in the election of 1896, Brewer spoke of the defeated Democratic presidential candidate in complimentary terms: "I have known Mr. Bryan personally for a great many years, and he is a pleasant man, and a dangerous one, too, to meet in an argument."[79] In a letter to his daughters from Paris in 1899, he was less complimentary: "I should judge from the little American news to be found in papers here that there was getting to be some trouble in political affairs. I hope it don't mean Bryan in 1900."[80]

There were some who believed Brewer himself should be elected president. This boom, such as it was, arose in 1896 when he was receiving increased national attention through his work on the Venezuelan boundary commission. It was mostly confined to some of his fellow Kansans, notably Albert H. Horton.[81] Even this small band had doubts about Brewer's eligibility to become president: the Constitution requires that the president be a natural-born citizen. Brewer himself was interested enough in the talk about the presidency to inquire about the latter point. According to Mayor George B. McClellan, Jr., of New York (who had presidential aspirations and was also foreign-born), Brewer told him that he asked the other members of the Court if they thought he was eligible. Making a distinction between "native-born" and "natural-born," they were unanimously of the opinion that he was not constitutionally barred from serving as chief executive.[82]

One of Brewer's remarks on political matters aroused the ire of the *New York Times*. When addressing the legislature of New York, he congratulated the lawmakers on their recent choice of Edward Murphy, Jr., for United States senator. A *Times* editorial fumed that Murphy's election came about because he had the support of Tammany boss Richard Croker and that Brewer's comment must have been either sarcastic or naive. "[I]f he was in earnest in saying what he deemed the polite thing on the occasion, he must be very ignorant of New York politics or must have derived from his Kansas experience a low idea of the qualifications necessary for United States Senators and the proper method of selecting them."[83]

His only other political activities of note were discrete attempts to secure federal jobs for others. He wrote President Harrison endorsing H. V. Hinckley of Topeka for chief of the commission to survey a proposed Pan-American railroad and Assistant Attorney General William A. Maury for justice of the supreme court of the District of Columbia. Later in the decade he wrote to President McKinley's secretary, supporting C. W. Ogden's bid for a district judgeship in Texas.[84]

Brewer much preferred the social affairs of Washington to its political ones. And at the center of his social life was his family. The Brewer household in Washington at first consisted of Lulu and three daughters. The eldest, Harriet, had married Aaron P. Jetmore in 1889. Etta became the bride of James Lawson Karrick in 1892, leaving only Fanny and Bessie at home. One of the many criticisms leveled at the federal judiciary over the years has been that the judges' social contacts tended to be with the wealthy and powerful, which removed them from the common people and their concerns. Certainly the Brewers moved within the upper reaches of Washington society. Brewer told Etta of her mother's lunching off gold plates with the wife of railroad magnate Senator Leland Stanford and of her dining with the president that same day.[85] Among others with whom they dined were Secretary of War Stephen B. Elkins (one of the principal figures in the Maxwell Land Grant Company) and George M. Pullman (whose labor policies triggered the Pullman Boycott, which in turn produced the *Debs* case).[86] In 1895 Brewer reported to Etta: "Last night I was at a dinner at Judge Shiras'. Saturday night I go to the Gridiron banquet, so you see I am getting my share of dissipation."[87] The Brewers hosted affairs of their own. For example, on December 21, 1893, they gave a tea in honor of Bessie's debut. The womenfolk of several prominent leaders attended.[88]

For relaxation Brewer went to the theater. A more democratic pleasure was strolling with the family pet, which he fondly referred to as "that *worthless* dog Rex."[89] He also enjoyed the lovely garden in the rear of their home, which he could view from his library in the basement. Leading to the library was a "dark and uncertain" stairway, which a newspaperman feared might "cause a vacancy some day on the bench." There Brewer did much of his work at a large three-sided desk.[90]

His only conspicuous vice was smoking cigars. Despite his poetical promise to smoke "my last cigar" when courting his "Anti-tobacco Friend Lulu Landon," he seems never to have broken the habit completely, much to the dismay of Lulu and the girls. When he stopped smoking in 1892—temporarily it turned out—Lulu wrote to Etta of the good news and suggested that she write "Papa" to congratulate him.[91] By 1896 he had quit again and complained to his daughters that "[t]his giving up tobacco is a terrible thing." He reported also that Justice Harlan had stopped chewing and smoking "and says now he is a *model man*."[92] Unfortunately for his despairing family, Brewer resumed smoking, for later newspaper accounts mentioned his habit.

In Leavenworth his friend Arthur Simmons produced "Our Judge" cigars, and the boxes in which they were sold featured Brewer's likeness. Once, when checking into the Copeland Hotel in Topeka, a bellboy asked him if he was the man who manufactured the cigars. A much amused Brewer replied affirmatively.[93]

A favorite means of escaping from the burdens of work was hunting in the Far West. Once, in Wyoming, the camp cook, a black man known as "Bill Goat," went berserk and threatened the hunting party with an axe. Brewer persuaded the others not to shoot him and bravely snatched the weapon out of his hand.[94]

On another of these expeditions, in the Medicine Bow range in Wyoming, his western informality brought about an amusing incident. His companions were W. H. Munger (later a federal district judge for Nebraska), Henry D. Estabrook (a Western Union attorney), and one or two others. The sheriff of Natrona County chanced upon their camp and heard one of the party call Brewer "Kansas

Dave," the nickname given him by the hunters. Brewer, "in a straggling growth of chin whiskers, wearing high topped boots, a blue flannel shirt, a broad-brimmed hat and a cartridge belt, looked about as much like a jurist as Dynamite Dick himself." The lawman grew suspicious and told Kansas Dave he was taking him to Casper for questioning about a recent robbery of the Union Pacific. Munger informed the sheriff that his suspect was Justice Brewer of the United States Supreme Court. "Ah, hell," retorted the lawman, "I seen his picture before I left town, and he's wanted for blowin' open an express car." When he pulled his gun on Brewer and reiterated his intention to take him into custody, the other hunters dissuaded him with "liberal drafts of our camp supply of snake bite antidote." Still convinced that the distinguished jurist was a desperado, the tipsy officer told the others as he rode off: "Him a jedge! Looks a devil of a sight more like an Arizona stage robber."[95]

Less dangerous were family vacations in Vermont, not far from Lulu's old home at Burlington. The family became part of "a small company of cottagers" who leased land at Thompson's Point, on Lake Champlain. The Brewers christened their cottage "Liberty Hall."[96] He published an article in a Vermont magazine in which he extolled the state's scenery and the character of its people.[97] Brewer regularly visited Kansas also. In 1892 he gave the address for the Republicans' annual observance of Kansas Day.[98] No matter how much he rubbed shoulders with the Washington elite, he still relished mingling with all classes of Kansas citizenry. Also close to his heart and the scene of occasional stays was Yale University. In 1893 he was elected president of its alumni association.[99]

These years, so full of achievement and honors, also brought on a large share of sorrow. Shortly before he addressed Philadelphia's Yale alumni chapter at a "Brewer dinner" in 1896, he learned that Fanny was critically ill in San Antonio, Texas.[100] She died of tuberculosis on May 11 at age twenty-five. He told of his grief in a letter to his wife and Etta: "Two weeks ago last night the little girl said 'good night & good bye'—I can not get used to it. Life seems very dark & vacant without her."[101] Adding to his burden was knowing how hard Fanny's death was on Lulu, who was then in Colorado. "Your mother's letter of Sunday came last night & I could not withhold tears as I read it. Poor woman, how lonely she feels & how the loss of our dear little Fanny does rest upon her."[102] He told Etta that he wanted to attend the Yale graduation and other gatherings because a "broken summer" would permit him to dwell less on the loss. Still, he felt a need to have several pictures of Fanny about the house.[103] At the beginning of 1897 he and Lulu declined a dinner invitation from President Cleveland because the death of their daughter meant that they would not be "going into society this season."[104]

On October 3, 1896, on the occasion of their thirty-fifth anniversary, Brewer penned a love letter to Lulu, saying that although she was no longer the "lithe & slender" bride of 1861, the years had given her face "a gentleness & sweetness which your husband at least sees, & which make you to him more beautiful than ever." He closed with: "My dear wife, God Bless you. If I have succeeded in life, your loyalty & devotion have made it possible. I have little of life before me, but my dying thought is of blessing to you." The letter was signed, "Lovingly, Dave."[105]

Brewer was certain that he would die before Lulu, and soon. But she passed away on April 3, 1898, a year and a half after her husband had written his tender sentiments. She was interred at Leavenworth's Mount Muncie Cemetery. Upon arrival back in Washington, Brewer sent a black-bordered note to Benjamin Harrison: "Have just returned from burying my dead. Have no heart to write."[106]

Death came also to three of his distinguished Field uncles in this decade. In 1890 he visited Cyrus W. Field in New York and wrote a three-stanza poem to commemorate the golden anniversary of Field's marriage (" 'Midst the music celestial hear the anthem of glory, / We twain are still one forever and aye.").[107] Two years later the father of the Atlantic cable was dead. In 1891 Brewer had suggested to Simeon E. Baldwin, president of the American Bar Association, that the association award its gold medal for law reform to David Dudley Field.[108] The ABA's decision to give it to Lord Selbourne instead no doubt added to Brewer's sorrow over Field's passing in 1894.

Surely the declining years of Stephen J. Field were hard for Brewer to bear. The powerful mind of the Supreme Court's last living Lincoln appointee had slipped badly in the 1890s, and he was unable to handle even a fraction of his normal share of Court business. Yet despite strong hints that he retire, he stubbornly refused to do so. Thanks in large part to the tactful efforts of his brother Henry M. Field and Brewer, Justice Field was gradually persuaded to leave the bench. Brewer was party to a plan whereby president-elect William McKinley was to appoint Joseph McKenna (like Field, a Californian) as his attorney general, with the understanding that Field resign soon after McKinley's inauguration in 1897 and that McKenna be elevated to the Supreme Court to take Field's place. Field himself may have participated in making this arrangement.[109]

In April of 1897 Field submitted a private letter of resignation to McKinley, stipulating, however, that the resignation would not take effect until December 1; this would make his tenure longer than that of any previous member of the Court. But in August an anxious Brewer informed Chief Justice Fuller that Field was feeling better and having second thoughts about retirement. Brewer advised that "the less said or done the better. It may only call his attention to the matter & suggest the doing of that which ought not to be done." Such patient dealing with the proud old man worked. On October 9 McKinley publicly announced that Fuller and Brewer had handed him Field's letter of resignation and that it was accepted. In accordance with the original agreement, the formal departure from the bench took place on December 1.[110]

While these arrangements were being made, Brewer informed the press that his uncle was "very feeble" and would retire soon. The news story noted that when Brewer "spoke about his venerable uncle, now 81 years old, his musical voice softened a little." In the same story Brewer professed to having no idea who would replace Field on the Court—which may not have been strictly true. In any case McKenna received the appointment early in 1898. Field died the following year, with his wife and Brewer among those at his side.[111]

The deaths of family members and six of his Court colleagues during the nineties inclined Brewer's thoughts toward his own passing, which by the end of the century he felt was imminent even though he was only in his early sixties. In his papers for the later years of the 1890s is a poem in manuscript, perhaps written by him, entitled "Faith." Its closing stanza read:

> Were it not better, strong, and true, and brave,
> To live our lives, letting what comes befall;
> Than quail through life, and cower in the grave,
> At empty echoes from a painted wall?[112]

In his 1899 speech on "The Twentieth Century from Another Viewpoint," he regretted that he would not live long into the new era and witness the wonders he prophesied for it: "I see the morning but I cannot hope to enter largely into the great revelations of the next century."[113] Such melancholy thoughts were entirely premature; he was to put in another full decade of service to the Court and the nation.

RATES, TRUSTS, AND TAXES
The Court and the Commerce, Police, and Taxing Powers, 1901–1910

T HE EARLY YEARS of the twentieth century, the so-called Progressive Era, were conspicuously an age of reform. But the period did not represent a sharp break with the last one-third of the previous century. Virtually none of the reform movements of the Progressive Era were new. True, a new generation led them, and there were differences in the spirit in which the reforms were advocated. And some historians have advanced strong arguments that "progressivism" at the federal level, for example, the regulation of big business, was often for the benefit of the corporations rather than for the public good.[1] Still, in matters of reform, there was much continuity between the late nineteenth and early twentieth centuries. This is evident in the sameness of the types of cases involving state and federal reform measures that came before the Supreme Court in both periods.

The Court itself was fairly consistent in its responses in the two periods. This despite the fact that there were four new faces on the Fuller Court between 1901 and 1910: Oliver Wendell Holmes, Jr., replaced Gray, who died in 1902; William R. Day took the place of Shiras, who resigned in 1903; Brown resigned in 1906 and was replaced by William H. Moody; and following Peckham's death in 1909 Horace H. Lurton was appointed to the Court.

One approach for analyzing the Court's response to the reforms of those years is to note which of the justices tended to defer to state and national legislatures and to uphold legislation and which of them tended to show the least deference and voted often to void legislation. According to one historian, the first group included Holmes, Day, Gray, and Brown; in the second group were Shiras, Harlan, White, and Peckham. The men in the first group were also more prone to cite precedent than those of the second group.

A third or middle group overlapping the other two consisted of Brewer, McKenna, and Fuller.[2] The same study shows that Brewer was in the middle of another category, length of opinion: his opinions averaged 8.75 pages, which for this period was closest to the Court's average of 8.93 pages.[3]

Certainly it is impossible to say that Brewer, in the twentieth century, was markedly hostile or friendly to reform. As in the 1890s, there are plenty of examples of his voting both to sustain and to invalidate reform efforts. This is not to say that he was inconsistent. His constitutional principles and biases remained largely the same throughout his career on the various levels of the state and national judicial systems: corporations were persons within the meaning of the Fourteenth Amendment;[4] businesses devoted to a public use were subject to regulation—but *only* if they were "*quasi* public agencies" and *only* if regulation did not deprive the business of its property or the use of property without compensation; and these same considerations placed definite limits upon the commerce power of the federal government and the police power of the states.[5] Running through all this was his deep antagonism to centralized power, particularly as it threatened the ownership and enjoyment of property.

Of the many large economic interests with which the reform-minded public concerned itself, railroads continued in the early twentieth century to maintain a prominent place. And Brewer's judicial responses to railroad matters figure prominently among his opinions in this period also. He insisted that railroad corporations had both rights and duties. On one hand, he wrote that a railroad "was not a benevolent association, but a railroad doing a business for profit."[6] On the other hand, he said that the Union Pacific and other lines built with government aid "in furtherance of the public interests" were subject to whatever reasonable restrictions and rules the government might wish to impose.[7] But they had to be reasonable; such restrictions and rules must not prevent a business from making a fair return on the investment.

He remained cool toward the ICC's attempts to regulate rates. For a unanimous Court he disagreed with the commission's contention that a railroad could not charge higher rates for shipping livestock than for dressed meats and other products of packinghouses.

The differences between the rates, he wrote, was the result of "genuine competition," not unlawful conspiracy. While he again affirmed the public's right to regulate rates, he also maintained that railroads were private property and that "in no proper sense is the public a general manager." He went on to make the curious suggestion that the railroads, by charging more for the shipment of cattle than for dressed meat, were perhaps discouraging such shipment in an effort to reduce the suffering of the livestock and would therefore "deserve to be commended rather than condemned."[8]

In another decision that went against the beleaguered ICC, the Court, speaking through Brewer, overturned the commission's ruling that the Chicago Great Western Railway's terminal charge was unreasonable.[9] Although he could usually be counted upon to favor railroads over the ICC, he argued for a broad interpretation of the federal government's power to regulate interstate commerce. A majority opinion by White held that a federal district attorney could not, upon the request of the ICC, initiate a suit against a railroad for violating the Interstate Commerce Act's prohibition against long haul–short haul discrimination. Brewer, joined by Harlan, dissented: the suit had been brought, he wrote, "to enforce a duty cast upon carriers of interstate commerce, and the right of a government to maintain such a suit does not depend upon the request of any individual or board."

Citing *In re Debs* as authority, he declared that the United States had the right "even in the absence of a statute specially authorizing such action" to go to the federal courts in order "to restrain parties from obstructing and interfering with interstate commerce." Brewer pointed out that the logic of *Debs* had implications for railroad companies as well as railroad workers: "It seems to me singular that the government can maintain a bill to prevent others from obstructing and interfering with interstate commerce and yet cannot maintain a bill to carriers to fully discharge their duties in respect to such commerce." He then asked: "Can it be that the government has power to protect carriers of interstate commerce and not power to compel them to discharge their duties?"[10]

Brewer's reaction in a case involving yet another railroad practice against which the public complained—rebates to favored shippers—was quite different. In an effort to strengthen the Interstate Commerce Act, Congress passed the Elkins Antirebating Act of 1903. The

Supreme Court, in an opinion written by Day, upheld the conviction of the Armour Packing Company for violating the act. Brewer, speaking for himself, Fuller, and Peckham, disagreed. The packing company and a railroad had, he believed, "entered into a fair and reasonable contract." The majority's position shocked his "sense of justice" because it authorized the carrier to break a valid contract and thereby punish the shipper. Such interference with freedom of contract created uncertainty in the business world, which in turn tended "to destroy and not promote commerce." He further believed that the framers of the Elkins Act had not intended it to be used in this way.[11]

Congress was then extending federal control over commerce in areas other than common carriers. In *Champion* v. *Ames*, the Court sustained legislation of 1895 that prohibited the interstate shipment of lottery tickets. In effect, the decision sanctioned Congress's right to exercise the police power (hitherto considered a state power) through the commerce power. No doubt Brewer's usual opposition to the extension of federal power induced him, along with Shiras and Peckham, to join the dissenting opinion written by the chief justice.[12]

Although Brewer tended in the twentieth century to be as cautious about broadening federal power over commerce as he had been in the nineteenth, he was showing a greater willingness to approve state regulation of railroads in the new century than he had shown in the previous one. When the majority in 1902 ruled that Kentucky's regulation of long and short haul rates interfered with federal regulation of interstate commerce because the state had used interstate long haul rates as the standard for setting the intrastate short haul rates, Brewer, joined by Gray, expressed his disagreement. The state, he asserted, had "full power over local rates" and using an interstate standard for establishing local rates in no way encroached upon Congress's regulation of interstate commerce.[13]

In 1906 Brewer wrote the opinion of a unanimous Court in two cases involving rates set by Florida's railroad commission. In both it was held that the rates did not deprive the railroad of property without due process of law, that is, the rates allowed a reasonable return for the railroad.[14] That same year another Brewer decision upheld Mississippi's right to compel a railroad to charge equal rates for all those who shipped over the same route. His opinion distinguished this case from *Texas & Pacific Railway* v. *ICC* (1896), in which the Court's interpretation of the Interstate Commerce Act concluded that "mere inequality of rate" was not necessarily proof of discrimination. But in the Mississippi case at hand it was decided that a state "may insist on equality."[15]

True to his long acceptance of the doctrine that a business devoted to a public *use* (as opposed to a business in which the public merely had an *interest*) had duties that the public could enforce, Brewer's opinion for the majority in *Missouri Pacific Railway Co.* v. *Larabee Flour Mills Co.* stated that the railroad could not refuse service to a company when it was offering the same service to all other businesses in a community. The very fact that it was a common carrier, said Brewer, obliged it to offer equal service; no specific statute or ruling by a regulatory agency compelling it to do so was necessary. He dismissed the railroad's contention that this was a matter subject only to federal regulation; but Moody (joined by White) noted that three-fifths of the cars involved were used for interstate shipments and saw merit in that point.[16]

Although Brewer was now more amenable to state regulation of railroad rates, he remained steadfast in his opposition to regulation of businesses other than railroads and public utilities. In *Cotting* v. *Kansas City Stock Yards Co.*, he handed down the decision that voided a Kansas law regulating stockyards. The act, passed by the Populist-dominated legislature of 1897, applied only to the Kansas City company. The rest of the Court agreed with Brewer that it was a violation of the Fourteenth Amendment's equal protection clause. But Brewer went beyond this and attempted unsuccessfully to convince the others that the law might also be a denial of due process. In reviewing the major decisions on state regulation from *Munn* onward, he reiterated the views he had put forth in his *Budd* and *Brass* dissents: not all businesses in which the public was interested should have their rates (as long as they were reasonable) regulated; to do so was to take away property without due process.[17]

No less than six of the justices were having none of it. In a paragraph by Harlan (joined by Gray, Brown, Shiras, White, and McKenna), they announced their concurrence with Brewer's assertion that the statute was invalid insofar as it denied equal protection, but they saw the due process argument as "unnecessary."[18]

This rebuke from his colleagues notwithstanding, one of Brewer's eulogists deemed *Cotting* to be "the leading case as to the rights in the use and the limitation upon his use of property which the individual has devoted to a public purpose."[19]

The issue of equal protection came up again in a case in which a railroad challenged a South Carolina law penalizing only common carriers for failure to adjust damage claims within forty days. Brewer's opinion for the majority (Peckham dissented without opinion) sustained the statute, even though common carriers alone were the targets of the law. Reasonable classification, Brewer had always maintained, was a legislative prerogative and was not inherently a denial of due process. In the course of his remarks, he also emphasized the fairness of the law because it protected the small shipper from the expense of lengthy litigation.[20]

Resolving conflicts between the states' police power and the federal government's commerce power continued to be a regular part of the Court's business in the early twentieth century. Speaking through Brewer, it upheld an Idaho statute for preventing the importation of scabrous sheep into the state.[21] Nor was New York's regulation and taxation of the cab service operated by a railroad an encroachment upon federal power, even though the cabs carried interstate passengers to the station.[22] But a Kentucky statute barring COD shipments of liquor into the state fared otherwise. The majority opinion by Brewer found the law invalid because it would "nullify or tend to weaken the power vested by the Constitution in Congress over interstate commerce." Harlan's dissent defended his state's right to foil the "devices and tricks by the [Adams] express company to defeat the laws of Kentucky."[23]

Harlan also dissented from a Brewer opinion that struck at another Kentucky liquor law. The law forbade the sale of alcoholic beverages to intoxicated persons or to habitual inebriates. Brewer and the majority said it was invalid insofar as it applied to interstate shipment of liquor, which was, according to *Leisy* v. *Hardin*, "a recognized article of commerce" even though "obnoxious and hurtful . . . in the judgment of many."[24]

The Court never doubted the constitutionality of the Sherman Antitrust Act. Yet in *E. C. Knight* (1895) the justices had interpreted the act so narrowly as to make it an ineffective weapon for combating "restraint of trade." Also, the public had been disappointed by the small number of antitrust cases initiated by the Justice Department in the 1890s. Thanks to a new administration and a changing attitude on the Court, the act appeared to have new life in the first years of the twentieth century.

In a dramatic move, President Theodore Roosevelt's Justice Department brought suit against the Northern Securities Company in 1902. This was a holding company formed by J. P. Morgan, Edward H. Harriman, and James J. Hill for the purpose of ending competition between the railroads they controlled in the Northwest. A circuit court decree agreed with the government's charge that the company was restraining trade and enjoined it from making further stock transactions and from controlling the railroad companies whose stock it held.

The railroad men appealed it to the Supreme Court, arguing that the company was engaged in stock transactions, not interstate commerce, and that it existed by virtue of a charter from New Jersey, which made its activities a state rather than a federal matter. Speaking for Brown, McKenna, and Day, Harlan's opinion affirmed the lower court's decree.[25] Holmes, White, Fuller, and Peckham dissented. Brewer's concurring opinion made it five to four against the company and for the government.

A leading authority on this era of the Court has stated that "[p]erhaps no opinion Brewer wrote during his long tenure on the Court better illustrates his integrity, competence, and sophistication than this short [three and one-half page] concurring opinion."[26] Fuller thought otherwise. A month before the Court's various opinions were announced, the chief justice informed Holmes: "I had an interesting interview with Brewer yesterday & he is inclined to write out his own views—Yours [that is, Holmes's dissent] will hit him between wind and water."[27]

Brewer began his opinion by acknowledging that although he had been of the majority in *United States* v. *Trans-Missouri Freight Association, Addyston*, and other decisions that had broadened the meaning of the Sherman Act since *E. C. Knight*, he felt compelled to disagree with Harlan's "broad and sweeping" construction of the statute. For Brewer the object of the Sherman Act was not to break up all monopolistic businesses, only those that "unreasonably" restrained trade. "Reasonable" combinations, especially "minor contracts in partial restraint of trade" were not, in his reading of the act and the common law, illegal. But surely, he went on to say, the Northern Securities Company was the very sort of combination at which the

Sherman Act took aim: it was both an unreasonable and unlawful result of a conspiracy to eliminate competition, and it was very much involved in interstate commerce.

As for the company's argument that the suit invaded states' rights, Brewer's reply was that the lower court, in putting the company out of business, had enforced state law and policy: "This merging of control and destruction of competition was not authorized, but specifically prohibited by the State which created one of the railroad companies, and within whose boundaries the lines of both were largely located and much of their business transacted." To the assertion that the government was seeking to infringe the holding company's Fourteenth Amendment rights, Brewer, who had long held that a corporation was a legal person and entitled to the amendment's protection, answered that a corporation was merely an artificial person, "created and existing only for the convenient transaction of business" and was "not endowed with the inalienable rights of a natural person."[28]

This opinion is a good illustration of Brewer's attitudes toward business. He admired persons such as Hill for building such a grand public enterprise as the Great Northern, and he had always sought to protect property rights, including those of corporate property. But when Hill and the others ceased to be builders and became stock-manipulating financial buccaneers, Brewer could no longer admire them or find them deserving of the protection of the courts. Without using Thorstein Veblen's terms "captains of industry" and "captains of business," Brewer saw the distinction between the two and was clearly unsympathetic to the latter. Also, the *Northern Securities* opinion reflected his desire to protect from federal regulation those small, local businesses that did no harm to the public.[29] In other words, his views in the *Northern Securities* case were perfectly consistent with his *Budd* and *Brass* dissents.

Roosevelt was bitter over the fact that his appointee Holmes had been conspicuous among the dissenters. There is even more irony in Brewer's position in the case. Roosevelt had privately castigated him as a reactionary, yet in *Northern Securities* he had not only supported the government's case but had also outlined a position on trusts that was close to Roosevelt's. Roosevelt, at heart, was not a "trustbuster," for he saw big business, even monopoly, as inevitable. Mere bigness was thus not in itself evil; only the "bad" trusts needed to be punished. "Good" trusts were to be regulated in the public interest. The similarity between his good trust/bad trust dichotomy and Brewer's distinction between "reasonable" and "unreasonable" restraints of trade seems to have escaped the Rough Rider. Quite possibly Brewer was more opposed to big monopolistic corporations than was Roosevelt.

Brewer did not invent the "rule of reason" (that is, the construction of the Sherman Act that holds that the act applied only to unreasonable restraints of trade) as an approach to antitrust cases. In his dissent in *United States* v. *Trans-Missouri Freight Association* (1897), White was actually the first of the justices to develop it.[30] Still, Brewer's emphasis on it in *Northern Securities* did much to further it, and it soon became a doctrine that the majority of the Fuller Court embraced.

The Roosevelt administration quickly enjoyed another antitrust victory. In 1905, with Holmes writing the unanimous opinion, the Supreme Court upheld a lower court's injunction against the Swift packing company for violating the Sherman Act. The decision introduced the "stream of commerce" doctrine, which allowed the Court to move even further from *E. C. Knight's* restrictive definition of commerce.[31]

Despite the increased vigor of federal antitrust activity, a number of cases arising out of state antitrust laws came before the Court in the early twentieth century. Brewer wrote opinions in some of them, most notably in *Smiley* v. *Kansas*, which upheld the antitrust statute passed by the Populists in his home state. He found no merit in the claim that the act violated freedom of contract, which, he wrote, did not extend to a "secret arrangement, by which . . . an apparently existing competition in a community of one of the necessaries of life [wheat] is substantially destroyed." Such practices, he wrote, were legitimate objects of the police power.[32] Later that year, however, he and McKenna dissented without opinion in a case that arose from the enforcement of the Kansas antitrust act. The majority had ruled that a witness in an antitrust investigation had not been denied constitutional guarantees against self-incrimination.[33]

Speaking through Brewer, the Court reversed a circuit court ruling that had allowed the city of Peoria to impose certain rates on a gas company because the company had earlier violated Illinois's antitrust law. This, said Brewer, was trying a case on one theory and deciding it on another: "The punishment adheres to the offense and stops when the offense itself stops."[34] Similarly, Brewer, in concurring with a dissenting opinion written by Holmes, objected to a decision delivered by Harlan that found a contract between two companies void because one of them was in violation of the Sherman Act.[35] These positions in minor antitrust cases do not alter the fact that Brewer stood firmly behind such legislation in the major cases.

As in the later nineteenth century, Brewer, in common with most of his colleagues, continued to view federal and state taxation favorably in the new century. His most noteworthy opinion in this regard was that written for the majority in *South Carolina* v. *United States*,[36] which upheld a federal license tax on agents of South Carolina's state-operated liquor dispensaries. He acknowledged that South Carolina had the right to establish a state monopoly on the sale of liquor but speculated that state ownership of public utilities and other businesses might jeopardize a state's republican form of government. On more concrete grounds he contended that if the trend toward state ownership of business continued and if the states claimed immunity from federal taxation upon these enterprises, "the National Government would be largely crippled in its revenues." Only state property that was "of a strictly governmental character" was exempt from federal taxation.[37] White, in a dissent concurred in by Peckham and McKenna, argued that the majority's ruling hindered the police powers of a state. Moreover, said White, according to Brewer's logic, a state could tax the nongovernmental operations of the federal government and "the distinct powers belonging to both the National and state Governments are reciprocally placed the one at the mercy of the other, so as to give to each the potency of destroying the other."[38]

Brewer was part of the majority that upheld a federal tax on bequests to states and municipalities.[39] Another questionable form of federal taxation, on cheese manufactured for export, was declared in a Brewer decision (against which Harlan and Fuller dissented) to be valid, on the grounds that it was not a tax on exports.[40]

Fairbank v. *United States*, for which Brewer wrote the majority opinion, struck down that portion of the War Revenue Act of 1898 that levied a stamp tax on foreign bills of lading, because, in the Court's view, it was a tax on exports and therefore in conflict with Article I, section 9, of the Constitution.[41] It was a difficult matter to justify that conclusion because the Congress had imposed such stamp duties from 1797 to 1802 and from 1862 to 1872 without any challenge as to their constitutionality. Brewer sought to explain this away by saying that during the first period the exports were so limited and the rates so low that no serious objection arose and that "during the second period we were passing through the stress of a great civil war or endeavoring to carry its enormous debt; so that it is not strange that the legislative actions in this respect passed unchallenged."[42] The four dissenters, speaking through Harlan, found this reasoning unacceptable; they believed that the tax in question was upon pieces of paper, not exported goods.[43]

State and local taxation produced a number of opinions by Brewer in this period and most of them sustained the taxes: Connecticut's taxation of shares of stock in local corporations and Florida's collection of delinquent railroad taxes were found not to be violations of the Fourteenth Amendment's equal protection clause; Virginia's tax on ships and Philadelphia's license fee for a telegraph company were held not to be interferences with interstate commerce;[44] and New York's inheritance tax law's provision for taxing the personalty of nonresident decedents who had owned real estate in New York did not deny due process and equal protection. In the latter opinion Brewer wrote that "[t]he power of the State in respect to matters of taxation is very broad, at least as far as the Federal Constitution is concerned."[45] In similar tones, in a decision upholding Michigan's system of railroad taxation, he insisted that "[t]here is no general supervision on the part of the Nation over state taxation, and in respect to the latter the State has, speaking generally, the freedom of a sovereign both as to objects and methods."[46]

In 1904 McKenna's majority opinion held that a bank previously exempted from paying a state tax on its capital could not be charged a license tax because this constituted impairment of a contract, that is, the bank's charter. Joined by Fuller, Brewer dissented on the grounds that the license tax was distinct from the taxation spoken of in the charter.[47] The next year a unanimous Court, speaking through Brewer, decided that it was not an impairment of contract for New York to levy a tax on street railways, even though such taxes had not been imposed previously. Escaping the tax for many years had been simply the companies' "good fortune," which "in no manner discharges them from the ordinary burdens of taxation which the present law imposes."[48]

On the other hand, Brewer's majority opinion in *Powers* v. *Detroit, Grand Haven and Milwaukee Ry. Co.* declared a 1901 Michigan tax invalid because it violated the Constitution's contract clause. In 1885 the state had enacted a law that exempted the company from all taxes except an annual levy of 1 percent on its capital stock; the old tax law, said Brewer, was a contract and the new law amounted to an impairment of that contract.[49] Another exception to Brewer's usual willingness to interpret state taxing power liberally came in 1910 when he was of the majority that struck down a Kansas tax on a telegraph company. The decision, delivered by Harlan, concluded that in basing the tax upon the entire capital of a firm doing an interstate business, Kansas had sought to tax property outside the state and thus encroached upon the commerce power of the federal government.[50]

Brewer has been categorized as an adherent of the doctrine of natural law, the dominant school of thought in American jurisprudence from colonial times into the nineteenth century. It held that there were natural rights belonging to all mankind and that those rights were fixed, universal, and timeless. Brewer and other legal minds of his generation believed that the Declaration of Independence, the Constitution, the common law, and the Christian religion affirmed elements of natural law.[51] Closely related to this older school of thought was legal formalism, a doctrine propounded in the late nineteenth century, principally by Christopher C. Tiedeman, Thomas M. Cooley, and John Forrest Dillon. They proclaimed a belief in universal, eternal verities that judges should apply in defending property interests against the attacks by legislatures. They were antilegislative, antiregulatory, and staunch defenders of judicial review and of the federal courts (which were in a better position to resist assaults on property than were popularly elected state judiciaries). Brewer, with much justification, has been identified with this doctrine also.[52]

In his defense of property and individual rights, Brewer's commitment to natural law and legal formalism is indeed evident. And yet, in his responses to several issues of his time, it will be seen that he was among those who led the way to acceptance of sociological jurisprudence and legal realism. These related forms of jurisprudence, which were to triumph in the twentieth century, would provide more flexible, factual, results-oriented, and pragmatic approaches to legal and constitutional interpretation, and thus facilitate judicial validation of reform measures.

II

FACTS AND LAW
Responses to Reform, 1901–1910

THE DECISIONS for which Brewer is best known historically are *In re Debs* (1895) and *Muller* v. *Oregon* (1908). For the first he has been roundly damned as an enemy of labor; for the second he has been praised for advancing the cause of prolabor legislation. In the years between the two decisions his record in labor-related cases is mixed. In most of them, however, he was opposed on various grounds to legislation designed to protect working people.

In many of the labor cases the main issue was liberty of contract.[1] The Court had developed this doctrine in the 1890s, most conspicuously in *Allgeyer* v. *Louisiana* (1897), a case concerning insurance contracts. Peckham's opinion for the majority, which included Brewer, held that liberty of contract was included within the Fourteenth Amendment's due process clause.[2]

Soon thereafter opponents of labor legislation began using the doctrine as an argument. In 1898 they failed to convince the Court in *Holden* v. *Hardy* that Utah's eight-hour law for miners violated the rights of the miners to contract for as many hours as they and their employers would agree to. The majority found the law to be a legitimate exercise of the state's police power. Brewer and Peckham dissented without opinion.[3]

In 1901 he and Peckham again dissented without opinion in two cases in which the majority declared that a Tennessee law aimed at the practice of paying workers in scrip did not infringe upon freedom of contract.[4] Joined by Fuller, Brewer and Peckham did the same in *Atkin* v. *Kansas* (1903), in which their brethren, speaking through Harlan, validated a Kansas law that established an eight-hour day for employees of the state and its local governments.[5] Yet that same year Brewer wrote the Court's opinion that a federal statute of 1898 outlawing the paying of seamen in advance was not abridging liberty of contract. Indeed, he found it a desirable measure. Brewer wrote feelingly of the "bad men" who lured sailors to "haunts of vice," advanced them money for drink, and placed them on board ships; the unfortunate sailors were then obligated to work off the debt. "It was in order to stop this evil, to protect the sailor, and not to restrict his liberty, that this statute was passed." Nor did it make any difference to Brewer that in this particular case the ship was British.[6]

Brewer was part of the majority for which Peckham spoke in the notorious case of *Lochner* v. *New York* (1905). Here the Court voided a state law that had imposed a ten-hour day for bakers. The majority, with Harlan, White, Day, and Holmes dissenting, found the statute to be an unreasonable exercise of the police power (baking, unlike mining, was deemed to be a relatively safe occupation) and a violation of a baker's liberty of contract.[7] Even though the decision may have been a temporary aberration among the Court's usually favorable responses to labor legislation in this period, reformers saw it as a major blow against maximum hours laws.[8] They anxiously looked forward to its reversal or modification.

They found cause for hope in 1907 when a divided Court gave its qualified approval to a federal law providing an eight-hour day for laborers and mechanics employed by the United States or by contractors and subcontractors engaged in public works for the federal government.[9] Brewer was with the majority, but he was also with the five-man majority that, in a decision handed down by Harlan in 1908, killed the statute that outlawed the "yellow dog" contract (in which a worker, as a condition of employment, pledged not to join or remain a member of a labor union). Since this was a federal law, here the supposed liberty of contract was protected by the Fifth Amendment.[10]

Small wonder that labor reformers viewed Brewer as hostile to measures designed to improve the lot of working people. Thus, it came as a pleasant surprise when he wrote the opinion of a unanimous Court in *Muller* v. *Oregon*.[11]

At issue was the constitutionality of an Oregon law of 1903 that made it illegal for a woman to be "employed in any mechanical establishment, or factory or laundry . . . more than ten hours during any one day." Muller, the owner of a Portland laundry, had been convicted of requiring one of his employees, Mrs. Elmer Gotcher, to work more than ten hours. His lawyers, with the seemingly firm *Lochner* precedent on their side, challenged the law's constitutionality.

Arguing the case for Oregon was the brilliant lawyer—reformer Louis D. Brandeis. Brandeis had won victories before the Supreme Court in decisions delivered by Brewer in two railroad land-grant cases in 1895.[12] But *Muller* was an entirely different matter, and considering the *Lochner* decision, there appeared to be little hope for a favorable outcome.

Aware that precedent was not squarely on the side of the Oregon law, Brandeis framed a bold and novel argument. The famous "Brandeis brief" consisted mostly of a review of American and foreign legislation protecting women in industry, and extracts from several public reports that showed that long hours by women in certain occupations were injurious to their health, safety, welfare, and morals. The brief accordingly concluded that the Oregon ten-hour law was a valid and desirable exercise of the police power. Brewer's opinion was almost as surprising for its brevity—seven pages—as for its conclusions. He and his colleagues were duly impressed with the data compiled by Brandeis (with the aid of his sister-in-law Josephine Goldmark and the eminent reform advocate Florence Kelley). Brewer took the unusual step of mentioning the attorney by name in the opinion: "In the brief filed by Mr. Louis D. Brandeis . . . is a very copious collection of all these matters."[13] The opinion explained that the case differed from *Lochner*, and the difference was that women, as shown in the brief, were different physically from men and thus in need of special legislative protection.[14] As for liberty of contract, which counsel for Muller emphasized, Brewer wrote that it was not absolute and that some conditions required limitations upon it.[15] Based upon those considerations, the opinion concluded that the Oregon statute was not in conflict with any portion of the Constitution.

We need not find Brewer's wording and viewpoints in *Muller* all that startling.[16] First, his responses to previous labor issues before the Court were not uniformly negative and those that were, for example, *Holden* and *Lochner*, are not proof that he was antagonistic to working people or indifferent to their problems. His objections to other laws to protect workers stemmed in large part from a reluctance to see the state's police power extended, not a desire to see laborers exploited.

Secondly, Brandeis's factual approach could hardly fail to provoke a response from Brewer. He had long insisted that courts had the right and the duty to look beyond the law, examine social and economic reality, and to consider "expressions of opinion from other than judicial sources."[17] He had always believed that judges were as fit as anyone to examine and act upon facts. His remarks in the *Muller* opinion that "[w]e take judicial cognizance of all matters of general knowledge" is often quoted.[18] We must also keep in mind that he believed judges to be capable of dealing with *specialized* knowledge as well, such as the technical information inherent in patent cases. Indeed, early in the *Muller* opinion he likened the Brandeis brief to the briefs in patent cases, wherein "counsel are apt to open the argument with a discussion of the state of the art."[19] Also, Brewer had maintained throughout his judicial career that lawmakers had the power to classify, as long as the classifications were reasonable. Thus, he would have little difficulty with legislation that placed females in a separate category.

In later years much has been made of Brewer's "patronizing" attitude toward women, as seen in *Muller*. Those who would condemn him on that basis need to be aware that he was a forthright proponent of women's rights. Then, too, we need to consider the impact of the *Muller* decision upon the Mrs. Gotchers of that time, not just the sensibilities of middle-class women in later years.

Not long after delivering the decision, Brewer, in an article published in a journal for social workers, emphasized that he had meant "no disrespect" to women and that he had not written it "in the sneering spirit in which it has been sometimes said, that women, like infants and lunatics, are not fit to vote." Rather, it had been "written with the utmost respect for them, by one who knows the blessings which come from the sex, and in the firm belief that there was something in her place and work in life which justified the legislature in forbidding her to contract for factory work beyond a limited time." More in the spirit of humanitarianism than paternalism, he continued: "The race needs her; her children need her; her friends need her, in a way that they do not need the other sex."[20]

In the twentieth century Brewer showed somewhat more willingness to support the claims of injured workingmen than before. In one case he announced the Court's opinion that a laborer was entitled to recover damages because the negligence had been on the part of the foreman, who was not a fellow servant.[21] Another Brewer decision upheld a verdict for a workingman, finding that the trial court had properly instructed the jury on the employer's duty regarding the safety of an employee and the employee's duty to take "reasonable care of himself."[22]

More consistent with his usual stand in this category of litigation, other opinions by him opposed the awarding of damages. One held that a telegraph operator and a station agent were fellow servants of an injured railroad worker. White (joined by Fuller, Harlan, and McKenna) dissented from what they believed was Brewer's too-narrow interpretation of the fellow servant rule.[23] Joined by Peckham, McKenna, and Day, Brewer dissented from a decision written by Holmes that awarded damages to the heirs of a dead brakeman; the dissenters believed that there had been contributory negligence.[24]

Of greater consequence were the *Employers' Liability Cases*, in which a narrow and uncohesive majority declared most of the federal Employers' Liability Act of 1906 invalid. White, joined by Day, wrote that the law invaded the area of intrastate commerce, over which the states had power. Peckham, joined by Brewer and Fuller, concurred but went further to say that Congress had no power to enact legislation dealing with master and servant. Moody, Harlan (joined by McKenna), and Holmes wrote separate dissents.[25]

In yet another area of labor legislation, a majority upheld an Arkansas "screen law," which required "coal to be measured for payment of miners' wages before screening." Brewer and Peckham dissented without opinion.[26] Although the unity of the two justices has been exaggerated by historians, they were usually together in labor questions.

The Progressive Era had few positive results for American blacks. In fact, the period was perhaps their bleakest hour since emancipation. Lynching and segregation in the South, and discrimination and race riots everywhere, were the order of the day. Harlan remained the Supreme Court's only consistent friend of the blacks. Brewer's opinions in cases involving blacks more accurately reflected the national mood. Within a few years he managed to restrict the potential benefits of all three Reconstruction era amendments to the Constitution.

Federal anti-peonage legislation, based upon the Thirteenth Amendment, received a severely narrow interpretation in Brewer's majority opinion in *Clyatt* v. *United States* (1905).[27] Clyatt, a white Georgian, had been convicted of returning two blacks to debt peonage and the Circuit Court of Appeals upheld the conviction. Brewer's decision for the Supreme Court sustained the constitutionality of the act in question (which the Roosevelt administration was committed to enforcing) but reversed the lower courts and ordered a new trial on the grounds that there was no proof that a prior state of peonage had existed; therefore, he reasoned, the blacks could not have been returned to peonage. Brewer and the majority also believed that the trial court had erred in not taking the case from the jury. Harlan dissented and scolded his brethren for being insensitive to the "barbarities of the worst kind against these negroes." He also believed that there was adequate proof of Clyatt's violation of the statute.[28]

An even more notorious decision by Brewer was *Hodges* v. *United States* (1906).[29] Here three whites were charged with violating the Civil Rights Acts of 1866 and 1870 by forming a conspiracy to prevent blacks, by intimidation, from fulfilling a work contract. Speaking for the majority, Brewer found no violation of the Thirteenth Amendment, the adoption of which was "not an attempt to commit [blacks] to the care of the nation";[30] nor did the acts charged against the accused constitute attempts to reduce the blacks to a condition of servitude. Furthermore, the actions of the whites were not violations of the Fourteenth Amendment, which forbids states, not individuals, from depriving persons of rights. In making these points, Brewer was echoing the *Civil Rights Cases* decision (1883), in which the Court largely invalidated the Civil Rights Act of 1875.[31] Once again Harlan, with Day in agreement, protested against the majority's refusal to take cognizance of the realities of southern life.[32]

Harlan did not participate in an otherwise unanimous decision written by Brewer wherein the Court affirmed the ruling of Florida's supreme court that exclusion of blacks from a jury trying a black man for murder was not a denial of equal protection of the laws. Brewer wrote that discrimination could not be presumed: "It must be proved or admitted."[33]

Harlan, however, did issue characteristically strong arguments against the Court's opinion, written by Brewer, in *Berea College* v.

Kentucky.[34] The decision upheld the state's prohibition against blacks and whites attending the same college. The law was obviously aimed at Berea, an integrated institution. Brewer accepted the reasoning of Kentucky's courts, which had held that the state had the power to alter the college's charter. Holmes and Moody concurred, and Day dissented, all without opinion. Harlan spoke his mind, calling the statute "an arbitrary invasion of the rights of liberty and property guaranteed by the Fourteenth Amendment against hostile state action."[35]

Another of Brewer's decisions placed limits on the meaning of the Fifteenth Amendment's protection of voting rights. It voided that section of the Civil Rights Act of 1870 that prohibited bribery in elections. In this case, *James* v. *Bowman*, blacks had been bribed not to vote. Brewer held that the amendment restrained states and not individuals from denying or abridging voting rights on the bases of race, color, and previous condition of servitude. Besides, he added, those bribed had been bribed because they were voters, not because they were black. Harlan and Brown dissented without opinion from Brewer's tortured reasoning.[36]

A decision delivered by Holmes tacitly upheld provisions of Alabama's constitution that disfranchised blacks through literacy and property requirements. Holmes wrote that if the black plaintiff were entitled to relief, it had to come from the "political" branches of the federal government, not from the courts. Harlan of course dissented. Less predictably, so did Brewer, whose separate opinion asserted that the federal courts had jurisdiction and that "it appears that the plaintiff was entitled to a place on the permanent registry [of voters]."[37]

In a somewhat later Brewer decision, a unanimous Court found against blacks who had been disfranchised in Virginia. They had sought to enjoin the state board of canvassers from conducting an election in which they had been prevented from voting. The decision was based upon a precedent that ruled that there could be no relief from the Court because the election had already been held.[38]

Another case in which race was a factor elicited an opinion by Brewer that upheld the right of a white man to will property to a black man who had been "his business and household companion for years." "Such continued intimacy," wrote Brewer, "is satisfactory evidence that he at least was not motivated by [race] prejudice." The testator's relatives had appealed to "the potency of blood relation-ship," but Brewer dismissed this with the observation that "affection between cousins is often not very strong."[39] Here Brewer was proba-bly less concerned with aiding a black man than with upholding the right of one to dispose of his property as he saw fit.

United States v. *Shipp* was the first time that the Supreme Court initiated a contempt proceeding. In the three hearings of the infamous case, Brewer voted with the majority. Shipp was a Tennessee sheriff accused of complicity with a mob that had lynched a black federal prisoner who had been accused of rape. A decision delivered by Holmes upheld the Court's power to issue a contempt citation against Shipp and others. An opinion written by Fuller found Shipp guilty of contempt. The final hearing resulted in jail sentences for Shipp and his accomplices.[40] Brewer's votes were no doubt motivated as much by a desire to uphold judicial power as by outrage over the crime itself, but off the bench he had earlier spoken out against the rising tide of lynch law.[41]

Brewer's inclination to countenance southern racial attitudes is in marked contrast to his steadfast opposition to intolerance as practiced against orientals. Although prejudice against the Chinese was abating somewhat in the early twentieth century, the Court was still deciding cases involving their rights. And the majority continued to find that they had few rights.

Usually joined by Peckham, Brewer dissented without opinion in a number of cases in which the majority upheld either the exclusion or expulsion of Chinese and Japanese.[42] Some decisions did not allow him to remain silent. In *United States* v. *Sing Tuck*, Brewer (joined by Peckham) chastised his brethren for denying access to the federal courts to a Chinese claiming American citizenship. After detailing the injustices suffered by Sing Tuck, Brewer concluded with a warn-ing that China could not reasonably be expected to stay on friendly terms with the United States if the Americans persisted in such officially sanctioned bigotry.[43] Equally outrageous to him was Holmes's majority opinion in *United States* v. *Ju Toy*, which held that there was no denial of due process if an immigration official, rather than a court, was given the authority to decide the claim of a Chinese seeking reentry into the United States. Here again he was joined by Peckham; Day dissented separately without opinion.[44]

Once legally in the country, however, an oriental was obliged to behave himself. Brewer (but not Peckham) was of the majority that denied Fourteenth Amendment protection to Chinese convicted of violating San Francisco's antigambling ordinance. The decision, written by Holmes, rejected the claim that enforcement of the ordinance discriminated against the Chinese.[45] If Brewer's opinions tended to be unfavorable to blacks and favorable to orientals, those concerning Indians were decidedly mixed. In most of them land was the principal issue. Among them were decisions holding that the sale of an Ottawa girl's land by her guardian was void; California mission Indians had no claim to lands now part of the public domain because they had made no earlier claim; Indians in Minnesota held certain lands in severalty even though they lay in townships usually ceded to the state for public school purposes; a Choctaw woman could not be required to accept lands in lieu of the forty acres allotted to her (Indians "were the principal beneficiaries, and their titles to the lands they selected should be protected against efforts of outsiders to secure them"); and lands granted to Indians in severalty under the Dawes Act of 1887 were no longer exempt from taxation.[46]

Matter of Heff also called for an interpretation of the Dawes Act.[47] The case involved a white man who had sold liquor to an Indian in Kansas. Since the Indian had received land under the Dawes Act, the central question was whether he was a full citizen of the United States or still a ward of the government; if the former, there was no grounds for convicting the seller of the liquor.

The Court's reporter, Charles H. Butler, later recalled the flamboyant attire of the young Kansas attorney who argued the petitioner's case: "a yellow tweed suit—no vest, flowing necktie, pink shirt and tan shoes—the most unique costume any lawyer ever wore during my time." He delivered his arguments while pacing up and down and gesticulating before the justices. Brewer interrupted him to ask what he believed the status of an Indian "allottee" to be. The young man responded: "If you fellows up there don't know, how do you think us fellows down here should know?"

Never before addressed as "you fellows up there," the stunned members of the Court (except for Harlan, who dissented without opinion) decided in favor of the outlandish lawyer's client. Brewer's opinion for the majority asked—and answered in the negative—this question: "Can it be that because one has Indian, and only Indian blood in his veins, he is to be forever one of a special class over whom the General Government may in its discretion assume the rights of guardianship which it has once abandoned, and this whether the State or the individual himself consents?"

Butler was perplexed by the decision and could only explain that the outcome "was largely owing to [the] lawyer's sheer audacity and his pink shirt." Soon the Court began ignoring *Matter of Heff* as a precedent and, in 1915, overturned it. Butler told the Court's marshal: "Well, they got his tan shoes and necktie long ago, and now they have his pink shirt." Despite his disagreement with the *Heff* decision, Butler looked upon Brewer as the Court's authority on Indian matters.[48]

Brewer himself delivered one of the decisions that distinguished—and thereby modified—the *Heff* ruling. In *United States* v. *Celestine* the Court, speaking through Brewer, decided that the federal government retained jurisdiction over Indians, even allottees under the Dawes Act, who committed crimes on a reservation.[49]

Questions of race and ethnicity also underlay the momentous series of decisions known as the *Insular Cases*, which the Fuller Court heard between 1901 and 1905.[50] At issue was the constitutional status of the new island possessions and their non-Anglo-Saxon peoples acquired as a result of the Spanish-American War, along with the recently annexed Hawaiian Islands. At the conclusion of the war, imperialists and anti-imperialists debated the wisdom and desirability of retaining the former Spanish Colonies. After the Treaty of Paris made them American property, the argument—ultimately to be decided by the Supreme Court—was over whether the new overseas territories enjoyed all, some, or none of the benefits and guarantees of the United States Constitution. Most of the *Insular Cases* involved the collection of customs duties; some pertained to jury trials and grand jury indictments. By the time the last of the *Insular Cases* was decided, the Court, by the narrowest of majorities, had concluded that the Constitution did not fully and automatically apply to the new possessions. Justice White emerged as the leader of those whose view eventually prevailed: that the Philippines, Puerto Rico, Guam, and Hawaii were "unincorporated" territories, entitled only to the most fundamental constitutional rights (for example, freedom of religion). According to this interpretation the Constitution would apply fully to those territories only when and if Congress chose to "incorporate" them and give them the status traditionally enjoyed by territories on the mainland.

Brewer consistently voted with those who rejected White's incorporation doctrine, namely, Fuller, Harlan, and Peckham. In none of the cases, however, did he write an opinion. Perhaps influencing him to be silent was the scolding from Republican newspapers, even some in Kansas, for his anti-imperialist remarks at Buffalo and elsewhere. Just as the Supreme Court was beginning to hear the early *Insular Cases*, the *Topeka Capital* noted that, according to current rumors, Brewer had "been set down as in favor of the Democratic [that is, anti-imperialist] contention" because he had "violated the traditions and habits of the judges of the highest court of the land by taking a hand in the political battle against expansion." The objectionable Buffalo speech, furthermore, had been "widely circulated by the 'aunties.'" The "mistake in taking part in a political discussion," said the *Capital*, had come to haunt Brewer now that he would be participating in the cases that were to decide the constitutional relations of the United States to its new empire.[51]

Privately, William H. Taft, the governor general of the Philippines, let Brewer know of his displeasure over one of the *Insular* decisions, in which a unanimous Court ruled that some of the import duties levied by the Philippine Commission had to be refunded. Taft told Brewer that the decision (delivered by Holmes) benefited "a lot of Englishmen who had been at the bottom of the [Filipino] insurrection." Brewer explained that he, Fuller, Harlan, and Peckham "had paid no attention to the case at all and let the other five run it." Taft grumpily concluded that "certainly the other five ran it into the ground."[52] The strong feeling behind Brewer's voting in the *Insular Cases* is abundantly evident in a letter to Fuller in which he urged the chief justice to "stay on the court till we over-throw this unconstitutional idea of colonial supreme control."[53]

Charles H. Butler remembered a Washington social affair where someone asked about the authenticity of the legend that John Marshall allowed the members of the Supreme Court to drink wine together only when it was raining—and the rain could be falling anywhere within the Court's jurisdiction. Brewer, with perhaps a touch of bitterness in his humor, replied that "the story is not only true, but you ought to know that the Supreme Court sustained the constitutionality of the acquisition of the Philippines so as to be sure of having plenty of rainy seasons."[54]

Taking his out-of-Court remarks together with his voting on the cases amounts to this: he opposed imperialism, but after the overseas empire became an established fact, he believed with equal conviction that the inhabitants of the islands were entitled to the benefits of the Constitution enjoyed by citizens of mainland territories.

Off the bench, Brewer objected to Theodore Roosevelt's acquisition of the Panama Canal Zone, yet he helped to sustain this particular venture in imperialism. Speaking for the Court in *Wilson* v. *Shaw*, he turned down a citizen's attempt to block the building of the Panama Canal. He found "the magnitude of the plaintiff's demand . . . somewhat startling," the more so because Wilson had not "disclose[d] the amount of his interest" in the project. The United States's title to the Canal Zone was held to be valid. The opinion further stated that just as the government had the power to build interstate highways, it had the power to construct this canal.[55] Brewer did not often agree with claims of broad federal power, but when he did, as in the *Debs* and *Wilson* decisions, his views could be expansive indeed.

His more usual inclination to interpret federal power narrowly is much in evidence in *Kansas* v. *Colorado*.[56] This 1907 decision emerged from a dispute between the two states over the waters of the Arkansas River. Kansas claimed that irrigation projects in Colorado diminished the flow of the Arkansas, to the detriment of agriculture in southwestern Kansas. The state based its arguments mainly upon the doctrine of riparian rights, a doctrine that obtained in the well-watered eastern states. Colorado defended her irrigation projects on the basis of prior appropriation, a water rights doctrine that the subhumid states and territories of the Far West had adopted. Colorado's case rested in part also on the Harmon doctrine, which held that a sovereign power could use the water within its borders as it saw fit.

A third party, the United States, entered a petition of intervention, claiming control over the river "to aid in reclamation of arid lands," as well as the authority to regulate interstate streams. The arguments of the three parties generated a mass of testimony and a number of constitutional questions.

Employing his usual mastery of facts, Brewer diligently studied the 8,559 typewritten pages of testimony and 122 exhibits. There are indications in his opinion that he went beyond what was presented to the Court and did some research of his own. At one point he cited a conversation with Bayard Taylor, recalling the noted traveler's views on irrigation in northern Africa.[57]

Brewer's majority opinion (White and McKenna concurred without opinion) maintained that Colorado's use of the river did indeed diminish its flow and that agriculture in Kansas had suffered as a result; yet it was necessary to weigh the harm done there against the harm that would come to Colorado should the latter be compelled to discontinue its unquestionably beneficial irrigation projects. Brewer noted also that Kansas's case was weakened by the fact that water for irrigation was taken from the Arkansas in Kansas too.[58] Kansas was, however, encouraged to return to the Court later if it could prove substantial injury to its interests. Even though the decision was a victory for Colorado, Brewer dismissed Colorado's claim to sovereign rights over the waters within her boundaries. Yet he acknowledged that principles of international law were applicable to disputes between states.[59]

The big loser in the case was the federal government. The solicitor general's petition of intervention advanced the argument that no state could prescribe rules for another and that the federal courts had no jurisdiction in matters of competing state interests; the Constitution "implied" that only Congress had the power to resolve conflicts over interstate waters.

Brewer rejected those claims of exclusive congressional power. He wrote that the Court, not Congress, was the proper agency to settle the question because federal judicial power encompassed "all controversies of a justiciable nature arising within the territorial limits of the Nation." He declared furthermore that Congress had only those powers delegated to it by the Constitution. He agreed that there were implied federal powers but insisted that they needed limitations. Regarding specific powers, he acknowledged that the Constitution granted Congress authority over navigable streams, and earlier, in *United States* v. *Rio Grande Dam and Irrigation Co.* (1899), he had interpreted this power broadly.[60] But the question now before the Court did not concern navigability. He based much of his rejection of the government's petition on his reading of the Tenth Amendment ("The powers not delegated to the United States by the Constitution, nor prohibited by it to the States, are reserved to the States respectively, or to the people.").

Since the Constitution, congressional acts, or the common law of the two states did not provide a solution to the matter at hand, Brewer wrote that "interstate common law" (as pronounced by the federal courts) had guided the Court to its decision. The doctrine of an interstate or "general" common law, distinct from that formulated by the state courts, derived from Justice Story's opinion in *Swift* v. *Tyson* (1842).[61] A decision delivered by Brewer in 1901, *Western Union Telegraph Co.* v. *Call Publishing Co.*, had advanced the doctrine that federal courts could decide questions of general commercial law without being bound by state decisions.[62]

Brewer's readiness in *Kansas* v. *Colorado* to deny the expansion of federal power was of course characteristic of him. Such judicial insistence on a limited role for the federal government did not survive many years beyond Brewer's tenure on the Court. But the decision was hailed by many then and since as a classic analysis of the federal system.[63] Its importance at the time entitles it to rank as one of his major opinions. Moreover, courts ever since have cited those portions of it that pertain to water rights and interstate common law. The decision also established the principle of an "equitable apportionment of benefits," which the Court would employ in later cases concerning interstate streams.

A later treatise on *Kansas* v. *Colorado* urged that it was better to settle disputes between states by means of compacts, as sanctioned by Article I, section 10, of the Constitution, rather than by litigation.[64] In a case to settle the boundary between Washington and Oregon, Brewer gave the same advice to those states.[65]

Kansas v. *Colorado* met with the hearty approval of states' rights advocates. Brewer's opinion in *South Dakota* v. *North Carolina*, however, caused unhappiness in that same quarter. The decision undermined the Eleventh Amendment, which forbids the federal courts from hearing suits brought against a state by a citizen of another state. The majority, through Brewer, held that it had not been a violation of the amendment for a person holding North Carolina bonds to donate them to South Dakota, which then sought to recover on them. White entered a long dissent, which Fuller, McKenna, and Day joined.[66]

The work of the Circuit Courts of Appeals and the demise of Isaac C. Parker contributed to a decrease of many types of criminal cases heard by the Supreme Court in the early twentieth century.

Yet in this age of expanding federal power Congress was passing legislation that imposed criminal penalties, thus increasing the criminal jurisdiction of the federal courts. In the criminal cases for which Brewer delivered opinions, he showed his usual firmness toward criminality, but balanced against this was a reluctance to endorse attempts by Congress to enter the realm of the police power, a power traditionally exercised by the states.

He had been part of the majority that, through White's opinion, upheld the federal Oleomargarine Act.[67] In a subsequent case Brewer's majority opinion held that a violator of the act, that is, one who sought to evade the tax imposed by it, was not entitled to a jury trial. He reasoned that the man had been charged not with a real crime but with a "petty offense." Harlan entered a long dissent, disputing the notion that the latter was not covered by the Constitution's guarantee of a jury trial.[68]

Brewer's dissent in *Patterson* v. *Colorado* showed more sensitivity to the Bill of Rights.[69] The plaintiff in error had published articles and a cartoon that "reflected upon the motives and conduct of the Supreme Court of Colorado." He was convicted for contempt of court. Holmes, for the majority, denied his appeal for want of federal jurisdiction. He saw no merit in Patterson's claim that his conviction violated First and Fourteenth Amendment rights to freedom of expression. Harlan's dissent challenged Holmes's contention that the First Amendment prohibited only prior restraint and went on to say that the Fourteenth Amendment incorporated the First Amendment's protection of freedom of the press and applied it to the states.[70] Brewer's dissent did not accept Harlan's view that the Fourteenth Amendment incorporated the Bill of Rights and applied those rights to the states (none of Harlan's colleagues shared his expansive interpretation of the amendment); but neither did Brewer accept Holmes's view that the case presented no federal question; Patterson's assertion of a constitutional right could not "be regarded as a frivolous one" and should have been addressed directly by the Court.[71]

The Immigration Act of 1907 made it a crime for one to bring an alien into the United States for purposes of prostitution and provided penalties for persons harboring such aliens. The majority, speaking through Brewer, held that it was within Congress's power to restrict immigration but also that the provision regarding the harboring of alien prostitutes was an unconstitutional invasion of the police power of the states. Brewer posed the question, "Can it be within the power of Congress to control all the dealings of our citizens with resident aliens?" He answered in the negative. Holmes, together with Harlan and Moody, disagreed, arguing for a broader view of federal authority.[72]

Even when Congress's power to enact criminal legislation was unquestioned, Brewer favored a narrow interpretation. United States Senator J. Ralph Burton of Kansas was convicted of receiving compensation from a company being investigated for fraud by the Post Office Department. Harlan's majority opinion upheld the lower court. Brewer, joined by White and Peckham, dissented on the grounds that neither Burton nor the government had a "pecuniary interest" in the matter being investigated.[73]

Brewer believed that there were certain kinds of cases that unnecessarily increased the justices' work load and should not be brought before them. He wrote opinions for a unanimous Court in which he expressed impatience with attempts to get cases before the Court by means of habeas corpus rather than on appeal through writs of error. In one he concluded by saying, "To permit every petty criminal case to be brought directly to this court upon *habeas corpus*, on the ground of alleged misconception or disregard of our decisions, would be a grievous misuse of our time, which should be devoted to a consideration of the more important legal and constitutional questions which are constantly arising and calling for our determination."[74] Appeals in civil cases could also waste the Court's time. In a decision for one of them Brewer noted that the plaintiff had filed thirty-seven assignments of error and the defendant thirty-nine. "It may be true, as the Scriptures have it," he observed, "that 'in the multitude of counsellors there is safety,' but it is also true that in a multitude of assignments of error there is danger."[75]

One scholar has described Brewer as "bitterly hostile" to collusive suits brought to the courts for the purpose of settling hypothetical questions.[76] Impatient though he was over attempts to bring unworthy cases before the Supreme Bench, he believed that once a legitimate matter was before the justices the lawyers were entitled to a generous allotment of time for making their oral arguments; along with Fuller and Harlan, he opposed attempts to limit them. Holmes, however, told Charles H. Butler that "he was never influenced by oral arguments, but considered the cases on the briefs" and therefore favored limiting the lawyers' verbal presentations.[77]

Several cases in the decade from 1901 to 1910 gave Brewer opportunities to admonish attorneys, as he had done throughout his judicial life, to mend their ways. The alleged misconduct of one of them prompted him to write that "[i]t is not enough that the doors of the temple of justice are open; it is essential that the ways of approach be kept clean."[78]

Brewer also saw to it, in his own case at least, that the temple of justice was kept busy. During his twenty years on the Supreme Court he wrote a total of 607 opinions. Five hundred thirty-three of these were the opinions of the Court; the remainder were 8 concurring, 57 dissenting, and 9 other opinions. On 36 occasions he concurred without opinion, and 169 times he dissented without opinion.[79] Of the first hundred men to serve on the Supreme Bench only eleven others have written more opinions of the Court, and only eight others have written more opinions altogether, nearly all of whom had longer tenures on the Court than did Brewer. Thus he ranks as one of the most prolific justices in the Court's history.[80]

Brewer's high percentage of dissenting opinions, as John E. Semonche has pointed out, shatters any notion that Brewer was an ideological leader of the Fuller Court.[81] Despite his frequent disagreement with his brethren, however, Brewer was generally in step with them. And the Fuller Court, contrary to shopworn interpretations of it, was generally in step with the nation. Far more often than not, Brewer and his colleagues gave their stamp of approval to state and federal legislation designed to meet the popular demand for reform. The relatively few instances when they did not caused no permanent damage to efforts to regulate and tax the great corporations nor to attempts to improve the lot of the laboring masses.

THE GREAT CIVIC APOSTLE
Reform Advocacy, 1901–1910

B Y THE END OF the nineteenth century Brewer was regularly referring to his own imminent demise. But his ten years of life in the
next century were to be as full of activity, both on and off the bench,
as were the first ten years as a member of the Supreme Court. In
the later period he seldom spoke of his impending departure from
this earth.

Contributing much to a brighter outlook was his second marriage.
Emma Miner Mott, a school principal, was a member of the Bible
class he taught at Washington's First Congregational Church. She
was a native of Chateaugay, New York, and had an unusually rich
educational background for a woman of that time, including graduation with honors from Oswego Normal School and training in vocal
music at Boston. Emma Mott moved to Washington after the death
of her father in 1887. There she and her invalid mother lived with
Emma's sister, Clara Mott, an examiner in the Pension Office.

In May of 1901, Brewer quietly informed the other members of
the Court of his engagement to Miss Mott. They assured him that
they would keep the news to themselves, but the word spread immediately throughout Washington and reached the newspapers.[1] Brewer,
then sixty-three years old, and Emma, about fifty, were married on
June 5 at the Burlington, Vermont, home of one of the bride's sisters.
Following the ceremony, which was attended by family members,
the couple went to his summer cottage at Thompson's Point on Lake
Champlain. In the fall they took up residence at Brewer's Washington
home at 1412 Massachusetts Avenue Northwest.[2] Later they lived at
1923 Sixteenth Street. The union proved as happy as his first marriage.

The marriage filled the void created by Lulu's death, and the birth of grandchildren helped to compensate for the departure of his married daughters and the loss of Fanny. One of his chief delights was to go to market in the morning with his grandchildren.[3]

Bessie, the last of the daughters to marry, once took her three-year-old child Henrietta Wells to a session of the Supreme Court. The little girl walked to the bench, where the justices were hearing arguments in an important case involving the Interstate Commerce Commission, and sat on Brewer's knee. Harlan gave her a rubber band to play with, which she used to snap her distinguished grandfather in the face.[4]

Beyond the pleasures of family life, Brewer also enjoyed the social whirl of the nation's capital. He remarked that "one can have as much of [Washington society] or as little of it as he wants" and added: "I take but little."[5] Nevertheless, the witty and outgoing justice was a popular guest at the city's numerous gatherings. At such occasions Washingtonians especially enjoyed "the good-natured badinage" between him and Justices Harlan and Brown. Brewer was a "constant and welcome guest at Gridiron Club dinners . . . where he never allow[ed] himself to get the worst of it in the interchange of jests and japes."[6]

His enjoyment of life in the upper social strata could not diminish his need to return regularly to the simpler pleasures of Leavenworth. In 1903 he took his new wife, who had never been west of the Mississippi, to Kansas.[7] Along the way he fulfilled several social engagements. Emma noticed that the manner of addressing her husband changed markedly as they progressed westward: in Washington he was the Honorable David Josiah Brewer, associate justice of the Supreme Court of the United States; in Chicago it was Mr. Justice Brewer; in Omaha he became David J. Brewer; in Kansas it was Dave. He professed to prefer the latter, but, according to a story he told, Emma feared that he would be called "Davie" if they went further west.[8] Nevertheless, they went to Colorado that year.

On January 29, 1910, he expressed his affection for his home state in a Kansas Day address before 175 members of the Kansas Society of New York at the Plaza Hotel. He began by recalling how the state had overcome earlier ravages by man and nature. Then he praised its tradition of producing reformers, "from the days of white-haired John Brown to those of red-haired Victor Murdock," the insurgent Republican congressman from Wichita. "While Kansas may not always have been wholly right, and while the stirring radicalism of her earlier days had softened a little, yet one thing remains as of old, and that is you always know what she believes in." He went on to point proudly to the state's high literacy rate, its large number of schools, the depth of religious feeling there, and its leadership in the temperance movement.[9]

Reform was the dominant theme in the many speeches he made elsewhere throughout the decade 1901–1910. As always, he was much in demand as a public speaker and, as always, he readily spoke his mind on the questions of the day.[10] In his addresses he gave at least a qualified endorsement to the multitude of reform efforts that characterized the era. He found in the various movements much to praise—and much to criticize.

His major speeches in this period included: addresses before the annual meetings of the agents of the Northwestern Mutual Life Insurance Company (of whose Board of Trustees he was a member from January 1872 until his death);[11] "Two Periods of the History of the Supreme Court," delivered to the Virginia State Bar Association; a series of lectures on "American Citizenship" at Yale; "Obedience to Law the First Civic Duty," at Chicago; and another series, "The United States a Christian Nation," at Haverford College.

In common with most other Americans of the time, Brewer decried the vast increase of wealth, both individual and corporate, because of the materialism and corruption that it engendered. The accumulation of wealth, unless accompanied by a sense of responsibility, he said, produced moral decay in persons and nations.[12] He pointed out one particularly odious example of the power of greedy and irresponsible use of money: "No one can be blind to the fact that these mighty corporations are holding out most tempting inducements to lawmakers to regard in their lawmaking those interests rather than the welfare of the nation." When he went on to charge that many members of Congress owed their offices to "corporate influence," the *New York Sun* scolded him for casting aspersions upon the nation's legislators.[13]

The remedy for corporate wrongdoing that he championed in this period was neither regulation nor trust-busting but rather the publicizing of questionable business practices. As early as 1880 he stated in a Kansas Supreme Court decision that "publicity prevents wrong."[14] In the Progressive Era he elaborated on this theme. Citing railroads as an example, Brewer argued that "the people have had reason to cry out, not so much against rates themselves as against the secret practices behind the management of transportation companies," that is, "rebates, the granting of special privileges that gave unfair advantages in competition and in the manipulations of stocks and bonds by those in control." Private corporations performing a public service "should be made subject to the same publicity" as would the government if it were performing these services. Publicizing of shady transactions would make it "dangerous for men to practice such things. Publicity is not a new force in our national life, but its power is greater today than in the past."[15]

Businesses other than railroads needed public scrutiny: "Think of the Standard Oil Company, that corporation whose assets are so great that they cannot be disclosed."[16] Even though he himself was an official of a large insurance company, he believed that the New York legislature's investigation of the insurance industry was desirable. "If there had been publicity of every act of the officers and directors of the New York insurance companies there could not have been the secret financial operations which netted so much profit for the men in charge."[17]

Brewer also insisted that corporations, like individuals, had the obligation to operate within the bounds of morality. "The organization of individuals into a corporate body . . . is not a movement outside the domain of morals, does not eliminate the matter of character, does not create a mere machine like a steam-engine unaffected by conscience, but simply puts into an organic whole the combined consciences, character and morality of all the individual members."[18]

Brewer's attitude toward corporations, as expressed in his public utterances in the early twentieth century, seems to be somewhat more critical than before. Also, he appears at this time to be less publicly hostile to labor organizations. He acknowledged that combinations of capital necessarily gave rise to combinations of labor and that industrialization and the greater reliance upon machinery had destroyed the old mutuality of interest between employers and employees.[19] He viewed concerted action by workers as not only necessary but desirable. "There is nothing more wholesome," he told an audience of Northwestern Mutual agents, "than the gathering of laborers into a union, with the collective bargains which they can make with their employers. It tends to secure higher wages, to give them a better standing, and that I heartily approve."[20]

But he remained firm in his opposition to compulsory unionism, the intimidation of nonstriking workers, and the violence, destruction of property, and other forms of lawbreaking that so often accompanied strikes. Replying to the denunciation of labor injunctions, he defended them as efforts by the courts to "prevent wrong and violence."[21]

In his eyes, both capital and labor engaged in reprehensible conduct: "[T]he black-list and boycott are alike equally damnable."[22] The excesses of capital and labor also injured individuals: "Capital too often fancies that the very magnitude of its undertakings and the beneficial results of what it is doing justifies the overriding of the rights of individuals. On the other hand labor relies on the mere physical force it can throw into the conflict."[23] His concern for individuals—laborers as well as owners—caused him to oppose compulsory arbitration as a means of ending labor-management conflicts.[24]

He continued to include governmental power, along with corporations and unions, as one of the dangers to liberty.[25] But his advocacy of a variety of reforms meant accepting—cautiously and selectively— the expansion of governmental activity. Before the Virginia bar association in 1906, he spoke at length on the role of the judiciary in contributing to, as well as limiting, "national enlargement." Included in his remarks was mention of two decisions that extended the federal judiciary's admiralty jurisdiction. In both he had dissented.[26]

In the same address he warned against the "never yet defined" police power of the states, which was "constantly broadening in its exercise, until it threatens to become an omnivorous governmental mouth, swallowing individual rights and immunities."[27] Yet a few years later in Washington, he spoke before the International Congress on Tuberculosis on "The Legitimate Exercise of the Police Power in the Protection of Health." In that address he stood by the *Lochner* decision, arguing that workers in jobs that were not unhealthy or unsafe should be free to contract for as many hours as they and their employers were agreeable to. Yet in apparent contradiction to his dissent in *Holden* v. *Hardy*, he endorsed the right of states to limit the hours of work in mining and other dangerous occupations. He even believed that the hours of railroad workers could be limited by law because the public's safety was involved. Of course, he spoke favorably of the upholding of the police power in *Muller* v. *Oregon*: "I had the honor to write the opinion of the court in that case. . . . I had and have no doubt that the decision was correct."[28]

Of all the issues that commanded his attention in the twentieth century, he spoke most passionately for that which appears closest to his heart: peace. Before a variety of audiences—lawyers, church groups, businessmen, and students—he spoke out on the same peace themes he had addressed previously: the promise and practicality of arbitration and adjudication; the evils of imperialism; the dangerous and expensive increase of armaments; the duty of Christians to work for peace; the Golden Rule as the guiding principle in diplomacy; the incompatibility of war and civilization; the rule of law in international relations; the progress being made in mitigating the horrors of war; and the role of commerce in promoting harmony between nations.[29]

Several of those public addresses were also printed as articles or pamphlets, thereby reaching still more people. His willingness to grant interviews to journalists gave him further opportunities to incline public opinion toward peace.

Brewer continued to be active at the Lake Mohonk conferences. At the 1904 meeting he spoke optimistically on the work of the Hague Conference in furthering the cause of arbitration. In later addresses at Lake Mohonk he urged that the United States assume leadership in the disarmament movement.[30] At the 1905 meeting, where he spoke on "The Enforcement of Arbitral Awards," he and other distinguished lawyers, jurists, and diplomats laid the groundwork for an organization, the American Society of International Law, which they formally established in 1907. Brewer was chosen as one of its vice presidents.[31]

With Charles H. Butler, he wrote a treatise on international law. In the preface they expressed their faith in international tribunals.[32] Brewer was one of many of his generation who saw the United States Supreme Court, with its history of successfully settling quarrels between states, as a "pattern for a future court of nations," which could similarly decide controversies between sovereign powers. "This method of determining causes," he believed, "will be extended throughout the world."[33]

Despite a growing sentiment for peace, Brewer was sadly aware that most Americans of the early twentieth century seemed to favor the aggressive foreign policies of the Roosevelt administration and a larger army and navy to back up such policies. He repeatedly and forthrightly condemned the Big Stick in general and, despite his opinion in *Wilson* v. *Shaw*, denounced in particular the wresting of Panama from Colombia. His views on militarism and imperialism of course came to Roosevelt's attention and may have been more important than his judicial responses to social and economic matters in shaping Roosevelt's privately expressed antipathy toward the justice.[34]

Most of Brewer's addresses, lectures, interviews, and articles covered more than one topic, not peace alone. His last major address, however, dealt with peace exclusively. "The Mission of the United States in the Cause of Peace," delivered before the New Jersey State Bar Association in 1909, was a forceful summing up of the peace themes he had long espoused, for example, arbitration and the Christian duty of the United States to lead the movement against war, but the major point was his opposition to increased armaments and the Big Navy thinking then so fashionable: "There never yet was a nation which built up a maximum of army and navy that did not get into war, and the pretense current in certain circles that the best way to preserve peace is to build up an enormous navy shows an ignorance of the lessons of history and the conditions of genuine and enduring peace." Brewer blasted those "interests which profit by naval construction" for being "active and clamorous" in the Big Navy movement.[35]

He then decried other manifestations of the martial spirit: "From the football field to the ironclad, from the athlete to the admiral the thought and the talk is fight." The increasingly military aspect of the nation's capital, so evident since the Spanish-American War, disturbed him. He considered the global voyage of the Great White Fleet to have been so much "parade and frolic," which contributed nothing to the promotion of peace. Also, he pointed out the disadvantages of war for both businessmen and the working classes; in time of war the former lost money and property, while the latter bore the brunt of the destruction of life.[36]

In some respects Brewer was typical of the peace advocates of his day: a conservative member of an elite class who saw war as destructive to property and the social order and who had a legalistic faith in the efficacy of arbitration and adjudication.[37] Yet in other important ways, Brewer went beyond the typical antiwar spokesman of that period. Unlike them, he was not content to work only within the small elitist peace groups. Although he did not attempt to reach a mass audience, he did take his message to many diverse groups of middle-class Americans. Several of his colleagues in the peace movement accepted imperialism and even embraced Big Navy thinking. Not Brewer. To him imperialism was both the evil fruit of past wars and productive of future ones. And increased armaments in any form, he believed, inevitably resulted in war.

One recent student of early twentieth century peace movements has written that the peace advocates of that time "refused to accept militarism as a growing evil of modern life. Rather they regarded it as an anachronistic survival of an earlier, unenlightened era and as incompatible with modern industrialism."[38] If this generalization is valid, Brewer again is an exception. He was acutely aware that militarism was on the rise and said so repeatedly.

On the other hand, he was not a thorough pacifist. He believed that the Civil War had been necessary because it preserved the union and ended slavery and that the freeing of Cuba had given the Spanish-American War a measure of respectability. When American lives and property were in jeopardy, armed force, he conceded, was justified. Brewer even stated that an American citizen owed military service to his country in time of war, even if the war itself was not altogether a just one.[39] Those qualifications aside, we must recognize that he was a tireless, dedicated, and eloquent spokesman for peace and among the most visible and vocal critics of militarism in his time.

His advocacy of peace reinforced his commitment to the women's movement because "the heart of the sex is against the terrible destruction of war." With the coming of female suffrage, which he considered both desirable and inevitable, "it may be affirmed that the ironclad will be seen only in pictures and known only in history."[40]

Brewer made those remarks in an article on women's suffrage for *The Ladies' World*. The periodical's editor prefaced the piece with the declaration that "Justice Brewer is the first great public man in America who has considered this question fairly and squarely, and written what he thinks. I consider it a great privilege to present such a paper to the readers." In the article Brewer commented on the arguments for and against equal suffrage and reviewed its record in the states that had by then adopted it. He predicted that it would be adopted throughout the country and that the country would be better for it.[41] To the graduating class of Vassar College he stated that a female president of the United States was a possibility within their lifetimes.[42]

Brewer saw the increasing influence of women as a beneficial force in other areas of American life. He singled out one female in particular for her work among the urban poor: "What man is doing more, if as much, for human betterment than Miss Jane Addams of Chicago. Her womanly sympathy does not blind her judgment, and multitudes feel that their uplift in life is due to her."[43]

Brewer, who was no social Darwinist (at least not in the commonly accepted sense of the term today), himself played a conspicuous rôle in charitable endeavors. By the time of his death he had served for over five years as president of the Associated Charities of Washington. It had been more than just lending his prestigious name to the organization. He regularly attended and participated in the monthly meetings of its board of managers, and his counsel was appreciated by its members. They valued also his attention to details, frequent financial contributions, and "unfailing devotion to the cause of the poor and helpless."[44]

Brewer divided the recipients of charity into three classes: those not able to help themselves ("the sick, the injured, all without friends, money or home"); "those who are destitute, but can help themselves if a door of opportunity be opened"; and "professional mendicants." The latter were "quasi-criminals" upon whom charity was wasted. But humanity and the good of society required that the first two groups receive aid. An official of the Associated Charities wrote feelingly of Brewer's special sympathies for those of the second group. Nevertheless, he insisted that "charity should be dispensed to them with great care lest it cause them to lose self-respect" and that all applicants be thoroughly investigated in order to prevent fraud.[45]

He did not confine his concern for the lowly to those living in Washington. The other main object of his humane feelings, the nation's orientals, resided mostly on the Pacific Coast. In keeping with his record on the Court and his earlier pronouncements, he championed their rights to enter and stay in the United States. He lashed out at "Denis Kearney, and men like him, who have just been welcomed to our shores, and who have not yet washed the brogue off their lips, stand on the street corners and cry out 'America for

the Americans; the Chinese must go.' "[46] Nor did he spare his colleagues on the Court from criticism: "Even the Chinese and Japanese
may learn that in America we know the meaning of the fatherhood
of God and the brotherhood of man, the case of Ju Toy to the
contrary notwithstanding." He was happy to note the modifying of
some of the more "brutal and barbaric" rules designed to keep orientals out of the country.[47] His support for blacks was less enthusiastic.
As a jurist he had rather consistently upheld the racial policies of the
white South. Off the bench he wished the American black well—
within a segregated society. In his oration for the Yale bicentennial,
with President Roosevelt and Booker T. Washington in the audience,
he thanked the Almighty that "there have always been in this country
college men able to recognize a true Washington whether his name be
George or Booker."[48] No doubt Washington's program of education,
self-help, and acceptance of racial separation appealed to Brewer. At
Hampton Institute in 1906, on the occasion of the presenting of a
bust of the school's founder, Samuel Chapman Armstrong, Brewer
noted that there was much talk of the government giving the citizen
a "square deal," but he emphasized that "the only square deal which
is worth anything is that deal in which the individual is himself the
active, persistent, and unconquerable factor."[49]

Washington's "accomodationist" strategy—and the endorsement
of it by men of Brewer's stature—did nothing to abate the wave of
racial violence that swept America in the early twentieth century. Its
most obvious manifestation, lynching, provoked some blunt words
from Brewer, who called it "a blot on our national life" and told a
reporter that "every man who participates in the lynching or burning
of a negro is a murderer, pure and simple."[50]

Among his colleagues on the Court, only Harlan stood out as a
supporter of black rights. In a speech at a gathering to honor the
Kentuckian, Brewer cited Harlan's bold dissent in the 1883 *Civil Rights
Cases*, in which he had argued eloquently against the majority's assault
on the Civil Rights Act of 1875. Since it was a lone dissenting opinion,
it was, said Brewer, "a mistake," but not one to be regretted: "[I]t
was a mistake on the side of equal rights, and no act done or word
said in behalf of liberty and equality ever fails to touch humanity
with inspiring, prophetic thrill." In this regard Brewer likened his
brother Harlan to John Brown but refrained from saying whether
he agreed fully with Harlan's stand.[51]

He prided himself on his Old American antecedents and, as with others of his generation, had no doubts about the superiority of Anglo-Saxon blood.[52] Yet he spoke favorably of America as "the great composite photographer of nations, with a duty to take all the various races of the earth, with all the various elements of those nations, and put them on the canvas to make one picture, one race." The *New York Times* objected to this advocacy of hybridization: "Judge Brewer's composite American, or universal mongrel . . . would be the equivalent of a yellow dog."[53]

Brewer had reservations of his own concerning some newcomers to America, particularly the ever-swelling ranks of those who came from eastern and southern Europe. He feared they lacked an understanding of true liberty—which they too often confused with license—and that they brought with them Old World notions that the law and its agents were their enemies.[54]

Obedience to the law was a persistent theme in the public remarks made in his last years. Among the lawbreakers that he singled out for special condemnation were violence-prone strikers and overly militant proponents of prohibition and women's suffrage.[55]

Even those who practiced and interpreted the law did not escape his criticism. He urged improvements in the legal profession. The nation, he repeatedly observed, needed well-trained, ethical, public-spirited, and articulate lawyers.[56] Although he defended the courts—especially the one on which he sat—from the brickbats hurled by those he termed demagogues or well-intentioned reformers,[57] he acknowledged that jurists fell short of infallibility: "Even the Supreme Court of the United States, which, barring one member is supposed to be very wise, often makes mistakes. I know it, for they overrule me, and of course they are wrong." Or as he told the Court's reporter, "[Y]ou don't know how tiresome it is to have to discuss legal problems with eight other men, none of whom knows any law."[58]

In a more serious vein he urged specific changes in the judicial system, including the controversial suggestion that the right of appeal in criminal cases be abolished. He pointed out that the English courts allowed no such appeals, and, earlier, neither had the federal courts in America. He believed that appeals in criminal cases existed as a "statutory privilege," not as a constitutional right, and that they often obstructed the punishment of criminals. The practice of lynching, he argued, would end if the crimes which incited it were punished swiftly and if the malefactors had no right of appeal. Brewer also wanted the right of appeal limited in civil cases because wealthy corporations had an unfair advantage when litigation was thus protracted.[59]

In the interest of swifter, surer justice, he wanted reform of the jury system, such as the elimination of the rule of unanimity. He also wanted courts to cease treating jurors like criminals by confining them for hours on end.[60]

Of the many recommendations he made for improving the American system of justice was one for a "better education" for members of the bar. Indeed, his faith in the salutary effects of education embraced all of society, not just lawyers: "I care not how great may be the success in material development, the greatest thing that America has produced or can produce is a free, honest, educated American citizen." For Brewer, the "Christian citizen" was especially obligated to promote education.[61]

He called for executing the provision of George Washington's will that left a bequest for a national university.[62] Among the specific educational reforms he advocated was a simplified system of spelling (for example, "altho," thru").[63]

Helping to explain his lifelong support of education is the fact that his three sisters, Mary Adele, Emilia, and Elizabeth, were teachers. So too was his second wife, who, beginning on July 1, 1906, served a three-year term as a member of the District of Columbia's Board of Education.[64] Given his strong commitment to learning, it was fitting that a number of colleges and universities bestowed honorary degrees upon him.[65]

Brewer's religious beliefs were central to his espousal of various causes—peace, charities, education, women's rights, and the rights of minorities. Some of his major public utterances in his last decade of life focused primarily upon religion. One was an address before the Old South (Congregational) Church of Boston, which was published in *The Outlook* with the title "The Religion of a Jurist." After commenting on the inherent imperfectability of human justice, he concluded: "[O]ut of my judicial experience, and looking through the glass of my life-work, I have learned to see in the cross the visible symbol of faultless justice, and in the resurrection of Christ the prophecy and truth of its final triumph."[66] A year later, in 1905, he delivered a series of lectures before the senior class of Haverford

College. In them he elaborated upon the "Christian nation" doctrine, which he had announced in the *Holy Trinity* decision.[67]

The publication of the Haverford lectures in book form called forth an accusation from *The Jewish Tribune* that he was "sowing the seeds of Anti-Semitism."[68] Brewer certainly had not consciously intended to do so. Speaking in New York before the Inter-Church Conference on Federation in 1905, he urged that subsequent meetings be broadened to include Jews as well as Christians. He was on good terms with at least two prominent Jews. Earlier he had thanked Oscar S. Straus for sending a copy of his lecture on religious liberty. In 1910 he accepted Simon Wolf's invitation to be among the speakers at a B'nai B'rith conference.[69] Less controversial than his Christian nation utterances was a brief article in *The Sunday School Times*, in which he concluded that the trial and execution of Christ were contrary to both Jewish and Roman law.[70]

As in earlier years, he continued to be a steadfast supporter of numerous church-related activities and organizations, including the dissemination of the Bible at home and abroad, Sunday schools, the American Missionary Association, and the Young Men's Christian Association.[71] In 1908 he returned to Leavenworth to participate in the observance of the semicentennial of the First Congregational Church, being then the only living original member.[72]

His concern for religion appeared to be greater than any interest in such worldly matters as politics. But his readiness to comment on public questions and his support of several causes made it impossible to divorce himself from political concerns entirely. In fact, Brewer spoke frankly to reporters in 1906 regarding Republican presidential possibilities. He predicted correctly that Roosevelt would groom Secretary of War William H. Taft as his successor rather than seek reelection in 1908. Although he paid tribute to Roosevelt's honesty and fearlessness, he believed that Taft would carry out national policies with "less friction" than had the "impulsive" and "brusque" Roosevelt. Lest he appear too partisan, Brewer had kind words also for the probable Democratic candidate for 1908, William J. Bryan, whom he described as "an honest, pure, clean man."[73]

By 1907 Roosevelt had not made his intentions clear. This provoked Brewer into condemning "the spectacle of our strenuous President playing a game of hide-and-seek with the American people."[74] This remark, according to the press, angered Roosevelt. Either this statement or some other equally public and candid criticism by Brewer—with the president in the audience—made the latter "so mad he hopped up and down forty-seven times, gnashing his teeth fourteen times on each hop and chopping even the shortest words— which were the kind he used almost exclusively—into fragments."[75]

Roosevelt was not in a position to vent his spleen against Brewer publicly, but he did so privately. When Brewer's friend Justice Brown resigned from the Court in 1906, Roosevelt considered Horace H. Lurton, a Tennessee Democrat, as a successor to Brown. He told Henry Cabot Lodge that Lurton "is really a better Republican than Brewer or Holmes." After leaving the presidency, Roosevelt opined to Henry L. Stimson that he had "seen upright well meaning judges, such as Peckham, Fuller, and Brewer, whose presence on the Supreme Court was a menace to the welfare of the Nation, who ought not to have been left there a day."[76] Holmes recalled that Roosevelt had once said that Brewer had "a sweet-bread for a brain."[77]

Nevertheless, Roosevelt consulted with Brewer, as well as other members of the Court, on the Lurton matter. In a letter to the president, Taft reminded him that Brewer had advised Roosevelt against the appointment of Lurton because he was from the Sixth Circuit, which was already overrepresented on the Court.[78] Roosevelt decided against Lurton, but not on geographical grounds; a Republican, William Henry Moody, received the appointment.

Roosevelt sought information from Brewer on another appointment, that of one Porter, who was being considered for membership on a federal commission.[79] Brewer involved himself in another patronage matter in this period: writing to William A. Johnston of the Kansas Supreme Court, he asked if Johnston thought that his court's reporter, Thomas E. Dewey, should be considered for appointment as reporter of the United States Supreme Court.[80]

A more important appointment was increasingly on his mind— the man who would succeed himself as associate justice. His health had been worsening at least since the beginning of the century, and he knew that death or retirement must come soon. A letter apparently written by a member of the Brewer family—perhaps one of his sisters—frankly declared that "Emma is determined David shall not give Roosevelt a chance to name David's successor."[81]

Surely Brewer himself wanted Roosevelt's heir apparent to have the opportunity to fill the impending vacancy. He was genuinely fond of Taft, a Yale man and a former federal circuit judge. Brewer made a witty and affectionate reference to his considerable bulk when he told an audience in 1906 that "Secretary Taft is the most polite man I ever saw in my life. Why, the other day I was in a street car with him and he got up and gave his seat to three women."[82]

When Taft received the Republican presidential nomination in 1908, a delighted Brewer wired his congratulations: "[O]ld Yale's the place in the nominative case."[83] Taft's triumph in the November election was no doubt a source of comfort to Brewer: a man far closer to his own temperament and constitutional philosophy than either Roosevelt or Bryan would in all probability name his replacement on the nation's highest tribunal.

As he approached his seventieth year, Brewer informed his wife that he would be eligible to retire at that age with a full pension "and do no more work for the balance of my life." Emma replied that he would find it impossible to do so.[84] She was right. In early June of 1907, a few weeks before his seventieth birthday, Brewer announced his intention to remain on the bench; "I am too young in spirit. I look ahead with hope, with optimism, with faith in the happy future of our country." If optimism was an attribute of youth, he said, "then I am indeed young, and can look with confidence at the years to come."[85] Two years later, newly inaugurated President Taft, in whose election Brewer had rejoiced, had an entirely different view of the justice's "youthful" qualities. Writing to Horace Lurton, he included Brewer among the "old fools" on the Supreme Court who "hold on with a tenacity that is most discouraging." Fuller was "almost senile; Harlan does no work; Brewer is so deaf that he cannot hear and has got beyond the point of the commonest accuracy; Brewer and Harlan sleep almost through all the arguments." The condition of the Court was "pitiable" and "most discouraging to the active men on the bench."[86]

Justice Brown, noting that Brewer had earlier announced his intention to retire at age seventy, privately wrote that "he pretends now that he is afraid he will lose his mind if he does so." "But," Brown added, "I think there is a much better reason than that for his remaining on the Bench. No one of them likes to take a back seat. Besides that, the wives cut an important figure, and, of course, they are always opposed to it."[87]

On the evening of March 27, 1910, Brewer, then age seventy-three, spoke to the members of Washington's Literary Club on labor relations and his dissenting opinions in cases involving regulatory legislation. For the past several days he had not felt well, having endured headaches and stomach trouble, but was in good spirits. After he had retired shortly past ten at night, Emma heard a thump. She found her husband on the bathroom floor. The only other family member present was her niece Clara Hall. Emma called Justice Ashley M. Gould of the District of Columbia Supreme Court, who lived nearby. Gould and two servants carried Brewer, whose pulse was still faintly beating, to his bed. Attempts to summon members of the Court to his bedside were unavailing. A neighboring physician, J. H. Taylor, arrived too late, as did two of the Brewer daughters. Dr. Taylor pronounced him dead at around 10:30, giving apoplexy as the cause of death.[88] Taft received the news while boarding a train. The newspapers reported that he was "much distressed." His only comment quoted at the time was that Brewer had been an "able judge."[89] A few weeks later he appointed Charles Evans Hughes, former governor of New York, to the vacancy on the Court.

The United States Senate, upon the motion of Charles Curtis of Kansas, adjourned on March 29 out of respect for Brewer's memory. The Kansas delegation in the House of Representatives issued an expression of sorrow on behalf of the people of the state.[90]

The Bar of the Supreme Court held a memorial meeting on April 30, presided over by Senator Curtis. Senator William E. Borah and other dignitaries gave addresses, and George Grafton Wilson presented the American Society of International Law's resolution of mourning. The Court's bar also organized a committee, chaired by Borah, which drew up resolutions to be presented to the Court by Attorney General George W. Wickersham.[91]

Wickersham read the resolutions and his own words of sorrow before the Supreme Court on May 31. Chief Justice Fuller responded with a brief statement on the Court's sense of loss.[92] Fuller himself passed away on July 4 of that year.

Brewer's body left Washington by rail at 3:40 P.M., March 31, and arrived at Leavenworth at 9:06 P.M., April 2. Accompanying it was William Bruce, his black messenger for over twenty years.[93] A crowd estimated at twelve hundred met the train at the Missouri Pacific depot. Several leading citizens escorted Brewer's remains to the First Congregational Church, where its pastor, the Reverend Brewer Eddy (the son of an old friend), conducted the simple service requested by the family. The choir sang a selection of Brewer's favorite hymns. The Leavenworth Bar Association had marched to the church from the courthouse. Most local businesses had either closed or were draped in mourning.

The body was then taken to Mount Muncie Cemetery. Two years earlier, on a visit to Leavenworth, Brewer had visited the cemetery and told the sexton that when he would be "brought home" he was to be buried beside his first wife and daughter Fannie.[94] The active pallbearers were prominent Leavenworth figures, including the mayor, Omar Abernathy. The fifteen honorary pallbearers (selected by Brewer's family) included: William C. Hook, judge of the Eighth Circuit; George F. Sharritt, former clerk of the federal district court, Henry W. Ide and James W. Gilpatrick, former judges of the first district court of Kansas; William Dill, current judge of the same court; Alexander Caldwell, former United States senator; and Dr. Tiffin Sinks.[95] Because army regulations had no provision for military escorts for funerals of associate justices of the Supreme Court, none was provided from Fort Leavenworth.[96] Considering the departed's antipathy toward things military, he would no doubt have preferred this.

Justice Holmes wrote Frederick Pollock, British jurist and legal scholar, that he was "rather sadly broken by Brewer's death" and expressed relief that the justices were not expected to disrupt Court business and brave a Kansas blizzard. This was largely because Emma Brewer, who had, said Holmes, "behaved like a heroine," insisted that they not make the journey. Holmes and others took comfort in reminding themselves that Brewer died while still relatively vigorous of mind. Memories of his uncle's last pathetic years were still fresh in the minds of the justices.[97]

Holmes's letter to Pollock provides us with a candid private appraisal of Brewer by a colleague. He described his late brother on the Court as a man who "came of strong blood and had been a man of great power, I believe, although I have not a very definite knowledge of his earlier work." Even though he found him to be "a very pleasant man," Holmes decried Brewer's "itch for public speaking and writing," which had caused Holmes to "shudder many times," especially when Brewer's utterances conveyed a "curious bitterness about some of the decisions of his brethren that he disagreed with.

Altogether I think he was rather an *enfant terrible*." Holmes added, in fairness to Brewer, that his penchant for speaking and writing came from a desire to provide financial security for Mrs. Brewer. Also, Holmes found it necessary to bear in mind that Brewer's unfortunate habit of too much "outside discourse" must not "blind one to great qualities, as it is apt to do."[98]

Twice in the foregoing remarks Holmes used the word "great" in his evaluation of Brewer. An eminent jurist of a later time has pointed out that "Holmes, in the unrestrained confidence of the letters to Pollock, was not likely to use the term 'great qualities' casually in referring to his judicial associates; and indeed, a perusal of the correspondence makes it clear that he felt otherwise as to some of them and said so." Taft, in his condolences to the widow, wrote that "[y]our husband was one of the great jurists and judges of this country" and spoke of "the great service which he has rendered this country."[99]

Eulogies of Brewer of course spoke favorably of his best-known attributes as a jurist and citizen: his defense of property rights; exaltation of the individual; caveats against centralization; eloquence as a public speaker; scholarship; sense of humor; broad human sympathies; and devotion to peace, education, and religion. Henry E. Davis, speaking to the Supreme Court bar, called him "the great civic apostle." The eulogists noted his wide knowledge of corporation, international, and Roman law, and of equity jurisprudence. Some lamented that his passing would impair the Court's ability to hand down strong decisions in the Standard Oil and American Tobacco Company antitrust cases then before it.[100] The Brewer opinions most often cited in obituaries and memorials were: *Kansas* v. *Colorado*, *In re Debs*, *Church of the Holy Trinity* v. *United States*, *Muller* v. *Oregon*, and *Northern Securities Co.* v. *United States*.

There were of course those who spoke less favorably. The obituary appearing in *The Outlook* (a journal for which Roosevelt was contributing editor) asserted that Brewer's long career as a judge had prevented him from knowing "those social conditions which judges are more and more compelled, through their decisions, to modify for good or for ill. In many cases a Constitutional decision is really an interpretation of social facts." Certainly Brewer would have agreed with the last sentence but, especially in light of the *Muller* decision, would have dissented vigorously with the statement that came next:

"In the interpretation of such facts Justice Brewer followed the standards of an individualistic age from which The Outlook believes the country is emerging."[101]

Others besides Holmes despaired of his readiness to mount the rostrum. Brewer had told a story on himself in this regard: The little daughter of the clerk of one of his courts refused to come to the parlor when he visited their home, telling her mother that she did not like Brewer. Upon being pressed for the reason, she replied "Judge Brewer talks too much."[102] A kinder but still critical view came later from Edward S. Corwin: "Justice Brewer was inordinately fond of the lecture platform, doing his best to restore the old Federalist conception of judges as moral mentors of the people."[103]

More recently Alan F. Westin described Brewer as "[a] conservative whose ideological bark was a bit worse than his decisional bite."[104] Others have been far more negative. Another of Holmes's British correspondents, the political theorist Harold J. Laski, told Holmes of "the rugged and ignorant feeling I always get in reading the opinions of Brewer and Peckham." He referred to John Marshall as one who would have been more at home with "sturdy Philistines like Field and Brewer and Peckham than with civilised creatures" such as Holmes. Laski recalled Roosevelt's remark that Brewer and Peckham had turned "private surmises into public decisions."[105]

In the 1930s two distinguished legal scholars, Felix Frankfurter and Jerome Frank, compiled lists of "great" justices of the Supreme Court; both included Brewer.[106] Frankfurter, later himself a member of the Court, believed that Brewer, of those who came to the Supreme Court with previous judicial experience, was "probably the most intellectually powerful of the lot." Frankfurter supposed that the "famous Field strain" accounted for "the weight of the strength he exerted on the Court," rather than his earlier service on the Kansas and circuit courts.[107]

Since the 1930s, however, writer after writer has routinely dismissed Brewer as a voice for laissez-faire. In nearly every instance it is apparent that they have based the judgment on a handful of his opinions and a few quotations from his speeches and articles, often taken out of context. Invariably, this negative view is arrived at with no clear understanding of the much-abused term *laissez-faire* and with but a superficial knowledge of the full range of Brewer's judicial and nonjudicial pronouncements.

A study based upon a poll of sixty-five law school deans and professors of history, political science, and law, published in 1972, rated the justices of the Supreme Court. Brewer was among those placed in the "average" category.[108] One suspects that the ratings were based upon notions held about the supposed liberalness or progressiveness of the individual justices. Two articles published in the 1960s presented favorable reevaluations of Brewer but did nothing to rescue him from the relatively undistinguished ranking received in the later survey.[109]

David Josiah Brewer, by the values of his day and even those of a later time, deserves to be remembered as an important figure of a much misunderstood period in the judicial history of the United States. Throughout his long service on the bench, he strove to fit the law to the new realities of an industrializing society. To do so he went beyond the dictates of legal formalism. Although committed to keeping to the law's "ancient roads," Brewer did much to establish a more pragmatic jurisprudence, one better suited to addressing the multitude of problems created by the rapid and unsettling changes of his time. Although more fearful than most of his Supreme Court colleagues that government expansion threatened property rights and individual liberties, he usually found that the Constitution could accommodate the new legislation called for by the public. More than that, he was a man of eloquence and humanitarian instincts who worked for his vision of a world of justice, material well-being, moral progress, and peace.

APPENDIX
NOTES
BIBLIOGRAPHY
INDEX

APPENDIX:
LIST OF CASES

Kansas Supreme Court:

Anthony v. Halderman, 7 Kan. 50 (1871): 33

Atchison, City of v. Jansen, 21 Kan. 560 (1879): 45

Atchison & Nebraska Rld. Co. v. Wagener, 19 Kan. 335 (1877): 45–46

Atchison Street Ry. Co. v. Missouri Pacific Ry. Co., 3 P. 284 (1884): 31

Atchison, Topeka & Santa Fe R. Co. v. Bobb, 24 Kan. 673 (1881): 31

Atchison, Topeka & Santa Fe Rld. Co. v. Brown, 26 Kan. 443 (1881): 31

Atchison, Topeka & Santa Fe Rld. Co. v. Commissioners of Jefferson County, 17 Kan. 29 (1876): 30

Avey v. Atchison, Topeka & Santa Fe R. Co., 11 Kan. 448 (1873): 30

Berg v. Atchison, Topeka & Santa Fe R. Co., 2 P. 639 (1883): 25

Blackistone v. Sherwood, 2 P. 874 (1883): 45

Board of Education of the City of Ottawa v. Tinnon, 26 Kan. 1 (1881): 43–44

Bodwell v. Crawford, 26 Kan. 292 (1881): 24

In re Bort, 25 Kan. 308 (1881): 41

Brown v. Steele, 23 Kan. 672 (1880): 43

In re Bullen, 28 Kan. 781 (1882): 40–41

Casterline v. Day, 26 Kan. 306 (1881): 45

Central Branch Rld. Co. v. Lea, 20 Kan. 353 (1878): 26

Central Branch Union Pacific R. Co. v. Smith, 23 Kan. 745 (1880): 28

Central Branch Union Pacific Rld. Co. v. Atchison, Topeka & Santa Fe Rld. Co., 26 Kan. 669 (1881): 24, 31

Chapsky v. Wood, 26 Kan. 650 (1881): 39–40

Clay v. Hoysradt, 8 Kan. 74 (1871): 45

Darling v. Rodgers, 7 Kan. 592 (1871): 26

In re Ebenhack, 17 Kan. 618 (1877): 46

Emporia, City of v. Soden, 25 Kan. 588 (1881): 38–39

Falloon v. Schilling, 29 Kan. 292 (1883): 44

Farlin v. Sook, 1 P. 123 (1883): 46

First National Bank of Parsons v. Franklin, 20 Kan. 264 (1878): 24

Francis v. Atchison, Topeka & Santa Fe Rld. Co., 19 Kan. 303: (1877): 31–32

Fretwell v. City of Troy, 18 Kan. 271 (1877): 32

Gilleland v. Schuyler, 9 Kan. 569 (1872): 33

Gossard v. Vaught, 10 Kan. 162 (1872): 32

Graham v. Board of County Commissioners of Chautauqua County, 2 P. 549 (1884): 32

Harris v. Harris, 5 Kan. 46 (1869): 20

Hays v. Rogers, 24 Kan. 143 (1880): 34

In re Holcomb, 21 Kan. 628 (1879): 34

Holthaus v. Farria, 24 Kan. 784 (1881): 42

Hudson v. Solomon, 19 Kan. 177 (1877): 45

Intoxicating Liquor Cases, 25 Kan. 751 (1881): 37–38

Kansas Pacific Rld. Co. v. Kessler, 18 Kansas 523 (1877): 30

Kansas Pacific Ry. Co. v. Dunmeyer, 24 Kan. 725 (1881): 31

Kansas Pacific Ry. Co. v. Mihlman, 17 Kan. 224 (1876): 45

Kansas Pacific Ry. Co. v. Mower, 16 Kan. 573 (1876): 25

Kansas Pacific Ry. Co. v. Reynolds, 8 Kan. 623 (1871): 24–25

Kansas Pacific Ry. Co. v. Wood, 24 Kan. 619 (1880): 25–26

Kirkpatrick v. Vickers, 24 Kan. 314 (1880): 33

Leavenworth County, Commissioners of v. Brewer, 9 Kan. 307 (1872): 24

Leavenworth County, Commissioners of v. Miller, 7 Kan. 479 (1871): 27

Leavenworth, Lawrence & Galveston Rld. Co. v. Commissioners of Douglas County, 18 Kan. 169, (1877): 28, 30

Lewis v. Commissioners of Bourbon County, 12 Kan. 186 (1873): 28

Marion County v. Hoch, 24 Kan. 778 (1881): 26

Memphis, Kansas & Colorado Ry. Co. v. Thompson, 24 Kan. 170 (1880): 28

Miami County, Commissioners of v. Brackenridge, 12 Kan. 114 (1873): 43

Millar v. State, 2 Kan. 175 (1863): 12

Missouri, Kansas & Texas Ry. Co. v. Weaver, 16 Kan. 456 (1876): 30

Missouri Pacific Rld. Co. v. Leggett, 27 Kan. 353 (1882): 26

Monroe v. May, 9 Kan. 466 (1872): 42

Morris v. Shew, 29 Kan. 661 (1883): 46

Morrow v. Commissioners of Saline County, 21 Kan 484 (1879): 30

Muse v. Wafer, 29 Kan. 279 (1883): 46

National Land Co. v. Perry, 23 Kan. 140 (1879): 44–45

Newton, City of v. Atchison, 1 P. 288 (1883): 32

Osterhout v. Osterhout, 2 P. 869 (1883): 43

Parmellee v. Knox, 24 Kan. 113 (1880): 29, 30

Perry v. Bailey, 12 Kan. 539 (1874): 46

Pfeiffer v. Union Evangelical Church, 20 Kan. 100 (1878): 45

Ex parte Phillips, 7 Kan. 48 (1871): 34

Plumb v. Bay, 18 Kan. 415 (1877): 52

Prohibitory Amendment Cases 24 Kan 704 (1881): 36–37

Prouty v. Stover, 11 Kan. 235 (1873): 33

In re Pryor, 18 Kan. 72 (1877): 46

Rahn v. King Wrought-Iron Bridge Manufactory, 16 Kan. 530 (1876): 46

Rice v. State, 3 Kan. 141 (1865): 12

Rolfs v. Shallcross, 1 P. 523 (1883): 35

Russell v. State, 11 Kan. 308 (1873): 32–33

St. Joseph & Denver City R. Co. v. Ryan, 11 Kan. 602 (1873): 25

Sarahass v. Armstrong, 16 Kan. 192 (1876): 43

Sawyer v. Sauer, 10 Kan. 466 (1872): 30

Scott v. Paulen, 15 Kan. 162 (1875): 32–33

Sherman v. Anderson, 27 Kan. 333 (1882): 26

Smith v. McNair, 19 Kan. 330 (1877): 30

Smith v. Smith, 22 Kan. 699 (1879): 41

Smith v. State, 1 Kan. 365 (1863): 11–12

Smith v. Woodleaf, 21 Kan. 717 (1879): 45

Solomon R. Co. v. Jones, 2 P. 657 (1883): 30

State v. Bancroft, 22 Kan. 170 (1879): 34

State v. Beebe, 13 Kan. 589 (1874): 34

State v. Commissioners of Shawnee County, 28 Kan. 431 (1882): 29

State v. Curtis, 29 Kan. 384 (1883): 38

State v. Elting, 29 Kan. 397 (1883): 33

State v. Furbeck, 29 Kan. 532 (1883): 35

State v. Mugler, 29 Kan. 252 (1883): 85

State v. Reddick, 7 Kan. 143 (1871): 24

State v. Wilson, 24 Kan. 189 (1880): 170

State ex rel. Griffith v. Osawkee Township, 14 Kan. 418 (1875): 29

State ex rel. St. Joseph & Denver City R. Co. v. Commissioners of Nemaha County, 7 Kan. 542 (1871): 27–28

State ex rel. St. Joseph & Denver City R. Co. v. Commissioners of Nemaha County, 10 Kan. 569 (1873): 28

State ex rel. Mitchell v. Stevens, 23 Kan. 456 (1880): 33

State ex rel., v. Gilmore, 20 Kan. 551 (1878): 33

Tennent v. Battey, 18 Kan. 324 (1877): 45

Tyler v. Safford, 3 P. 333 (1884): 46

Union Pacific Ry. Co. v. Milliken, 8 Kan. 647 (1871): 30

Union Pacific Ry. Co. v. Young, 19 Kan. 488 (1877): 31

Warner v. Warner, 11 Kan. 121 (1873): 41–42

Watson v. Balch, 1 P. 775 (1883): 34

Werner v. Edmiston, 24 Kan. 147 (1880): 36

Whitford v. Horn, 18 Kan. 455 (1877): 23

Wicks v. Mitchell, 9 Kan. 80 (1872): 42

Wicks v. Smith, 18 Kan. 508 (1871): 45

Wilkens v. Tourtellott, 29 Kan. 513 (1883): 46

Willets v. Jeffries, 5 Kan. 470 (1870): 20

Wolf v. Hough, 22 Kan. 659 (1879): 45

Wright v. Noell, 16 Kan. 601 (1876): 42

Wyandotte County v. First Presbyterian Church, 1 P. 109 (1883): 225n.23

Yandle v. Kingsbury, 17 Kan. 195 (1876): 31

United States Circuit Court

American Bell Telephone Co. v. Southwestern Telephone Co., 34 F. 795 (C.C.E.D. Ark. 1888): 66

Ames v. Union Pacific Ry. Co., 64 F. 165 (C.C.D. Neb. 1894): 88–89, 108, 118

Bard v. City of Augusta, 30 F. 906 (C.C.D. Kan. 1887): 58

Blair v. St. Louis, Hannibal & Keokuk R. Co., 23 F. 521 (C.C.E.D. Mo. 1885): 69

Block v. Atchison, Topeka & Santa Fe R. Co., 21 F. 529 (C.C.E.D. Mo. 1884): 58

Borgman v. Omaha & St. Louis Ry. Co., 41 F. 667 (C.C.S.D. Iowa 1890): 58

Burlington, Cedar Rapids & Northern Ry Co. v. Northwestern Fuel Co., 31 F. 652 (C.C.D. Minn 1887): 56

Central Trust Co. v. Wabash, St. Louis & Pacific Ry. Co., 26 F. 74 (C.C.E.D. Mo. 1886): 69

Central Trust Co. v. Wabash, St. Louis & Pacific Ry. Co., 29 F. 546 (C.C.E.D. Mo. 1886): 55

Central Trust Co. v. Wabash, St. Louis & Pacific Ry. Co., 29 F. 618 (C.C.E.D. Mo. 1886): 60

Chicago & N.W. Ry. Co. v. Dey, 35 F. 866 (C.C.S.D. Iowa 1888): 55–56, 85, 216n.20

Chicago, Burlington & Quincy R. Co. v. Dey, 38 F. 656 (C.C.S.D. Iowa 1889): 56

Chicago, Rock Island & Pacific Ry. Co. v. Union Pacific Ry. Co., 47 F. 15 (C.C.D. Neb. 1891): 102–103

Chicago, St. Paul, Minneapolis & Omaha Ry. Co. v. Becker, 35 F. 883 (C.C.D. Minn. 1888): 55–56

Cooke v. Bangs, 31 F. 640 (C.C.D. Minn. 1887): 69

Cowan v. Union Pacific Ry. Co., 35 F. 43 (C.C.D. Colo. 1888): 57

Davis v. St. Louis & San Francisco Ry Co., 25 F. 786 (C.C.D. Kan. 1885): 54

Denver & Rio Grande R. Co. v. United States, 34 F. 838 (C.C.D. Colo. 1888): 57

In re Deputy Sheriffs, 22 F. 153 (C.C.E.D. Mo. 1884): 69

In re Doolittle, 23 F. 544 (C.C.E.D. Mo. 1885): 62

Frank v. Denver & Rio Grande Ry. Co., 23 F. 757 (C.C.D. Colo. 1885): 63–64

Gilette v. City of Denver, 21 F. 822 (C.C.D. Colo. 1884): 68

Hakes v. Burns, 40 F. 33 (C.C.D. Colo. 1889): 55

Hedges v. Dixon County, 37 F. 304 (C.C.D. Neb. 1889): 58

Howard v. Denver & Rio Grande R. Co., 26 F. 837 (C.C.D. Colo. 1886): 58

Interstate Land Co. v. Maxwell Land Grant Co., 41 F. 275 (C.C.D. Colo. 1889): 65

Iowa v. Chicago, Burlington & Quincy R. Co., 37 F. 497 (C.C.S.D. Iowa 1889): 56

Jackson County Horse R. Co. v. Interstate Rapid Transit Ry. Co., 24 F. 306 (C.C.D. Kan. 1885): 59

Kansas v. Bradley, 26 F. 289 (C.C.D. Kan. 1885): 54, 67

Kansas v. Walruff, 26 F. 178 (C.C.D. Kan. 1886): 66–67, 68, 74, 85

Keyes v. Pueblo Smelting & Refining Co., 31 F. 560 (C.C.D. Colo. 1887): 66

Ex Parte Kieffer, 40 F. 399 (C.C.D. Kan. 1889): 67–68

Lyon v. Union Pacific Ry. Co., 35 F. 111 (C.C.D. Colo. 1888): 69–70

McCory v. Chicago, Milwaukee & St. Paul Ry. Co., 31 F. 531 (C.C.D. Minn. 1887): 57

McDonald v. Union Pacific Ry. Co., 35 F. 38 (C.C.D. Colo. 1888): 57

McElroy v. Kansas City, 21 F. 257 (C.C.W.D. Mo. 1884): 67

Mealman v. Union Pacific Ry. Co., 37 F. 189 (C.C.D. Colo. 1889): 58

Mercantile Trust Co. v. Missouri, Kansas & Texas Ry. Co., 36 F. 221 (C.C.D. Kan. 1888): 61

Mercantile Trust Co. v. Missouri, Kansas & Texas Ry. Co., 41 F. 8 (C.C.D. Kan. 1889): 61

Missouri v. Kansas City, Fort Scott & Gulf R. Co., 32 F. 722 (C.C.W.D. Mo. 1887): 58

Missouri ex rel. Baltimore & Ohio Telegraph Co. v. Bell Telephone Co., 23 F. 539 (C.C.E.D. Mo. 1885): 59–60

Newton v. Joslin, 30 F. 891 (C.C.D. Colo. 1887): 69

Northern Pacific R. Co. v. United States, 36 F. 282 (C.C.D. Minn. 1888): 57

Omaha Horse Ry. Co. v. Cable Tramway Co., 30 F. 324 (C.C.D. Neb. 1887): 59

Omaha Horse Ry. Co. v. Cable Tram Way Co., 32 F. 727 (C.C.D. Neb. 1887): 59

O'Rorke v. Union Pacific Ry. Co., 22 F. 189 (C.C.D. Colo. 1884): 57

Polsdorfer v. St. Louis Wooden-Ware Works, 37 F. 57 (C.C.E.D. Mo. 1888): 66

Pullman's Palace Car Co. v. Twombly, 29 F. 658 (C.C.S.D. Iowa 1887): 59

Rollins v. Lake County, 34 F. 845 (C.C.D. Colo. 1888): 55

St. Paul, Minneapolis & Manitoba R. Co. v. Greenhalgh, 26 F. 563 (C.C.D. Minn. 1886): 56

Sherwood v. Moelle, 36 F. 478 (1888): 22–23

Short v. Chicago, Milwaukee & St. Paul Ry. Co., 33 F. 114 (C.C.D. Minn. 1887): 55

Sullivan v. Chrysolite Silver Mining Co., 21 F. 892 (C.C.D. Colo. 1884): 66

Union Pacific Ry. Co. v. United States, 59 F. 813 (8th Cir. 1894): 103

United States v. Kane, 23 F. 748 (C.C.D. Colo. 1885): 62–63

United States v. Maxwell Land Grant Co., 21 F. 19 (C.C.D. Colo. 1884): 64–65

United States v. Maxwell Land Grant Co., 26 F. 118 (C.C.D. Colo. 1886): 65

United States v. Missouri, Kansas & Texas Ry. Co., 37 F. 68 (C.C.D. Kan. 1888): 57

United States v. Morrissey, 32 F. 147 (C.C.E.D. Mo. 1887): 55

United States v. Union Pacific Ry. Co., 37 F. 551 (C.C.D. Colo. 1889): 57

United States v. Western Union Telegraph Co., 50 F. 28 (C.C.D. Neb. 1892): 102–103

Washburn & Moen Manufacturing Co. v. Grinnell Wire Co., 24 F. 23 (C.C.S.D. Iowa 1885): 66

Western Union Telegraph Co. v. Brown, 32 F. 337 (C.C.E.D. Mo. 1887): 55

Westinghouse Air-Brake Co. v. Carpenter, 32 F. 484 (C.C.S.D. Iowa 1887): 66

Wheeler v. Sexton, 34 F. 154 (C.C.D. Neb. 1888): 55

United States Supreme Court

Acres v. United States, 164 U.S. 388 (1896): 112

Adair v. United States, 208 U.S. 161 (1908): 152

Adams Express Co. v. Kentucky, 206 U.S. 129 (1907): 146

Adams Express Co. v. Kentucky, 214 U.S. 218 (1909): 146

Adams Express Co. v. Ohio State Auditor, 166 U.S. 185 (1897): 93

Addyston Pipe and Steel Co. v. United States, 175 U.S. 211 (1899): 97, 145

Aerfetz v. Humphreys, 145 U.S. 418 (1892): 110

Ah How v. United States, 193 U.S. 65 (1904): 158

Ah Sin v. Wittman, 198 U.S. 500 (1905): 159

Alabama and Vickburg Ry. Co. v. Mississippi R.R. Commission, 203 U.S. 496 (1906): 142–143

Allgeyer v. Louisiana, 165 U.S. 578 (1897): 151

Ard v. Brandon, 156 U.S. 537 (1895): 101

Armour Packing Co. v. United States, 209 U.S. 56 (1908): 142

Atchison, Topeka & Santa Fe R.R. Co. v. Matthews, 174 U.S. 96 (1899): 97

Atkin v. Kansas, 191 U.S. 207 (1903): 151

Atlantic and Pacific Telegraph Co. v. Philadelphia, 190 U.S. 160 (1903): 149

Atlantic Coast Line R.R. Co. v. Florida, 203 U.S 256 (1906): 142

Austin v. Tennessee, 179 U.S. 343 1900): 91–92

Ballinger v. United States ex rel. Frost, 216 U.S. 240 (1910): 159

Baltimore & Ohio R.R. Co. v. Baugh, 149 U.S. 368 (1893): 110

Barden v. Northern Pacific R.R. Co., 154 U.S. 288 (1894): 100–101

Barker v. Harvey, 181 U.S. 481 (1901): 159

Bassett v. United States, 137 U.S. 496 (1890): 113

Beers v. Glynn, 211 U.S. 477 (1909): 149

Bellingham Bay & British Columbia Ry. Co. v. New Whatcom, 172 U.S. 314 (1899): 98

Bell Telephone Co. of Missouri v. Missouri ex rel. Baltimore & Ohio Telegraph Co., 127 U.S. 780 (1887): 60

Berea College v. Kentucky, 211 U.S. 45 (1908): 156–157

Bram v. United States, 168 U.S. 532 (1897): 113

Brass v. North Dakota, 153 U.S. 391 (1894): 87, 146

Brennan v. Titusville, 153 U.S. 289 (1894): 93

Brown v. United States, 164 U.S. 221 (1896): 112

Budd v. New York, 143 U.S. 517 (1892): 86–87, 118, 146

Burton v. United States, 202 U.S. 344 (1906): 166

Camou v. United States, 171 U.S. 277 (1897): 100

The Carlos F. Roses [*sic*], 177 U.S. 655 (1900): 113

Southworth v. United States, 161 U.S. 639 (1896): 113–114

Spencer v. McDougal, 159 U.S. 62 (1895): 153

Springer v. United States, 102 U.S. 586 (1881): 94

Stearns v. Minnesota, 179 U.S. 223 (1900): 98–99

Stone v. Farmers' Loan and Trust Co., 116 U.S. 307 (1886): 216n.20

Sullivan v. Iron Silver Mining Co., 143 U.S. 431 (1892): 80

Swift & Co. v. United States, 196 U.S. 375 (1905): 147

Swift v. Tyson, 16 Peters 1 (1842): 164

Talbott v. Silver Bow County, 139 U.S. 438 (1891): 94

Tamerling v. United States Freehold & Emigration Co., 93 U.S. 644 (1876): 65

Tarpey v. Madsen, 178 U.S. 215 (1900): 101

Tarrance v. Florida, 188 U.S. 519 (1903): 156

Taylor v. Beckham, 178 U.S. 548 (1900): 99

Texas & Pacific Ry. Co. v. Marshall, 136 U.S. 393 (1890): 102

Thompson v. Maxwell Land Grant and Railway Co., 168 U.S. 451 (1897): 100

Thompson v. Utah, 170 U.S. 343 (1898): 112

Travellers' Insurance Co. v. Connecticut, 185 U.S. 364 (1902): 149

Underwood v. Dugan, 139 U.S. 380 (1891): 101

Union Pacific Ry. Co. v. Botsford, 141 U.S. 250 (1891): 109

Union Pacific R.R. Co. v. Mason City and Fort Dodge R.R. Co., 199 U.S. 160 (1905): 140

United States v. American Bell Telephone Co., 167 U.S. 224 (1897): 99–100

United States v. Ballin, 144 U.S. 1 (1892): 114

United States v. California and Oregon Land Co., 148 U.S. 31 (1893): 222n.20

United States v. Celestine, 215 U.S. 278 (1909): 160

United States v. Colton Marble and Lime Co., 146 U.S. 615 (1892): 101

United States v. Des Moines Navigation and Railway Co., 142 U.S. 510 (1892): 100

United States v. E. C. Knight Co., 156 U.S. 1 (1895): 96, 109, 144, 145, 147

United States v. Hancock, 133 U.S. 193 (1890): 82

United States v. Ju Toy, 198 U.S. 253 (1905): 158, 177

NOTES

Introduction

1. DJB, "The Federal Judiciary," *Tenth Annual Meeting of the Bar Association of the State of Kansas* (Topeka: Crane & Co., 1893), 82.

2. See, for example, Henry J. Abraham, *Justices and Presidents: A Political History of the Appointments to the Supreme Court*, 2d ed. (New York: Oxford University Press, 1985), 145, 147–148, 150, 165, and Loren P. Beth, *The Development of the American Constitution, 1877–1917* (New York: Harper & Row, 1971), 185.

3. Especially important in this regard are Michael Les Benedict, "Laissez-Faire and Liberty: A Re-Evaluation of the Meaning and Origins of Laissez-Faire Constitutionalism," *Law and History Review* 3 (Fall 1985):293–331; Charles W. McCurdy, "Justice Field and the Jurisprudence of Government-Business Relations: Some Parameters of Laissez-Faire Constitutionalism," *Journal of American History* 61 (March 1975):970–1005; John E. Semonche, *Charting the Future: The Supreme Court Responds to a Changing Society, 1890–1920* (Westport, CN: Greenwood Press, 1978); and Melvin I. Urofsky, "Myth and Reality: The Supreme Court and Protective Legislation in the Progressive Era," *Yearbook Supreme Court Historical Society* (1983):53–72.

1. The Path to the Bench: From Smyrna to Kansas, 1837–1862

1. There are only a few scholarly treatments of Brewer's life and work: Francis Bergan, "Mr. Justice Brewer: Perspective of a Century," *Albany Law Review* 25 (June 1961):191–202; D. Stanley Eitzen, *David J. Brewer, 1837–1910: A Kansan on the United States Supreme Court*, Emporia State Research Studies, vol. 12, no. 3 (Emporia, KS: Kansas State Teachers College, 1964); Owen M. Fiss, "David J. Brewer: The Judge as Missionary," in *The Fields and the Law* (San Francisco: United States District Court for the Northern District of California Historical Society, 1986):53–63; Robert E. Gamer, "Justice Brewer and Due Process: A Conservative Court Revisited," *Vanderbilt Law Review* 18 (March 1965):615–641; Kermit L. Hall, "David J. Brewer," in *Encyclopedia of the American Constitution*, Leonard W. Levy et al., eds., 4 vols. (New York: Macmillan Publishing Co., 1986)1:152–153; Lynford A. Lardner, "The Constitutional Doctrines of Justice David Josiah Brewer" (Ph.D. diss., Princeton University, 1938); Brian J. Moline, "David Josiah Brewer, Kansas Jurist," *Journal of the Kansas Bar Association* 55 (January–February 1986):7–11; Arnold M. Paul, "David J. Brewer," in *The Justices of the United States Supreme Court, 1789–1969: Their Lives and Major Opinions*, Leon Friedman and Fred Israel, eds., 5 vols. (New York: Chelsea House Publishers, 1969)3:1515–1549. All of the above were useful in preparing the present study. Anyone seeking a fuller understanding of Brewer's career and

thought is urged to read especially Fiss's essay, Gamer's article, and Lardner's dissertation.

2. Details of Brewer's ancestry and parentage are found in *Eminent and Representative Men of Virginia and the District of Columbia in the Nineteenth Century* (Madison, WI: Brant & Fuller, 1893), 58; Henrietta Brewer Karrick, *David Josiah Brewer: A Biographical Sketch. . . .* (Washington, D.C.: n.p., 1912), 3, 4; F. P. Brewer, *Sketch of Rev. Josiah Brewer, Missionary to the Greeks* (n.p., 1880), 7–8; Josiah Brewer, "What must I do to be saved," ms. sermon, May 11, 1862, Brewer Papers, Yale University Library (all subsequent citations of the "Brewer Papers" are to this collection).

3. Carl Brent Swisher, *Stephen J. Field: Craftsman of the Law* (Washington, D.C.: Brookings Institution, 1930), 13–15.

4. Josiah Brewer, "What must I do to be saved"; F. P. Brewer, *Josiah Brewer*, 9–10; Clark A. Smith, "In Memoriam," 83 Kansas vi (1911).

5. DJB extolled the accomplishments of the Field family in an undated ms. poem, found in Box 10, Brewer Papers.

6. Gamer, "Justice Brewer and Due Process," 617–618; Karrick, *Brewer*, 4.

7. Josiah Brewer to Rev. E. P. Tyler, March 8, 1844, Brewer Papers.

8. DJB to Heman Field, November 2, 1846; "Minerals DJB, Middletown, Conn.," Box 8, Brewer Papers.

9. Warren Watson, "David Josiah Brewer," in *Distinguished American Lawyers*, by Henry W. Scott (New York: C. L. Webster, 1891), 76.

10. F. P. Brewer, *Josiah Brewer*, 13.

11. DJB, [Remarks at dinner given for John Marshall Harlan], *Beta Theta Pi* 18 (February–March 1891):254–256; Karrick, *Brewer*, 5; Charles Fairman, "The Education of a Justice: Justice Bradley and Some of His Colleagues," *Stanford Law Review* 1 (January 1949):243.

12. Chauncey M. Depew, *My Memories of Eighty Years* (New York: Charles Scribner's Sons, 1924), 4–5, 6, 8.

13. Ibid., 4; Fairman, "The Education of a Justice," 243–244.

14. Fairman, "The Education of a Justice," 243–244; *Kansas City Star*, March 3, 1910.

15. "Orations and Poems Presented for Commencement and Junior Exhibition Class of 1856," Yale Mss., Yale University Library.

16. Watson, "Brewer," 77.

17. Irving Browne, "The Albany Law School," *Green Bag* 2 (April 1890):153–157.

18. DJB to Etta (Henrietta Brewer, a sister), December 19, 1857.

19. Undated clipping, Box 9, Brewer Papers.

20. Dred Scott v. Sandford, 19 Howard 393 (1857).

21. Undated clipping, Box 9, Brewer Papers.

22. Undated clipping, Box 9, Brewer Papers. Another poem by Brewer, a New Year's Day carrier's address for the *Leavenworth Times* (quoted in part in Fairman, "The Education of a Justice," 245) also refers to the Dred Scott case.

23. Many of them are found in Box 135, Karrick Family Collection, Yale University Library.

24. Browne, "Albany Law School," 153; DJB's diploma is in the Yale Miscellaneous Mss., Yale University Library.

25. Bergan, "Mr. Justice Brewer," 195; Henry M. Field, *The Life of David Dudley Field* (New York: Charles Scribner's Sons, 1898), 61.

26. DJB, "Typescript of Speech Delivered to Congregational Club of Rhode Island," n.d., Brewer Papers, Box 4.

27. *Kansas City Times*, March 29, 1910.

28. *Topeka Commonwealth*, September 17, 1870.

29. *Topeka Capital*, August 1, 1897; Albert H. Horton, "David Josiah Brewer," *Green Bag* 2 (January 1890):1.

30. David G. Taylor, "Boom Town Leavenworth: The Failure of the Dream," *Kansas Historical Quarterly* 38 (Winter 1972):389–415.

31. Frank W. Blackmar, ed., *Kansas: A Cyclopedia of State History*, Supplementary Volume, Part I (Chicago: Crane & Co., 1902), 48; *Report of the Thirty-third Annual Meeting of the American Bar Association . . . 1910*, 660.

32. *Topeka Mail and Breeze*, July 6, 1910.

33. *Kansas City Star*, March 30, 1910; H. Miles Moore, *Early History of Leavenworth City and County* (Leavenworth: Sam'l Dodsworth Book Co., 1906), 303.

34. *Leavenworth Times*, November 3, 1859; Moore, *Early History of Leavenworth*, 321; *Leavenworth City Directory, and Business Mirror, for 1860–1861* (Leavenworth: James Sutherland, 1860), 33, 44, 164.

35. Brewer Papers.

36. *Portrait and Biographical Record of Leavenworth, Douglas and Franklin Counties, Kansas* (Chicago: Chapman Publ. Co., 1899), 592.

37. *Kansas City Star*, June 2, 1901.

38. The last professional "card" for Brewer and Hathaway appeared in the October 2, 1861, issue of the *Leavenworth Times*.

39. *Leavenworth City Directory, and Business Mirror, for 1862–1863* (Leavenworth: Buckingham and Hamilton, 1862), 21, 97.

40. *Collins' Business and Resident Directory of Leavenworth* (Leavenworth: C. Collins, 1868), 21; James C. Malin, "Notes on the Writing of General Histories of Kansas," Part 3, *Kansas Historical Quarterly* 21 (Spring 1955):361–365; *The United States Biographical Dictionary, Kansas Volume* (Chicago and Kansas City: S. Lewis & Co., 1879), 85.

41. *Portrait and Biographical Record of Leavenworth, Douglas and Franklin Counties*, 591.

42. Undated clipping, c. 1881, Scrapbook, Box 9, Brewer Papers.

43. *Kansas City Star*, March 30, 1910.

44. DJB, "The Federal Judiciary," 81–82.

45. John D. Bright, ed., *Kansas: The First Century*, 4 vols. (New York: Lewis Historical Publishing Co., 1956)3:100; *Leavenworth Times*, November 6, 1862.

2. Judge and Citizen: Leavenworth, 1863–1870

1. *Topeka Mail and Breeze*, July 6, 1900.

2. Albert H. Horton, "The State Judiciary," *Kansas Law Journal* 3 (March 20, 1886):87.

3. *Leavenworth City Directory, and Business Mirror, for 1863–64* (Leavenworth: James Sutherland, 1863), 25, 195.

4. Unidentified clipping, Scrapbook, Box 135, Karrick Family Collection.

5. Smith v. State, 1 Kan. 365 (1863); Millar v. State, 2 Kan. 175 (1863).

6. Rice v. State, 3 Kan. 141, 170 (1865).

7. Lulu to DJB, April 23 and May 1, 1864, Brewer Papers.

8. Lulu to DJB, July 24, 1864, Brewer Papers.

9. F. P. Brewer, *Josiah Brewer*, 13; Henry M. Field, *David Dudley Field*, 64.

10. Letter from several attorneys to DJB, September 20, 1864, Brewer Papers; unidentified clipping, Box 9, Brewer Papers.

11. *Leavenworth Times*, October 11, November 4, 5, 6, 1864.

12. *Annual Report of the Secretary of State of the State of Kansas, 1864*, 17; DJB to M. W. Delahay, December 5, 1865, Delahay Papers, Kansas State Historical Society.

13. William E. Unrau, "Joseph G. McCoy and Federal Regulation of the Cattle Trade," *Colorado Magazine* 43 (Winter 1966):34–38; *Leavenworth Times*, August 19, 20, 1865.

14. Unidentified clipping, Scrapbook, Box 135, Karrick Family Collection.

15. Frank H. Betton, "The Genesis of a State's Metropolis," *Collections of the Kansas State Historical Society* 7 (1901–1902):117.

16. *Topeka State Journal*, March 28, 1910.

17. *Kansas City Times*, June 16, 1901.

18. *Collins' Leavenworth Directory for 1866–1867* (Leavenworth: C. Collins, 1866?), 11, 25, 28; Kansas Corporation Charters, vol. I, 234, Archives Division, Kansas State Historical Society; E. P. Wilson to H. Miles Moore, August 9, 1867, Moore Papers, KSHS (the letterhead lists DJB as one of the twenty-six incorporators of the Leavenworth Soldiers Monument Association).

19. *Leavenworth City Directory, and Business Mirror, for 1865–66* (Leavenworth: James Sutherland, 1865), 31, 202; DJB, *Second Annual Report of the Superintendent of Public Schools of Leavenworth City, Kansas. August 1, 1866* (Leavenworth: Clarke, Emery & Co., 1866), 3, 29, 30, 33.

20. D. W. Wilder, *The Annals of Kansas, 1541–1885* (Topeka: T. Dwight Thatcher, Kansas Publishing Co., 1886), 435.

21. DJB, *Second Annual Report*, 15, 17–18.

22. Ibid., 18.

23. Ibid., 19.

24. Ibid., 20–21.

25. Ibid., 22.

26. DJB, *Third Annual Report of the Superintendent of Public Schools of Leavenworth City, Kansas, August 1, 1867* (Leavenworth: Bulletin Co-operative Printing Co., 1867), 6–8, 15, 16.

27. Ibid., 14–15, 16–17.

28. Ibid., 18–20.

29. Ibid., 21, 22, 23–24.

30. Lyman B. Kellogg, "The Founding of the State Normal School," *Collections of the Kansas Historical Society* 12 (1911–1912), 89–90; the address,

entitled "The New Profession," was published in the *Emporia News*, July 8, 1865.

31. Lincoln and Washburn College, First Secretary's Book . . . 1865–1889 (microfilm copy), Manuscripts Division, Kansas State Historical Society, 39; Russell K. Hickman, "Lincoln College, Forerunner of Washburn University," *Kansas Historical Quarterly* 18 (May 1950):180, 188.

32. "Judge D. J. Brewer," *Agora* 5 (December 1895):295.

33. DJB, "Politics in the School Room," *Kansas Educational Journal* 4 (December and January, 1867–1868):173–174.

34. DJB, "Should Teachers Engage in Politics?" ibid. 5 (August 1868):88.

35. DJB, "The Woman of Samaria," ibid. 6 (February 1869):227–228.

36. *Leavenworth Times and Conservative*, September 27, October 2, 18, 22, 1868.

37. Ibid., October 29, November 7, 1868.

38. *Merwin's Leavenworth City Directory for 1870–71* (Leavenworth: Heman Merwin, 1870), 35, 148; vols. 5 and 6 of the *Kansas Reports*.

39. Harris v. Harris, 5 Kan. 46 (1869); S. A. Kingman, [Untitled address] *Seventh Annual Meeting of the Bar Association of the State of Kansas, 1890*, 41.

40. Willets v. Jeffries, 5 Kan. 470 (1870).

3. "A Coterie of Able Men": Brewer and the Kansas Supreme Court on Corporations, the Public Interest, Politics, and Crime, 1871–1884

1. Wilder, *Annals of Kansas*, 525.

2. *Annual Report of the Secretary of State of the State of Kansas, 1870*, 8.

3. Wilder, *Annals of Kansas*, 715–716, 736, 983, 1002.

4. Sherwood v. Moelle, 36 F. 478, 479 (1888).

5. Edwin A. Austin, "The Supreme Court of the State of Kansas," *Collections of the Kansas State Historical Society* 13 (1913–1914), 99.

6. Wilder, *Annals of Kansas*, 711.

7. Austin, "Supreme Court of the State of Kansas," 99.

8. *In the Supreme Court of Kansas, October 4, 1937, in Memory of William Agnew Johnston* (Topeka: Kansas State Printing Plant, 1937), 9.

9. DJB, "The Work of the Supreme Court," *Law Notes* 1 (March 1898):167.

10. Whitford v. Horn, 18 Kan. 455 (1877).

11. Bodwell v. Crawford, 26 Kan. 292, 297 (1881).

12. First National Bank of Parsons v. Franklin, 20 Kan. 264, 269 (1878); Central Branch Union Pacific Rld. Co. v. Atchison, Topeka & Santa Fe Rld. Co., 26 Kan. 669, 677 (1881).

13. State v. Reddick, 7 Kan. 143 (1871).

14. Commissioners of Leavenworth County v. Brewer, 9 Kan. 307 (1872); Moline, "David Josiah Brewer, Kansas Jurist," 9.

15. Kansas Pacific Ry. Co. v. Reynolds, 8 Kan. 623, 637 (1871).

16. Berg v. Atchison, Topeka & Santa Fe R. Co., 2 P. 639, 641 (1883).

17. St. Joseph & Denver City R. Co. v. Ryan, 11 Kan. 602, 609 (1873).

18. Kansas Pacific Ry. Co. v. Mower, 16 Kan. 573, 576 (1876). Subsequently,

many cases involving this law were appealed to the Kansas Supreme Court; Brewer wrote the court's opinion in several of them, usually agreeing with the juries and lower court judges who found against the railroads.

19. Kansas Pacific Ry. Co. v. Wood, 24 Kan. 619, 624 (1880).

20. Sherman v. Anderson, 27 Kan. 333, 335 (1882).

21. Kansas Pacific Ry. Co. v. Wood, 24 Kan. 619 (1880).

22. Missouri Pacific Rld. Co. v. Leggett, 27 Kan. 323 (1882); Central Branch Rld. Co. v. Lea, 20 Kan. 353 (1878).

23. Darling v. Rodgers, 7 Kan. 592 (1871).

24. Marion County v. Hoch, 24 Kan. 778, 779 (1881).

25. Commissioners of Leavenworth County v. Miller, 7 Kan. 479 (1871).

26. 7 Kan. 542 (1871).

27. Id. at 550.

28. Id. at 554–555.

29. Id. at 566.

30. Id. at 571.

31. Id. at 572.

32. Id. at 575.

33. Id.

34. "In Memoriam," 83 Kan. ix (1911).

35. Leavenworth, Lawrence & Galveston Rld. Co. v. Commissioners of Douglas County, 18 Kan. 169, 184 (1877).

36. State ex rel. St. Joseph & Denver City R. Co. v. Commissioners of Nemaha County, 10 Kan. 569 (1873).

37. Lewis v. Commissioners of Bourbon County, 12 Kan. 186 (1873).

38. Memphis, Kansas & Colorado Ry. Co. v. Thompson, 24 Kan. 170 (1880).

39. Central Branch Union Pacific R. Co. v. Smith, 23 Kan. 745 (1880).

40. State ex rel. Griffith v. Osawkee Township, 14 Kan. 418, 426, 428, 429 (1875).

41. William G. Cutler, ed., *History of the State of Kansas* (Chicago: A. T. Andreas, 1883), 218.

42. State v. Commissioners of Shawnee County, 28 Kan. 431, 433 (1882).

43. Parmellee v. Knox, 24 Kan. 113, 122 (1880).

44. Atchison, Topeka & Santa Fe Rld. Co. v. Commissioners of Jefferson County, 17 Kan. 29, 46 (1876). See also Morrow v. Commissioners of Saline County, 21 Kan. 484 (1879), and Leavenworth, Lawrence & Galveston Rld. Co. v. Commissioners of Douglas County, 18 Kan. 169 (1877).

45. Parmellee v. Knox, 24 Kan. 113, 122 (1880); Smith v. McNair, 19 Kan. 330 (1877).

46. Kansas Pacific Rld. Co. v. Kessler, 18 Kan. 523 (1877).

47. Avey v. Atchison, Topeka & Santa Fe R. Co., 11 Kan. 448, 455 (1873).

48. Missouri, Kansas & Texas Ry. Co. v. Weaver, 16 Kan. 456, 462 (1876).

49. Solomon R. Co. v. Jones, 2 P. 657 (1883); Sawyer v. Sauer, 10 Kan. 466 (1872).

50. Union Pacific Ry. Co. v. Milliken, 8 Kan. 647, 656 (1871).

51. Atchison, Topeka & Santa Fe Rld. Co. v. Brown, 26 Kan. 443, 460, 461 (1881).

52. Union Pacific Ry. Co. v. Young, 19 Kan. 488, 499–500 (1877).

53. Yandle v. Kingsbury, 17 Kan. 195, 198–203 (1876); Joseph G. Waters, "Samuel A. Kingman," *Collections of the Kansas Historical Society* 9 (1905–1906):53.

54. Atchison Street Ry. Co. v. Missouri Pacific Ry. Co., 3 P. 284 (1884).

55. Atchison, Topeka & Santa Fe R. Co. v. Bobb, 24 Kan. 673 (1881); Kansas Pacific Ry. Co. v. Dunmeyer, 24 Kan. 725 (1881).

56. Central Branch Union Pacific Rld. Co. v. Atchison, Topeka & Santa Fe Rd. Co., 26 Kan. 669 (1881).

57. Francis v. Atchison, Topeka & Santa Fe Rld. Co., 19 Kan. 303, 310 (1877).

58. 18 Kan. 271 (1877).

59. 1 P. 288, 290 (1883).

60. 2 P. 549 (1884).

61. Gossard v. Vaught, 10 Kan. 162, 168 (1872).

62. Russell v. State, 11 Kan. 308, 323 (1873); Scott v. Paulen, 15 Kan. 162 (1875).

63. State v. Elting, 29 Kan. 397, 400–401 (1883).

64. Gilleland v. Schuyler, 9 Kan. 569, 590 (1872).

65. Kirkpatrick v. Vickers, 24 Kan. 314, 319 (1880).

66. State ex rel. Mitchell v. Stevens, 23 Kan. 456, 458–459 (1880).

67. State ex rel., v. Gilmore, 20 Kan. 551 (1878).

68. Anthony v. Halderman, 7 Kan. 50 (1871); Prouty v. Stover, 11 Kan. 235 (1873).

69. 24 Kan. 143, 145 (1880).

70. Ex parte Phillips, 7 Kan. 48 (1871).

71. In re Holcomb, 21 Kan. 628 (1879).

72. State v. Beebe, 13 Kan. 589 (1874).

73. State v. Bancroft, 22 Kan. 170, 216 (1879).

74. Watson v. Balch, 1 P. 775, 778 (1883); Rolfs v. Shallcross, 1 P. 523 (1883).

75. State v. Furbeck, 29 Kan. 532, 534 (1883).

76. Kermit L. Hall, *The Magic Mirror: Law in American History* (New York: Oxford University Press, 1989), 185, 187.

4. The Substance of Right: Brewer and the Kansas Supreme Court on Prohibition, Family Law, Women's Rights, Race Questions, and the Legal Profession, 1871–1884

1. 24 Kan. 704 (1881). See also Robert Smith Bader, *Prohibition in Kansas: A History* (Lawrence: University Press of Kansas, 1986), chaps. 3 and 4.

2. Prohibitory Amendment Cases, 24 Kan. 704, 706 (1881).

3. Id. at 710.

4. Id. at 720.

5. Id. at 720.

6. Id. at 722–724; Werner v. Edmiston, 24 Kan. 147 (1880).

7. 25 Kan. 751 (1881).

8. Id. at 765.

9. Id. at 768.
10. State v. Curtis, 29 Kan. 384 (1883).
11. 29 Kan. 252 (1883).
12. Id. at 274.
13. Mugler v. Kansas, 123 U.S. 623 (1887).
14. City of Emporia v. Soden, 25 Kan. 588 (1881).
15. "In Memoriam," 83 Kan. x (1911).
16. 26 Kan. 650 (1881).
17. Id. at 652.
18. Id. at 656.
19. Id. at 658.
20. 28 Kan. 781 (1882).
21. Id. at 782, 783.
22. Id. at 786.
23. Id. at 787–788.
24. Id. at 789.
25. In re Bort, 25 Kan. 308, 311 (1881).
26. Hall, *The Magic Mirror*, 166.
27. Ibid., 165–166.
28. Smith v. Smith, 22 Kan. 699, 704 (1879).
29. Warner v. Warner, 11 Kan. 121, 123–124 (1873).
30. 16 Kan. 601 (1876).
31. *Kansas City Star*, January 30, 1910.
32. Wicks v. Mitchell, 9 Kan. 80, 90 (1872).
33. Holthaus v. Farria, 24 Kan. 784 (1881). See also Monroe v. May, 9 Kan. 466 (1872).
34. Hall, *The Magic Mirror*, 160.
35. Osterhout v. Osterhout, 2 P. 869, 870 (1883).
36. Sarahass v. Armstrong, 16 Kan. 192, 195 (1876).
37. Commissioners of Miami County v. Brackenridge, 12 Kan. 114, 116 (1873).
38. 23 Kan. 672 (1880).
39. 26 Kan. 1 (1881).
40. Paul E. Wilson, "Brown v. Board of Education Revisited," *University of Kansas Law Review* 12 (May 1964):508–515, reviews the laws and decisions on segregation in early Kansas, as does Randall B. Woods, "Integration, Exclusion, or Segregation? The 'Color Line' in Kansas, 1878–1900," *Western Historical Quarterly* 14 (April 1983):186–189.
41. Board of Education v. Tinnon, 26 Kan. 1, 19 (1881).
42. Id. at 23–26.
43. Falloon v. Schilling, 29 Kan. 292, 297 (1883).
44. National Land Co. v. Perry, 23 Kan. 140, 141 (1879).
45. Tennent v. Battey, 18 Kan. 324 (1877).
46. Michael J. Brodhead, *Persevering Populist: The Life of Frank Doster* (Reno: University of Nevada Press, 1969), 114.
47. Wolf v. Hough, 22 Kan. 659 (1879); Hudson v. Solomon, 19 Kan. 177, 186 (1877); Smith v. Woodleaf, 21 Kan. 717, 721 (1879); Casterline v. Day, 26 Kan. 306, 308 (1881); City of Atchison v. Jansen, 21 Kan. 560, 577 (1879).

48. Kansas Pacific Ry. Co. v. Mihlman, 17 Kan. 224, 236 (1876).

49. Pfeiffer v. Union Evangelical Church, 20 Kan. 100, 101–102 (1878).

50. Wicks v. Smith, 18 Kan. 508, 516 (1871).

51. Blackistone v. Sherwood, 2 P. 874 (1883).

52. Clay v. Hoysradt, 8 Kan. 74, 81 (1871).

53. Atchison & Nebraska Rld. Co. v. Wagener, 19 Kan. 335, 337 (1877).

54. Farlin v. Sook, 1 P. 123, 128–129 (1883).

55. Muse v. Wafer, 29 Kan. 279, 281 (1883).

56. Perry v. Bailey, 12 Kan. 539, 546–547 (1874); Tyler v. Safford, 3 P. 333, 336 (1884).

57. In re Ebenhack, 17 Kan. 618, 621–622 (1877).

58. Morris v. Shew, 29 Kan. 661, 664 (1883).

59. In re Pryor, 18 Kan. 72, 75 (1877).

60. Id. at 76.

61. Wilkens v. Tourtellott, 29 Kan. 513, 515 (1883); Rahn v. King Wrought-Iron Bridge Manufactory, 16 Kan. 530, 531–534 (1876).

62. Box 12, Brewer Papers.

63. DJB to Etta, July 7, 1872, Brewer Papers.

64. *Kansas City Times*, March 29, 1910; *Topeka Capital*, April 13, 1883.

65. DJB's certificate of membership in the Kansas Bar Association, dated January 10, 1883, is in the Yale Miscellaneous Mss., Yale University Library.

66. DJB, "Constitutional Convention," *The Western Homestead* 3 (November 1881), 70–71.

67. DJB, "Increase of Litigation—Its Causes and Cure," ibid., 2 (January 1880), 193–194.

68. DJB, "Preferential Voting," *Kansas Educational Journal* 9 (August 1872):105–107.

69. DJB, "The Scholar in Politics," in *Commencement Exercises of Washburn College, June, '83* (Manhattan, KS: College Press, E. H. Perry, 1885), 9.

70. Ibid., 13.

71. Ibid., 19–20.

72. Ibid., 20.

73. Ibid., 21–22.

74. Ibid., 22–23.

75. Ibid., 23–24.

76. Ibid., 27.

77. DJB, "Dedicatory Address of Hon. D. J. Brewer . . . Delivered at Emporia, Kansas, June 16, 1880," in *Catalogue of the Officers and Students of the Kansas State Normal School, Emporia, 1879–80* (Emporia: Rowland Bros., 1880), 26, 27, 28–29.

78. *Topeka Commonwealth*, May 15, 1880.

79. DJB to John A. Anderson, January 4, 1875, Anderson Papers, Kansas State Historical Society; *Industrialist* (Manhattan, KS), October 2, November 13, 20, 1875.

80. DJB to John A. Anderson, February 12, 1876, Anderson Papers, KSHS; *Industrialist*, April 8, 15, 1876.

81. DJB to John A. Anderson, October 19, 1876, Anderson Papers, KSHS; *Industrialist*, February 24, March 17, 1877.

82. *Collins, Lynch & Edge's Leavenworth City Directory and Business Mirror, for the Years 1871–72* (Leavenworth, 1871), 12; *Corbett, Hoye & Co's III Annual City Directory of the . . . City of Leavenworth* (Leavenworth: Commercial Steam Book and Job Printing House, 1874), 49.

5. "An Empire in Itself": The Eighth Circuit, 1884–1889

1. Plumb v. Bay, 18 Kan. 415 (1877).
2. St. John et al. to Hayes, May 30, 1879, Brewer Papers.
3. Wilder, *Annals of Kansas*, 1043, 1053.
4. Unidentified clipping, Scrapbook, Box 8, Brewer Papers.
5. DBJ to Arthur, April 9, 1884, Chester A. Arthur Papers, ser. 1, reel 2, Presidential Papers Microfilm, Manuscript Division, Library of Congress.
6. *Topeka Capital*, April 9, 1884; L. B. Kellogg, "The Supreme Court," *Minutes of the Third Annual Meeting of the Bar Association of the State of Kansas* (Topeka: Geo. W. Crane & Co., 1886), 47–48.
7. DJB, "Growth of the Judicial Function," *Report of the Organization and First Annual Meeting of the Colorado Bar Association. . . .* (Denver: Smith-Brooks Printing Co., 1898), 83.
8. DJB to John Guthrie, February 4, 1889, Guthrie Papers, Kansas State Historical Society.
9. Kansas v. Bradley, 26 F. 289, 292 (C.C.D. Kan. 1885).
10. Davis v. St. Louis & San Francisco Ry. Co., 25 F. 786, 788 (C.C.D. Kan. 1885).
11. Hall, *Magic Mirror*, 230, 234.
12. Short v. Chicago, Milwaukee & St. Paul Ry. Co., 33 F. 114 (C.C.D. Minn. 1887); Hakes v. Burns, 40 F. 33 (C.C.D. Colo. 1889).
13. Western Union Telegraph Co. v. Brown, 32 F. 337 (C.C.E.D. Mo. 1887); United States v. Morrissey, 32 F. 147 (C.C.E.D. Mo. 1887).
14. Wheeler v. Sexton, 34 F. 154 (C.C.D. Neb. 1888); Rollins v. Lake County, 34 F. 845, 852 (C.C.D. Colo. 1888).
15. 94 U.S. 113 (1877).
16. Central Trust Co. v. Wabash, St. Louis & Pacific Ry. Co., 29 F. 546, 559–560 (C.C.E.D. Mo. 1886).
17. 35 F. 866 (C.C.S.D. Iowa 1888).
18. Chicago, St. Paul, Minneapolis & Omaha Ry. Co. v. Becker, 35 F. 883, 886 (C.C.D. Minn. 1888).
19. Chicago, Burlington & Quincy R. Co. v. Dey, 38 F. 656, 660 (C.C.S.D. Iowa 1889).
20. Arnold M. Paul, *Conservative Crisis and the Rule of Law: Attitudes of Bench and Bar, 1887–1895* (Ithaca: Cornell University Press, 1960), 42. Also, two years before the *Dey* ruling, Chief Justice Waite (the author of the *Munn* opinion) paved the way to *Dey* by stating that the Fourteenth Amendment limited the power of a state to regulate rates: "Under pretense of regulating fares and freights, the State cannot require a railroad corporation to carry persons or property without reward; neither can it do that which in law amounts to a taking of private property for public use without just compensa-

tion, or without due process of law." Stone v. Farmers' Loan and Trust Co., 116 U.S. 307, 331 (1886).

21. Iowa v. Chicago, Burlington & Quincy R. Co., 37 F. 497 (C.C.S.D. Iowa 1889).

22. 31 F. 652, 657, 659 (C.C.D. Minn. 1887).

23. United States v. Union Pacific Ry. Co., 37 F. 551 (C.C.D. Colo. 1889); United States v. Missouri, Kansas & Texas Ry. Co., 37 F. 68 (C.C.D. Kan. 1888); Northern Pacific R. Co. v. United States, 36 F. 282 (C.C.D. Minn. 1888); Denver & Rio Grande R. Co. v. United States, 34 F. 838 (C.C.D. Colo. 1888).

24. Cowan v. Union Pacific Ry. Co., 35 F. 43 (C.C.D. Colo. 1888).

25. McDonald v. Union Pacific Ry. Co., 35 F. 38 (C.C.D. Colo. 1888); McCory v. Chicago, Milwaukee & St. Paul Ry. Co., 31 F. 531 (C.C.D. Minn. 1887).

26. O'Rorke v. Union Pacific Ry. Co., 22 F. 189 (C.C.D. Colo. 1884).

27. Chicago, Milwaukee & St. Paul Ry. Co. v. Ross, 112 U.S. 377 (1884); Charles W. McCurdy, "Justice Field and the Jurisprudence of Government-Business Relations," 979n.

28. Howard v. Denver & Rio Grande R. Co., 26 F. 837, 845 (C.C.D. Colo. 1886); Mealman v. Union Pacific Ry. Co., 37 F. 189 (C.C.D. Colo. 1889).

29. Borgman v. Omaha & St. Louis Ry. Co., 41 F. 667 (C.C.S.D. Iowa 1890).

30. Block v. Atchison, Topeka & Santa Fe R. Co., 21 F. 529 (C.C.E.D. Mo. 1884).

31. Bard v. City of Augusta, 30 F. 906 (C.C.D. Kan. 1887); Hedges v. Dixon County, 37 F. 304 (C.C.D. Neb. 1889).

32. Missouri v. Kansas City, Fort Scott & Gulf R. Co., 32 F. 722, 723, 727 (C.C.W.D. Mo. 1887).

33. Hall, *Magic Mirror*, 361.

34. Omaha Horse Ry. Co. v. Cable Tramway Co., 30 F. 324 (C.C.D. Neb. 1887); Jackson County Horse R. Co. v. Interstate Rapid Transit Ry. Co., 24 F. 306 (C.C.D. Kan. 1885); Omaha Horse Ry. Co. v. Cable Tram Way Co., 32 F. 727, 732 (C.C.D. Neb. 1887).

35. Pullman's Palace Car Co. v. Twombly, 29 F. 658, 662, 627 (C.C.S.D. Iowa 1887).

36. Missouri ex rel. Baltimore & Ohio Telegraph Co. v. Bell Telephone Co., 23 F. 539, 541–543 (C.C.E.D. Mo. 1885).

37. Bell Telephone Co. of Missouri v. Missouri ex rel. Baltimore & Ohio Telegraph Co., 127 U.S. 780 (1887).

38. "The Wabash Swindle," *Nation* 40 (April 16, 1885):316–317; "The Wabash Receivership Case," *American Law Review* 21 (January–February 1887):141–145; ibid. (September–October 1887):798–804; "A Chapter of Wabash," *North American Review* 146 (February 1888):178–193.

39. Central Trust Co. v. Wabash, St. Louis & Pacific Ry. Co., 29 F. 618, 620, 621, 623–628 (C.C.E.D. Mo. 1886).

40. Swayne to Gresham (typed copy), March 8, 1888, Brewer Papers; George W. Smith to Swayne (typed copy), March 8, 1888, ibid.

41. "A Chapter of Wabash," 185–186.

42. Matilda Gresham, *Life of Walter Quintin Gresham*, 2 vols. (Freeport, NY: Books for Libraries Press, 1970)2:530–549, 550–560, 621–626.

43. White, *The Autobiography of William Allen White* (New York: Macmillan, 1946), 439–440.

44. Mercantile Trust Co. v. Missouri, Kansas & Texas Ry. Co., 36 F. 221, 226, 227 (C.C.D. Kan. 1888).

45. Unidentified clipping, probably 1910, Biographical Clippings 18, Kansas State Historical Society, 235.

46. Mercantile Trust Co. v. Missouri, Kansas & Texas Ry. Co., 41 F. 8, 12–13 (C.C.D. Kan. 1889).

47. DJB, *American Citizenship* (New York: C. Scribner's Sons, 1902), 50.

48. Charles Fairman, *Mr. Justice Miller and the Supreme Court* (Cambridge: Harvard University Press, 1939), 245–246; Kneeland v. American Loan & Trust Co., 136 U.S. 89, 97 (1890).

49. In re Doolittle, 23 F. 544, 547 (C.C.E.D. Mo. 1885).

50. Id. at 548, 549.

51. United States v. Kane, 23 F. 748 (C.C.D. Colo. 1885).

52. Id. at 755, 756, 757.

53. Id. at 757.

54. Frank v. Denver & Rio Grande Ry. Co., 23 F. 757 (C.C.D. Colo. 1885).

55. Id. at 758, 759, 760–761, 761–762.

56. St. Paul, Minneapolis & Manitoba R. Co. v. Greenhalgh, 26 F. 563, 568 (C.C.D. Minn. 1886).

57. United States v. Maxwell Land Grant Co., 21 F. 19 (C.C.D. Colo. 1884).

58. United States v. Maxwell Land Grant Co., 26 F. 118 (C.C.D. Colo. 1886); Jim Berry Pearson, *The Maxwell Land Grant* (Norman: University of Oklahoma Press, 1961), 90–91; Morris F. Taylor, *O. P. McMains and the Maxwell Land Grant Conflict* (Tucson: University of Arizona Press, 1979), 108, 112, 138, 140–141, 157, 164, 178–179, 239, 271, 277, 278.

59. Interstate Land Co. v. Maxwell Land Grant Co., 41 F. 275 (C.C.D. Colo. 1889).

60. American Bell Telephone Co. v. Southern Telephone Co., 34 F. 795, 796 (C.C.E.D. Ark. 1888).

61. Westinghouse Air-Brake Co. v. Carpenter, 32 F. 484, 485 (C.C.S.D. Iowa 1887).

62. Washburn & Moen Manufacturing Co. v. Grinnell Wire Co., 24 F. 23, 24 (C.C.S.D. Iowa 1885).

63. Polsdorfer v. St. Louis Wooden-Ware Works, 37 F. 57, 58 (C.C.E.D. Mo. 1888).

64. Keyes v. Pueblo Smelting & Refining Co., 31 F. 560, 561–562 (C.C.D. Colo. 1887).

65. Sullivan v. Chrysolite Silver Mining Co., 21 F. 892, 893 (C.C.D. Colo. 1884).

66. 26 F. 178 (C.C.D. Kan. 1886).

67. Kansas v. Bradley, 26 F. 289 (C.C.D. Kan. 1885).

68. The text of the *Walruff* opinion, with editorial comment, is printed in *Kansas Law Journal* 2 (January 30, 1886):401; James M. Mason, "The Walruff Case," ibid. 3 (February 27, 1886):33–38.

69. Mugler v. Kansas, 123 U.S. 623 (1887). See also Kidd v. Pearson, 128 U.S. 1 (1888).

70. Mugler v. Kansas, 123 U.S. 623, 675–678 (1887); Eitzen, *David J. Brewer*, 18.

71. McElroy v. Kansas City, 21 F. 257 (C.C.W.D. Mo. 1884).

72. Ex parte Kieffer, 40 F. 399 (C.C.D. Kan 1889).

73. Hall, *Magic Mirror*, 199.

74. Kansas v. Walruff, 26 F. 178, 199 (C.C.D. Kan. 1886); Gilette v. City of Denver, 21 F. 822, 823 (C.C.D. Colo. 1884).

75. Details, as given by one of the participants in the affair, are found in A. J. Sawyer, "History of the Incarceration of the Lincoln City Council," *Proceedings and Collections of the Nebraska State Historical Society*, 2d ser. 2 (1902):105–137.

76. Ibid., 121–122.

77. In re Sawyer, 124 U.S. 200, 222, 223–225 (1888).

78. In re Deputy Sheriffs, 22 F. 153, 155 (C.C.E.D. Mo. 1884).

79. Cooke v. Bangs, 31 F. 640, 642 (C.C.D. Minn. 1887).

80. Newton v. Joslin, 30 F. 891, 893 (C.C.D. Colo. 1887).

81. Central Trust Co. v. Wabash, St. Louis & Pacific Ry. Co., 26 F. 74, 77 (C.C.E.D. Mo. 1886).

82. Blair v. St. Louis, Hannibal & Keokuk R. Co., 23 F. 521, 522 (C.C.E.D. Mo. 1885).

83. Lyon v. Union Pacific Ry. Co., 35 F. 111 (C.C.D. Colo. 1888).

84. "Retirement of the Honorable Samuel Treat. . . ." 29 F. iv (1887).

85. *Topeka Capital*, December 2, 1884.

86. DJB, "Libel," *Minutes of the Third Annual Meeting of the Bar Association of the State of Kansas (1886)*, 55–59.

87. "Hattie" (Harriet?) to "My dear Sister," March 12, 1888, Brewer Papers; *Edwin Greene's City Directory of the . . . City of Leavenworth, 1885* (n.p., n.d.), 65; ibid., 1889, 87.

88. DJB to Etta, August 7, 1889, Brewer Papers.

89. Unidentified clipping, Scrapbook, Box 8, Brewer Papers.

90. Watson, "David Josiah Brewer," 84.

6. A Centennial Justice: Elevation to the United States Supreme Court

1. J. J. Brown and M. M. Hurley to Harrison, March 28, 1889 (telegram), Benjamin Harrison Papers, ser. 2, reel 64, Presidential Papers Microfilm, Manuscript Division, Library of Congress.

2. *New York Times*, December 5, 1889 (1:1); DJB to Plumb, January 19, 1889, Harrison Papers, ser. 1, reel 16.

3. Watson, "David Josiah Brewer," 80, 81.

4. Plumb to Harrison, September 15 and October 7, 1889, Brewer file, "Personnel Records of U.S. Supreme Court Justices," Record Group 60,

220
Notes to Pages 72–77

National Archives; Harry J. Sievers, *Benjamin Harrison, Hoosier President* (Indianapolis: Bobbs-Merrill, 1968), 137.

5. Horton to Harrison, April 5, 1889, and Horton et al. to Harrison, October 10, 1889, Brewer file, "Personnel Records of U. S. Supreme Court Justices."

6. *New York Times*, December 11, 1889 (1:7); Edward C. Wade et al. to Harrison, March 29, 1889, Harrison Papers, ser. 1, reel 19.

7. Shelby M. Cullom, *Fifty Years of Public Service* (Chicago: A. C. McClurg, 1911), 248.

8. Harrison to R. S. Taylor, July 23, 1889, Harrison Papers, ser. 1, reel 21; Harrison to Francis B. Stockbridge, October 17, 1889, ibid., reel 23; *Topeka Capital*, December 5, 1889.

9. *New York Times*, December 5, 1889 (1:1); *American Law Review* 24 (January–February 1890):140.

10. White, *Autobiography*, 358–359.

11. Sievers, *Harrison*, 138; Brown to Harrison, December 12, 1889), Brewer file, "Personnel Records of U.S. Supreme Court Justices."

12. *Topeka Capital*, December 5, 1889.

13. A. J. Kynett to Harrison, December 4, 1889, and January 14, 1890, "Personnel Records of U. S. Supreme Court Justices"; *Topeka Capital*, December 18, 1889; *American Law Review* 24 (January–February 1890):139–140.

14. Gustavus Myers, *History of the Supreme Court of the United States* (Chicago: Charles H. Kerr, 1912), 591; *New York Times*, December 18, 1889 (1:7).

15. Kirk Mechem, *The Annals of Kansas, 1886–1925*, 2 vols. (Topeka: Kansas State Historical Society, 1954–1956):2:83; *New York Times*, December 11, 1889 (4:1).

16. *New York Times*, December 10, 1889 (1:2), December 17, 1889 (2:1), December 18, 1889 (1:7), December 19, 1889 (1:1); "Papers re Nominations, Sen. 51B-A4, Brewer, David J.," RG 46, National Archives; *American Law Review* 24 (January–February 1890):140; *Topeka Capital*, December 19, 1889.

17. Harrison to DJB, December 18, 1889, and DJB to Harrison, December 19, 1889 (telegram), Harrison Papers, ser. 1, reel 24. The certificate of appointment, dated December 18, 1889, is in the Yale Miscellaneous Mss.

18. *New York Times*, December 19, 1889 (4:1).

19. *American Law Review* 24 (January–February 1890):138, 139; ibid. (March–April 1890), 313.

20. Horton, "David Josiah Brewer," *Green Bag* 2 (January 1890):1–2.

21. Thomas J. Bain to John J. Ingalls, December 18, 1889, "Papers re Nominations, Sen. 51B-A4, Brewer, David J."; *Minutes of the Seventh Annual Meeting of the Bar Association of the State of Kansas* (1890), 10.

22. Watson, "David Josiah Brewer," 87–88.

23. 132 U.S. iiin (1889); *Official Register of the United States, Containing a List of Officers and Employees in the Civil, Military, and Naval Services on the First of July, 1895*, 2 vols. (Washington, D.C.: Government Printing Office, 1895):1:971. Salaries of associate justices were raised to $12,500 in 1903.

24. *Topeka State Journal*, March 28, 1910.

25. Willard L. King, *Melville Weston Fuller: Chief Justice of the United*

States, 1888–1910 (New York: Macmillan, 1950; Chicago: University of Chicago Press, Phoenix Books, 1967), 150–151.

26. 133 U.S. 712 (1889); 137 U.S. 713 (1890); 168 U.S. 719 (1897).
27. King, *Fuller*, 153, 155.
28. Swisher, *Stephen J. Field*, 438–439; Ernest Sutherland Bates, *The Story of the Supreme Court* (Indianapolis: Bobbs-Merrill, 1936), 210; Fiss, "David J. Brewer," 55.
29. Semonche, *Charting the Future*, 1–8; 134 U.S. 729–746 (1890).
30. 134 U.S. 741, 743.
31. DJB, "The Work of the Supreme Court," 167.
32. Ibid., 168.
33. Ibid.
34. Semonche, *Charting the Future*, 165.
35. 143 U.S. 394, 407 (1892).
36. Sullivan v. Iron Silver Mining Co., 143 U.S. 431, 436 (1892).
37. King, *Fuller*, 155, 340, 341.
38. *Kansas City Times*, June 16, 1901.
39. *Topeka State Journal*, March 29, 1910.
40. DJB, "The Work of the Supreme Court," 168.
41. Ibid.
42. DJB, "The Federal Judiciary," 81.
43. *Kansas City Times*, March 29, 1910; R. W. Apple, Jr., "The Case of the Monopolistic Railroadmen," in *Quarrels That Have Shaped the Constitution*, John A. Garraty, ed. (New York: Harper Torchbooks, 1975), 170.
44. Watson, "David Josiah Brewer," 87.
45. Clipping from the *New York Recorder*, February 18, 1891, in U.S. Supreme Court Clerk's Scrapbook, vol. 3, p. 32, RG 267, National Archives; George Shiras, 3rd, *Justice George Shiras of Pittsburgh* (Pittsburgh: University of Pittsburgh Press, 1953), 118–119.
46. DJB to Etta, October 25, 1890, and May 22, 1891, Brewer Papers.
47. 133 U.S. 193 (1890); 133 U.S. 198 (1890).
48. 135 U.S. 286, 302–303 (1890); King, *Fuller*, 155.
49. DJB, [address to] *Thirty-third Annual Meeting of the Agents of the Northwestern Mutual Life Insurance Company* (n.p., 1909), 5–6.
50. *Topeka Capital*, July 30, 1897.

7. The Court and the Economic Realm: Regulation, Public Finance, Trusts, Patents, and Land, 1890–1900

1. 118 U.S. 394 (1886).
2. Alfred H. Kelly and Winfred A. Harbison, *The American Constitution: Its Origins and Development*, 5th ed. (New York: W. W. Norton, 1976), 473.
3. 118 U.S. 557 (1886).
4. Three studies of railroad regulation, each with widely different emphases and conclusions, are Gabriel Kolko, *Railroads and Regulation, 1877–1916* (New York: W. W. Norton, 1965); Albro Martin, "The Troubled Subject of Railroad Regulation in the Gilded Age—A Reappraisal," *Journal of American*

History 41 (September 1974):339–371; Ari and Olive Hoogenboom, *A History of the ICC: From Panacea to Palliative* (New York: W. W. Norton, 1976).

5. Chicago & Grand Trunk Ry. Co. v. Wellman, 143 U.S. 339, 344, 345 (1892).

6. Budd v. New York, 143 U.S. 517, 548–552 (1892). Field's biographer suggested that Field and Brewer may have collaborated in writing the dissenting opinion.

7. Budd v. New York, 143 U.S. 517, 550–551 (1892).

8. Id. at 551.

9. McCurdy, "Justice Field and the Jurisprudence of Government-Business Relations," 970–1005, passim.

10. Quoted in Paul, *Conservative Crisis*, 74n. Paul himself wrote that "[a]lthough Brewer did not base his opinion on the Declaration [of Independence] per se, he never did allege any specific provision of the Constitution to which he thought the [New York] act repugnant, not even deigning to notice the due process clause." Ibid., 89n. Yet Brewer's emphasis on compensation was certainly made with reference to the due process clause of the Fourteenth Amendment.

11. 153 U.S. 391, 405–410 (1894).

12. Id. at 408, 409, 410.

13. 142 U.S. 492, 509, 510 (1892).

14. 134 U.S. 418, 458, (1890).

15. 154 U.S. 362 (1894).

16. 64 F. 165 (C.C.D. Neb. 1894).

17. Id. at 173–174, 176.

18. Id. at 176.

19. Id. at 189.

20. Myers, *History of the Supreme Court*, 602–603. Myers also accused Brewer of similarly faulty reasoning in the opinion he wrote for United States v. California and Oregon Land Co., 148 U.S. 31 (1893).

21. *Topeka State Journal*, September 6, 1897.

22. 169 U.S. 466 (1898); Eric Monkkonen, "Can Nebraska or Any State Regulate Railroads?" *Nebraska History* 54 (Fall 1973):365–382.

23. Chicago, Milwaukee & St. Paul Ry. Co. v. Tompkins, 176 U.S. 167 (1900).

24. 158 U.S. 98, 105 (1895).

25. 167 U.S. 479 (1897).

26. ICC v. Cincinnati, New Orleans & Texas Pacific Ry. Co., 162 U.S. 184 (1896).

27. Bates, *The Story of the Supreme Court*, 225; Myers, *History of the Supreme Court*, 637.

28. ICC v. Alabama Midland Ry. Co., 168 U.S. 144 (1897).

29. 167 U.S. 447 (1897).

30. Wight v. United States, 167 U.S. 512 (1897).

31. ICC v. Brimson, 154 U.S. 447, and 155 U.S. 3, 4 (1894).

32. 135 U.S. 100, 125–160 (1890); King, *Fuller*, 168. On similar grounds Harlan and Brewer dissented in O'Neil v. Vermont, 144 U.S. 323, 366–371 (1892); Field wrote a vigorous separate dissent (pp. 337–366).

33. 155 U.S. 461, 480–482 (1894); King, *Fuller*, 239.
34. Austin v. Tennessee, 179 U.S. 343 (1900).
35. King, *Fuller*, 241.
36. Ibid., 367.
37. Austin v. Tennessee, 179 U.S. 343, 364–388 (1900).
38. Missouri, Kansas & Texas Ry. Co. v. Haber, 169 U.S. 613, 644 (1898).
39. Cleveland, Cincinnati, Chicago & St. Louis Ry. Co. v. Illinois, 177 U.S. 514, 523 (1900).
40. Erb v. Morasch, 177 U.S. 584, 585 (1900).
41. Brennan v. Titusville, 153 U.S. 289 (1894).
42. Postal Telegraph Cable Co. v. Adams, 155 U.S. 688, 701 (1895).
43. Adams Express Co. v. Ohio State Auditor, 166 U.S. 185, 211 (1897).
44. Pittsburgh, Cincinnati, Chicago & St. Louis Ry. Co. v. Backus, 154 U.S. 421, 437–438 (1894).
45. Illinois Central R.R. Co. v. Decatur, 147 U.S. 190 (1893).
46. St. Louis v. Western Union Telegraph Co., 148 U.S. 92 and 149 U.S. 465 (1893).
47. Talbott v. Silver Bow County, 139 U.S. 438 (1891).
48. 157 U.S 429, 158 U.S. 601 (1895).
49. 102 U.S. 586 (1881).
50. 157 U.S. 429 (1895).
51. Semonche, *Charting the Future*, 69–71; King, *Fuller*, 218–221; Allan Nevins, *Grover Cleveland, A Study in Courage* (New York: Dodd, Mead, 1932) 778–779; Shiras, *Justice George Shiras*, 168–183; Edwin S. Corwin, *Court Over Constitution: A Study of Judicial Review as an Instrument of Popular Government* (Princeton, NJ: Princeton University Press, 1938), 195–201.
52. Magoun v. Illinois Trust & Savings Bank, 170 U.S. 283, 301–303 (1898).
53. Knowlton v. Moore, 178 U.S. 41, 110 (1900).
54. 156 U.S. 1 (1895).
55. 166 U.S. 290 (1897).
56. Addyston Pipe and Steel Co. v. United States, 175 U.S. 211 (1899).
57. Gulf, Colorado & Santa Fe Ry. Co. v. Ellis, 165 U.S. 150, 154, 166–168 (1897).
58. Atchison, Topeka & Santa Fe R.R. Co. v. Matthews, 174 U.S. 96, 107–125 (1899).
59. Chicago, Burlington & Quincy R.R. Co. v. Chicago, 166 U.S. 226, 261 (1897).
60. Long Island Water Supply Co. v. Brooklyn, 166 U.S. 685, 689 (1897).
61. Monongahela Navigation Co. v. United States, 148 U.S. 312 (1893).
62. 172 U.S. 314 (1899).
63. Winona and St. Peter Land Co. v. Minnesota, 159 U.S. 526 (1895).
64. Stearns v. Minnesota, 179 U.S. 223, 253–254, 254–262 (1900).
65. L'Hote v. New Orleans, 177 U.S. 587, 595–596 (1900).
66. 178 U.S. 548, 581–585, 585–609 (1900).
67. United States v. American Bell Telephone Co., 167 U.S. 224, 250, 265 (1897); Homer Cummings and Carl McFarland, *Federal Justice: Chapters in the History of Justice and the Federal Executive* (New York: Macmillan, 1937), 310.

68. Patent Clothing Co. v. Glover, 141, U.S. 560, 561, 563 (1891).

69. Ely's Administrator v. United States, 171 U.S. 220, 223 (1898).

70. Russell v. Maxwell Land Grant Co., 158 U.S. 253 (1895); Thompson v. Maxwell Land Grant and Railway Co., 168 U.S. 451 (1897).

71. Camou v. United States, 171 U.S. 277 (1897); Myers, *History of the Supreme Court*, 608–611.

72. 142 U.S. 510 (1892); Myers, *History of the Supreme Court*, 605.

73. 154 U.S. 288, 349 (1894).

74. United States v. Southern Pacific R.R. Co., 146 U.S. 570 (1892); United States v. Colton Marble and Lime Co., 146 U.S. 615 (1892).

75. Ard v. Brandon, 156 U.S. 537 (1895); Whitney v. Taylor, 158 U.S. 85 (1895); Tarpey v. Madsen, 178 U.S. 215 (1900).

76. E.g., Moss v. Downman, 176 U.S. 413 (1900).

77. Underwood v. Dugan, 139 U.S. 380, 385 (1891).

78. 174 U.S. 690 (1899); Ira G. Clarke, "The Elephant Butte Controversy: A Chapter in the Emergence of Federal Water Law," *Journal of American History* 61 (March 1975):1024, 1032–1033.

79. McCurdy, "Justice Field and the Jurisprudence of Government-Business Relations," 981–985.

80. Pleasant Township v. Aetna Life Insurance Co., 138 U.S. 67, 69 (1891).

81. Texas & Pacific Ry. Co. v. Marshall, 136 U.S. 393 (1890).

82. Cummings and McFarland, *Federal Justice*, 283–285.

83. Ibid., 285; Chicago, Rock Island & Pacific Ry. Co. v. Union Pacific Ry. Co., 47 F. 15 (C.C.D. Neb. 1891).

84. United States v. Western Union Telegraph Co., 50 F. 28 (C.C.D. Neb. 1892); Union Pacific Ry. Co. v. United States, 59 F. 813 (8th Cir. 1894); United States v. Union Pacific Ry. Co., 160 U.S. 1 (1895).

8. The Court and Humanity: Minorities, Labor, Crime, and Legal Ethics, 1890–1900

1. 163 U.S. 537 (1896).

2. DJB, remarks delivered at a "Dinner Given by the Bar of the Supreme Court of the United States to Mr. John Marshall Harlan," in December 1902. Republished in Alan F. Westin, ed., *An Autobiography of the Supreme Court: Off-the-Bench Commentary by the Justices* (New York: Macmillan, 1963), 192–193.

3. 133 U.S. 587 (1890); Semonche, *Charting the Future*, 15.

4. 154 U.S. 116 (1894).

5. Chae Chan Ping v. United States, 130 U.S. 581 (1889).

6. Quock Ting v. United States, 140 U.S. 417, 424 (1891). For a discussion of the refusal of American courts to admit Chinese testimony in this period, see John R. Wunder, "Chinese in Trouble: Criminal Law and Race on the Trans-Mississippi Frontier," *Western Historical Quarterly* 17 (January 1986):25–41.

7. Fong Yue Ting v. United States, 149 U.S. 698 (1893).

8. Id. at 733, 737, 738, 744.

9. Nishimura Ekiu v. United States, 142 U.S. 651 (1892); Lem Moon Sing v. United States, 158 U.S. 538 (1895).

10. United States v. Wong Kim Ark, 169 U.S. 649 (1898).

11. Brewer Papers, Box 5; Semonche, *Charting the Future*, 111–114, 128.

12. Ames v. Union Pacific Ry. Co., 64 F. 165, 189 (C.C.D. Neb. 1894).

13. 158 U.S. 564 (1895).

14. Id. at 587–593.

15. Id. at 583.

16. Myers, *History of the Supreme Court*, 624–625.

17. Clune v. United States, 159 U.S. 590 (1895).

18. Union Pacific Ry. Co. v. Botsford, 141 U.S. 250, 258–259 (1891).

19. 149 U.S. 368, 391–411 (1893).

20. E.g., Aerfetz v. Humphreys, 145 U.S. 418 (1892), Kohn v. McNulta, 147 U.S. 238 (1893), and Elliott v. Chicago, Milwaukee & St. Paul Ry. Co., 150 U.S. 245 (1893).

21. 169 U.S. 366 (1898).

22. 143 U.S. 457 (1892).

23. Id. at 465–472. As a member of the Kansas Supreme Court, Brewer had asserted that the United States was a "Christian commonwealth." Wyandotte County v. First Presbyterian Church, 1 P. 109, 112 (1883).

24. Philip B. Kurland, *Religion and the Law of Church and State and the Supreme Court* (Chicago: Aldine, 1962), 26–27; William Addison Blakely, ed., *American State Papers Bearing on Sunday Legislation* (Washington. D.C.: Religious Liberty Assn., 1911), 487–488n, 500, 502n, 508–510n, 512n. Yet Justice William O. Douglas, in Zorach v. Clauson, 343 U.S. 306, 313 (1952), wrote that "[w]e are a religious people whose institutions presuppose a Supreme Being."

25. Parker to Harrison, November 29, 1889, "Personnel Records of U.S. Supreme Court Justices."

26. Semonche, *Charting the Future*, 51–56; Mary M. Stolberg, "The Evolution of Frontier Justice: The Case of Judge Isaac Parker," *Prologue: Quarterly Journal of the National Archives* 20 (Spring, 1988), 14–20.

27. 164 U.S. 221, 225 (1896).

28. Collins v. United States, 150 U.S. 62 (1893); Johnson *alias* Overton v. United States, 157 U.S. 320 (1895); Davis v. United States, 165 U.S. 372 (1897); Acres v. United States, 164 U.S. 388, 390 (1896).

29. 135 U.S. 1 (1890).

30. Ex parte Medley, 134 U.S. 160, 175–176 (1890); Fairman, *Mr. Justice Miller*, 324–325.

31. Thompson v. Utah, 170 U.S. 343 (1898).

32. Hawker v. New York, 170 U.S. 189 (1898).

33. 168 U.S. 532, 569 (1897).

34. 137 U.S. 496, 506 (1890).

35. E.g., The Pedro, 175 U.S. 354 (1899), and The Carlos F. Roses, 177 U.S. 655 (1900).

36. Dewey v. United States, 178 U.S. 510 (1900).

37. Kneeland v. American Loan and Trust Co., 138 U.S. 509, 513 (1891).

38. Southworth v. United States, 161 U.S. 639, 642 (1896).

39. Northwestern Fuel Co. v. Brock, 139 U.S. 216, 221 (1891).

40. Peake v. New Orleans, 139 U.S. 342 (1891); Clement v. Field, 147 U.S. 467 (1893).

41. Hartranft v. Myer, 149 U.S. 544, 547 (1893).

42. United States v. Ballin, 144 U.S. 1 (1892).

43. *Kansas City Star*, June 30, 1900.

9. Rostrum and Fireside: Off-the-Bench Activity, 1890–1900

1. *Topeka State Journal*, June 1, 1901; *Topeka Capital*, May 27, 1891.

2. Brewer, ed., *The World's Best Orations, from the Earliest Period to the Present Time*. 10 vols. (St. Louis: Ferd. P. Kaiser, 1899). Later editions appeared in 1901 and 1923.

3. Brewer, ed., *The World's Best Essays, from the Earliest Period to the Present Time*. 10 vols. (St. Louis: Ferd. P. Kaiser, 1900). Edward A. Allen and William Schuyler were the associate editors of both sets.

4. S. F. Neely to DJB, February 10, 1896, Brewer Papers.

5. *New Englander and Yale Review* 55 (August 1891):97–110.

6. Ibid., 106, 108.

7. Ibid., 107, 110.

8. DJB, *The Movement of Coercion. An Address by Mr. Justice Brewer . . . Before the New York State Bar Association, January, 1893* (Chicago: Building Contractors' Council, n.d.).

9. Ibid., 5.

10. Ibid., 5–6.

11. Ibid., 7.

12. Ibid., 8.

13. Ibid., 8–9.

14. DJB to Harrison, August 5, 1893, Harrison Papers, ser. 1, reel 38.

15. DJB, "Government by Injunction," *National Corporation Reporter* 15 (February 24, 1898), 848–850.

16. Ibid., 849.

17. DJB, *The Income Tax Cases. Address Delivered before the Graduating Class of the Law Department of the University of Iowa at the Annual Commencement, June 8, 1898* (n.p., n.d.).

18. Ibid., 3–4.

19. Ibid., 15.

20. Ibid., 15–16.

21. Ibid., 14.

22. Undated, unpaged "Typescript of Speech Delivered to Congregational Club of Rhode Island," Brewer Papers, Box 4.

23. *Minutes of the Twelfth Annual Meeting of the Bar Association of the State of Kansas* (1895), 61–72.

24. Ibid., 62–64.

25. Ibid., 64, 69.

26. DJB, "The Liberty of Each Individual," reported in *New York Times*, July 5, 1893 (9:2). Under the same title, the address was published in *Independent* 45 (July 13, 1893):938–939.

27. "Typescript of Speech Delivered to Congregational Club of Rhode Island."

28. DJB, *Jubilee Anniversary: An Address Delivered at the Fiftieth Annual Meeting of the American Missionary Association, October 21, 1896* (n.p., n.d.). Unpaged pamphlet.

29. DJB, "Address to the Law School," *Commencement Annual, University of Wisconsin, June 17–21, 1900* (Madison: Sommers & Reynolds, n.d.), xii-xiii.

30. DJB, *The Twentieth Century from Another Viewpoint* (New York: F. H. Revell, 1899), 9–10.

31. Henry M. Field, *David Dudley Field*, 219–242; *American Advocate of Peace* 55 (November 1893):243, 254.

32. Fairman, "The Education of a Justice," 244.

33. *Report of the First Annual Meeting of the Lake Mohonk Conference on International Arbitration* (n.p., 1895), 17.

34. Adjudication, as distinguished from arbitration, is the settlement of international disputes by a court, tribunal, or other judicial body.

35. DJB, "A Better Education the Great Need of the Profession," *American Lawyer* 4 (January 1896):13.

36. Leslie B. Rout, Jr., *Which Way Out? A Study of the Guyana-Venezuela Boundary Dispute* (East Lansing: Latin American Studies Center, Michigan State University, 1971), 18–21; Marcus Baker, "The Venezuela Boundary Commission and Its Work," *National Geographic Magazine* 8 (July–August 1897):195–197; George Lincoln Burr, "The Search for the Venezuela-Guiana Boundary," *American Historical Review* 4 (April 1899):470–477; Burr, "The Guiana Boundary: A Postscript to the Work of the Commission," *American Historical Review* 6 (October 1900):49–64.

37. *Report of the Special Commission . . . to Examine and Report upon the True Divisional Line between the Republic of Venezuela and British Guiana*. 4 vols. 55th Cong., 2d sess., S. Doc. 91, 1:x, 21–22 (1898).

38. DJB to Etta, February 3, 1896, Brewer Papers.

39. King, *Fuller*, 251–255.

40. Harrison to DJB, December 21, 1897, Harrison Papers, ser. 1, reel 41.

41. Burr, "The Guiana Boundary," 50; King, *Fuller*, 257.

42. DJB to Etta, January 19, 1899, Brewer Papers.

43. DJB to Etta, February 15, 1899, Brewer Papers.

44. "Address by Hon. David J. Brewer, Associate Justice of the United States Supreme Court, Before the Young Men's Club of the First Congregational Church [Washington, D.C.?], Friday Evening, December 15, 1905," Brewer Papers, Box 4.

45. DJB to "Dear Girls," July 19, 24, August 2, 6, and 19, 1899, Brewer Papers.

46. King, *Fuller*, 258–259; DJB to his daughters, July 10, 1899, Brewer Papers.

47. Otto Shoenrich, "The Venezuela-British Boundary Dispute," *American Journal of International Law* 43 (July 1949):529–530.

48. Ibid., 526; Marcus Baker, "The Anglo-Venezuelan Boundary Dispute," *National Geographic Magazine* 9 (April 1900):143.

49. Gust. J. Sanafria to Herbert W. Bowen, March 11, 1904, Brewer Papers.

50. James C. Malin, *Confounded Rot about Napoleon: Reflections upon Science and Technology, Nationalism, World Depression of the Eighteen-nineties, and Afterwards* (Lawrence KS: The author, 1961), 176.

51. DJB, *Address of David J. Brewer . . . at the Dedication of the Battle Monument, West Point, New York, May 31, 1897* (West Point?: U.S.M.A. Press and Bindery, 1897).

52. DJB, *The Twentieth Century from Another Viewpoint*, 23.

53. *Topeka Capital*, July 30, 1897.

54. *New York Times*, December 17, 1906 (7:2).

55. DJB, *The Income Tax Cases*, 17, 21–23.

56. *New York Times*, July 22, 1898 (12:5).

57. DJB, "What I Have Gained from Bible Teaching," unidentified magazine article, Brewer Papers, Box 3.

58. DJB, *The Spanish War: A Prophecy or an Exception?* (Buffalo: Liberal Club, 1899), 3–4.

59. Ibid., 12, 21–22.

60. Ibid., 11–12.

61. DJB, *The Twentieth Century from Another Viewpoint*, 54.

62. *Celebration of the Twenty-fifth Anniversary of the First Congregational Church, of Washington, D.C., November 9th to 16th, 1890* (Washington?: Press of H. I. Rothrock, 1891), 14.

63. DJB, "One Way of Conducting a Bible Class," *Sunday School Times*, July 17, 1897 (clipping in Scrapbook, Box 135, Karrick Papers).

64. *Proceedings of the Sixty-sixth Annual Meeting of the American Home Missionary Society, Held at the First Congregational Church, Washington, D.C., May 24–26, 1892* (Washington: Gibson Bros., 1892), 95.

65. Certificates of DJB's membership in these organizations are in the Yale Misc. Mss.

66. *Kansas City Star*, June 30, 1900.

67. Certificate in Yale Misc. Mss.

68. DJB, "The Pew to the Pulpit," ms. in Brewer Papers, Box 4, 17, 18. A published version of this address, not seen by the present writer, is: DJB, *The Pew to the Pulpit: Suggestions to the Ministry from the Viewpoint of a Layman* (New York: F. H. Revell, 1897).

69. DJB, *The Twentieth Century from Another Viewpoint*, 12, 15–17.

70. Ibid., 38, 44, 45.

71. Ibid., 51–52.

72. DJB, "The Patent System," *Yale Law Journal* 3 (May 1894):149–157.

73. DJB, "A Better Education," 10–11.

74. Ibid., 12.

75. Ibid., 12, 13.

76. *The Columbian University. The School of Comparative Jurisprudence and Diplomacy. Catalogue, 1899–1900. Announcements, 1900–1901* (Washington, D.C.: Judd & Detweiler, n.d.), 2; *Topeka State Journal*, June 1, 1901.

77. DJB to Etta, November 18, 1892, Brewer Papers.

78. R. Hal Williams, *The Democratic Party and California Politics, 1880–1896* (Stanford, CA: Stanford University Press, 1973), 70–81, 177n.

79. *Topeka Capital*, July 30, 1897.
80. DJB to "Dear Girls," July 19, 1899, Brewer Papers.
81. *Topeka State Journal*, January 23, 1896; unidentified clipping, Biographical Clippings, BR, III, 412, Kansas State Historical Society.
82. Harold C. Syrett, ed., *The Gentleman and the Tiger: The Autobiography of George B. McClellan, Jr.* (Philadelphia: J. B. Lippincott, 1956), 197.
83. *New York Times*, January 19, 1893 (4:1).
84. DJB to Harrison, July 26, 1890, ser. 2 reel 73, and September 27, 1892, Harrison Papers, ser. 1 reel 37; DJB to John Addison Porter, February 11, 1898, William McKinley Papers, ser. 2, reel 26, Presidential Papers Microfilm, Manuscript Division, Library of Congress.
85. DJB to Etta, February 16, 1892, Brewer Papers.
86. DJB to Etta, April 9, 1893, Brewer Papers.
87. DJB to Etta, January 23, 1895, Brewer Papers.
88. *New York Times*, December 22, 1893 (8:4).
89. DJB to Etta, February 15, November 18, 1892, Brewer Papers.
90. Shiras, *Justice George Shiras*, 119.
91. "Mama" to Etta, October 9, 1892, Brewer Papers.
92. DJB to Etta and Bessie, June 21, 1896, Brewer Papers.
93. *Kansas City Times*, March 29, 1910; *Kansas City Star*, March 30, 1910.
94. *Washington Post*, August 17, 1902.
95. *Kansas City Journal*, March 19, 1905.
96. DJB to Etta, July 12, 1901, Brewer Papers; *Kansas City Times*, June 16, 1901.
97. DJB, "The Green Mountain State," *The Vermonter* 1 (January 1896):125–126.
98. DJB, "Judge Brewer on Kansas," in F. H. Barrington, ed., *Kansas Day* (Topeka: G. W. Crane, 1892), 97–98.
99. DJB to Edward A. Bowers, 1893, Bowers Papers, Beinecke Library, Yale University.
100. *Beta Theta Pi Magazine* 23 (May 1896):336–339; DJB, "The True Greatness of American Citizenship," ibid., 314–320.
101. DJB to Lulu, May 26, 1896, Brewer Papers.
102. DJB to Etta, May 29, 1896, Brewer Papers.
103. DJB to Etta, May 30, 1896, Brewer Papers.
104. DJB to Cleveland, January 26, 1897, Grover Cleveland Papers, ser. 3, reel 142, Presidential Papers Microfilm, Manuscript Division, Library of Congress.
105. DJB to "My Dear Wife," October 3, 1896, Brewer Papers.
106. Note, postmarked April 13, 1898, Harrison Papers, ser. 1, reel 41.
107. DJB to Etta, October 6, 1890, Brewer Papers; the poem is in Box 5, Brewer Papers.
108. DJB to Thomas Semmes, July 6, 1891, Simeon Baldwin Papers, Yale University.
109. Swisher, *Field*, 444–445.
110. King, *Fuller*, 224–226.
111. *Topeka Capital*, June 30, 1897; Swisher, *Field*, 448.

112. "Faith," ms. poem in folder marked "Correspondence 1896–1898," Box 2, Brewer Papers.

113. DJB, *The Twentieth Century from Another Viewpoint*, 55.

10. Rates, Trusts, and Taxes: The Court and the Commerce, Police, and Taxing Powers, 1901–1910

1. The best known example of this view is Gabriel Kolko, *The Triumph of Conservatism: A Reinterpretation of American History, 1900–1916* (New York: Free Press, 1963).

2. Walter F. Pratt, "Rhetorical Styles on the Fuller Court," *American Journal of Legal History* 24 (July 1980):192, 213–218.

3. Ibid., 190n.

4. Hale v. Henkel, 201 U.S. 43, 83–84 (1906).

5. Chicago, Burlington and Quincy Ry. Co. v. Illinois *ex rel.* Drainage Commissioners, 200 U.S. 561, 599–600 (1906); United States v. Lynah, 188 U.S. 445 (1903).

6. Northern Pacific Ry. Co. v. Adams, 192 U.S. 440, 453 (1904).

7. Union Pacific R.R. Co. v. Mason City and Fort Dodge R.R. Co., 199 U.S. 160, 170 (1905).

8. ICC v. Chicago Great Western Ry. Co., 209 U.S. 108, 118–119, 121, 122 (1908).

9. ICC v. Stickney, 215 U.S. 98 (1909).

10. Missouri Pacific Ry. Co. v. United States, 189 U.S. 274, 288, 289 (1903).

11. Armour Packing Co. v. United States, 209 U.S. 56, 87, 88 (1908); Semonche, *Charting the Future*, 219.

12. Champion v. Ames, 188 U.S. 321, 364–375 (1903).

13. Louisville & Nashville R.R. Co. v. Eubank, 184 U.S. 27, 49 (1902).

14. Atlantic Coast Line R.R. Co. v. Florida, 203 U.S. 256 (1906); Seaboard Air Line Ry. v. Florida, 203 U.S. 261 (1906).

15. Alabama and Vicksburg Ry. Co. v. Mississippi R.R. Commission, 203 U. S. 496, 500 (1906).

16. Missouri Pacific Ry. Co. v. Larabee Flour Mills Co., 211 U.S. 612, 624–627 (1909).

17. Cotting v. Kansas City Stockyards Co., 183 U.S. 79 (1901).

18. Id. at 114–115.

19. "In Memoriam," 83 Kan. ix (1911).

20. Seaboard Air Line Ry. Co. v. Seegers, 207 U.S. 78 (1907).

21. Rasmussen v. Idaho, 181 U.S. 198 (1901).

22. Pennsylvania R.R. Co. v. Knight, 192 U.S. 21 (1904).

23. Adams Express Co. v. Kentucky, 206 U.S. 129, 138, 141 (1907).

24. Adams Express Co. v. Kentucky, 214 U.S. 218 (1909).

25. Northern Securities Co. v. United States, 193 U.S. 197 (1904).

26. Semonche, *Charting the Future*, 171.

27. King, *Fuller*, 294.

28. Northern Securities Co. v. United States, 193 U.S. 197, 360–364 (1904).

29. "The Death of Justice Brewer," *Independent* 68 (April 7, 1910):774.

30. 166 U.S. 290 (1897).

31. Swift & Co. v. United States, 196 U.S. 375 (1905); Semonche, *Charting the Future*, 185.

32. 196 U.S. 447, 456–457 (1905).

33. Jack v. Kansas, 199 U.S. 372, 382 (1905).

34. Peoria Gas and Electric Co. v. Peoria, 200 U.S. 48, 54, 56 (1906).

35. Continental Wall Paper Co. v. Louis Voight and Sons Co., 212 U.S. 227, 267–274 (1909).

36. 199 U.S. 437 (1905).

37. Id. at 454, 455, 461.

38. Id. at 464; Robert B. Highsaw, *Edward Douglass White: Defender of the Conservative Faith* (Baton Rouge: Louisiana State University Press, 1981), 191–192.

39. Snyder v. Bettman, 190 U.S. 249 (1903).

40. Cornell v. Coyne, 192 U.S. 418 (1904).

41. 181 U.S. 283 (1901).

42. Id. at 312.

43. Id. at 312–323.

44. Travellers' Insurance Co. v. Connecticut, 185 U.S. 364 (1902); Florida Central and Peninsular R.R. Co. v. Reynolds, 183 U.S. 471 (1902); Old Dominion Steamship Co. v. Virginia, 198 U.S. 299 (1905); Atlantic and Pacific Telegraph Co. v. Philadelphia, 190 U.S. 160 (1903).

45. Beers v. Glynn, 211 U.S. 477, 484 (1909).

46. Michigan Central R.R. Co. v. Powers, 201 U.S. 245, 292–293 (1906).

47. Citizens' Bank v. Parker, 192 U.S. 73, 86–93 (1904).

48. New York *ex rel.* Metropolitan Street Ry. Co. v. New York State Board of Tax Commissioners, 199 U.S. 1, 46 (1905).

49. 201 U.S. 543 (1906).

50. Western Union Telegraph Co. v. Kansas *ex rel.* Coleman, 216 U.S. 1 (1910).

51. Lardner, "Constitutional Doctrines of Justice Brewer," 31–32, 105, 206, 220–221, 222.

52. Hall, *Magic Mirror*, 221–223.

11. Facts and Law: Responses to Reform, 1901–1910

1. Charles W. McCurdy, "The Roots of 'Liberty of Contract' Reconsidered: Major Premises in the Law of Employment, 1867–1937," *Yearbook Supreme Court Historical Society* (1984):20–33.

2. 165 U.S. 578 (1897).

3. 169 U.S. 366, 398 (1898).

4. Knoxville Iron Co. v. Harbison, 183 U.S. 13, 22 (1901); Dayton Coal and Iron Co. v. Barton, 183 U.S. 23, 25 (1901).

5. 191 U.S. 207, 224 (1903).

6. Patterson v. Bark Eudora, 190 U.S. 169, 175 (1903).

7. 198 U.S. 45 (1905).

8. Urofsky, "Myth and Reality," 62.

9. Ellis v. United States, 206 U.S. 246 (1907).

10. Adair v. United States, 208 U.S. 161 (1908).

11. 208 U.S. 412 (1908).

12. Wisconsin Central R.R. Co. v. Forsythe, 159 U.S. 46 (1895); Spencer v. McDougal, 159 U.S. 62 (1895).

13. Muller v. Oregon, 208 U.S. 412, 419 (1908).

14. Id. at 422–423.

15. Id. at 421.

16. Urofsky, "Myth and Reality," 62–63.

17. Muller v. Oregon, 208 U.S. 412, 419 (1908).

18. Id. at 421.

19. Id. at 419.

20. DJB, "The Legitimate Exercise of the Police Power in the Protection of Health," *Charities and the Commons* 21 (November 7, 1908):241.

21. McCabe & Steen Construction Co. v. Wilson, 209 U.S. 275 (1908).

22. El Paso and Southwestern R.R. Co. v. Vizard, 211 U.S. 608 (1909).

23. Northern Pacific Ry. Co. v. Dixon, 194 U.S. 338, 347–356 (1904); Myers, *History of the Supreme Court*, 684.

24. Schlemmer v. Buffalo, Rochester and Pittsburg [*sic*] Ry. Co., 205 U.S. 1, 14–20 (1907).

25. 207 U.S. 463, 504–541 (1908).

26. McLean v. Arkansas, 211 U.S. 539, 552 (1909).

27. 197 U.S. 207 (1905).

28. Id. at 222–223; Semonche, *Charting the Future*, 180; Myers, *History of the Supreme Court*, 678.

29. 203 U.S. 1 (1906).

30. Id. at 16.

31. 109 U.S. 3 (1883).

32. Id. at 20–38; Harold M. Hyman and William M. Wiecek, *Equal Justice Under Law: Constitutional Development, 1835–1875* (New York: Harper & Row, 1982), 501–505.

33. Tarrance v. Florida, 188 U.S. 519, 520 (1903).

34. Berea College v. Kentucky, 211 U.S. 45 (1908).

35. Id. at 58, 67.

36. 190 U.S. 127 (1903).

37. Giles v. Harris, 189 U.S. 475, 488 (1903).

38. Jones v. Montague, 194 U.S. 147 (1904).

39. Leach v. Burr, 188 U.S. 510, 515 (1903).

40. United States v. Shipp, 203 U.S. 563 (1906); 214 U.S. 386 (1909); 215 U.S. 580 (1909); Semonche, *Charting the Future*, 233; King, *Fuller*, 323–327.

41. DJB, "Plain Words on the Crime of Lynching," *Leslie's Weekly* 97 (August 20, 1903):182.

42. E.g., Fok Yung Yo v. United States, 185 U.S. 296 (1902); Lee Gon Yung v. United States, 185 U.S. 306 (1902); Lee Lung v. Patterson, 186 U.S. 168 (1902); Ah How v. United States, 193 U.S. 65 (1904); Japanese Immigrant Case (Yamatoya v. Fisher), 189 U.S. 86 (1903).

43. 194 U.S. 161, 182 (1904); Semonche, *Charting the Future*, 175.

44. 198 U.S. 253, 264–280 (1905).

45. Ah Sin v. Wittman, 198 U.S. 500 (1905).

46. Wiggan v. Connolly, 163 U.S. 56 (1896); Barker v. Harvey, 181 U.S. 481 (1901); Minnesota v. Hitchcock, 185 U.S. 373 (1902); Ballinger v. United States *ex rel.* Frost, 216 U.S. 240, 249 (1910); Goudy v. Meath, 203 U.S. 146 (1906).

47. 197 U.S. 488 (1905).

48. Charles H. Butler, *A Century at the Bar of the Supreme Court of the United States* (New York: G. P. Putnam's Sons, 1942), 74–77.

49. 215 U.S. 278 (1909).

50. The leading Insular Cases are DeLima v. Bidwell, 182 U.S. 1 (1901); Dooley v. United States, 182 U.S. 222 (1901); Downes v. Bidwell, 182 U.S. 244 (1901); Hawaii v. Mankichi, 190 U.S. 197 (1903); Dorr v. United States, 195 U.S. 138 (1904); and Rasmussen v. United States, 197 U.S. 516 (1905).

51. *Topeka Capital*, December 22, 1900.

52. Henry F. Pringle, *The Life and Times of William Howard Taft*, 2 vols. (New York: Farrar & Rinehart, 1939)1:266. The case in question appears to be Lincoln v. United States, 197 U.S. 419 (1905) and 202 U.S. 484 (1906).

53. King, *Fuller*, 270–271.

54. Butler, *A Century at the Bar*, 90.

55. 204 U.S. 24, 30, 31 (1907).

56. 206 U.S. 46 (1907); James E. Sherow, "The Contest for the 'Nile of America,' " *Great Plains Quarterly* 10 (Winter 1990):48–61.

57. Id. at 105, 107.

58. Id. at 104–105.

59. Id. at 97.

60. 174 U.S. 690 (1899); Donald J. Pisani, "State vs. Nation: Federal Reclamation and Water Rights in the Progressive Era," *Pacific Historical Review* 51 (August 1982):273–274.

61. 16 Peters 1 (1842).

62. 181 U.S. 92 (1901).

63. *New York Sun*, July 6, 1907.

64. Robert D. Scott, "*Kansas* v. *Colorado* Revisited," *American Journal of International Law* 52 (1958), 454.

65. Washington v. Oregon, 214 U.S. 205, 218 (1909).

66. South Dakota v. North Carolina, 192 U.S. 286, 322–354 (1904); Butler, *A Century at the Bar*, 98–99; Charles Warren, *The Supreme Court in United States History*, rev. ed., 2 vols. (Boston: Little, Brown, 1926)2:665n; Highsaw, *White*, 144–145.

67. McCray v. United States, 195 U.S. 27 (1904).

68. Schick v. United States, 195 U.S. 65, 70, 72–100 (1904). The courts have continued to recognize the distinction between a crime and a petty offense and to hold that the latter is not covered by the constitutional right to a jury trial.

69. 205 U.S. 454 (1907).

70. Id. at 463–465.

71. Id. at 465–466.

72. Keller v. United States, 213 U.S. 138, 148–149, 149–151 (1909).

73. Burton v. United States, 202 U.S. 344, 390–400 (1906).

74. Whitney v. Dick, 202 U.S. 132 (1906); In re Lincoln, 202 U.S. 178, 183 (1906).
75. Fidelity and Deposit Co. v. L. Bucki & Son Lumber Co., 189 U.S. 135, 138 (1903).
76. Gamer, "Justice Brewer," 634n.
77. Butler, *A Century at the Bar*, 86–87.
78. Hatfield v. King, 184 U.S. 162, 168 (1902).
79. Albert P. Blaustein and Roy M. Mersky, *The First One Hundred Justices: Statistical Studies on the Supreme Court of the United States* (Hamden, CN: Archon Books, 1978), 144. The category "other opinions" includes "[s]eriatim opinions, judicial 'asides', opinions which concur in part and dissent in part, and other opinions difficult to classify." Ibid., 90.
80. Ibid., 99, 101.
81. Semonche, *Charting the Future*, 244–245.

12. The Great Civic Apostle: Reform Advocacy, 1901–1910

1. *Kansas City Journal*, May 31, 1901; *Kansas City Star*, June 2, 1901.
2. *Topeka Capital*, June 7, 1901.
3. *Topeka State Journal*, June 1, 1901.
4. "David Josiah Brewer: An Ideal American," *Case and Comment* 16 (May 1910):363; undated clipping from the *Washington Star*, U.S. Supreme Court Clerk's Scrapbook 3:12, RG 267, National Archives.
5. *Topeka Capital*, April 3, 1910.
6. *Topeka State Journal*, June 1, 1910; "A Sunflower Solon," *Saturday Evening Post* 182 (September 11, 1909):23.
7. DJB to Mary Adele Brewer, April 27 and July 27, 1903, Brewer Papers.
8. "David Josiah Brewer: An Ideal American," 363; "A Sunflower Solon," 23.
9. *Kansas City Star*, January 30, 1910.
10. *New York Times*, June 15, 1905 (8:3).
11. Margaret E. Winter, personal communication, April 8, 1985.
12. DJB, *Address of Justice David J. Brewer to the Association of Agents of the Northwestern Mutual Life Insurance Company, July 18, 1906* (n.p., 1906?), 6; DJB, *The United States a Christian Nation* (Philadelphia: J. C. Winston, 1905), 83; DJB, *Legal Ethics: Address Delivered at Commencement of Albany Law School, June First, 1904* Albany: (Union University, 1904), 18–19.
13. *New York Times*, June 2, 1904 (9:3); the *Sun's* response is printed in the *Wichita Eagle*, November 26, 1904.
14. State v. Wilson, 24 Kan. 189, 193 (1880).
15. *Kansas City Journal*, June 3, 1907.
16. E. F. Ware, "D. J. Brewer," *Proceedings of the Twenty-eighth Annual Meeting of the Bar Association of the State of Kansas* (1911):19–20.
17. *Kansas City Journal*, June 3, 1907; DJB, *Address to the Agents of the Northwestern Mutual Life Insurance Company, 1906*, 3–4.
18. DJB, *American Citizenship*, 40.
19. DJB, "The Supreme Court of the United States," *Scribner's Monthly* 33 (March 1903):277–278.

20. DJB, *Address of Justice David J. Brewer to the Association of Agents of the Northwestern Mutual Life Insurance Company, July 16, 1908* (n.p., 1908?), 5.

21. DJB, *American Citizenship*, 100; *New York Times*, July 18, 1903 (1:2).

22. DJB, *Address to the Agents of the Northwestern Mutual Life Insurance Company, 1908*, 5.

23. DJB, [address in] *Report. Colorado Bar Association, Sixth Annual Meeting, Colorado Springs, Colorado, July 1 and 2, 1903* (n.p., 1903?).

24. DJB, "The Supreme Court," 279.

25. Ibid., 280–281; *Kansas City Journal*, June 3, 1907; DJB, *Yale's Relation to Public Service: Address by David J. Brewer . . . at the Yale Bicentennial Celebration, New Haven, Conn., October 23, 1901* (New Haven: Tuttle, Morehouse & Taylor, 1901), 11.

26. DJB, "Two Periods in the History of the Supreme Court," in *Report of the Eighteenth Annual Meeting of the Virginia State Bar Association, Held at Hot Springs, August 7th, 8th and 9th, 1906* (Richmond: Richmond Press, 1906), 133, 145.

27. Ibid., 153.

28. DJB, "The Legitimate Exercise of the Police Power in the Protection of Health," 238–241.

29. DJB, "The Triumph of Justice" (University of Kansas commencement address), *Lawrence Journal*, June 10, 1903; DJB, *The United States a Christian Nation*, 63, 66, 68, 88–89; *New York Times*, November 21, 1905 (2:3); ibid., December 17, 1906 (7:2); DJB, *American Citizenship*, 43, 51–54, 125–127; DJB [address to] *Association of Agents of the Northwestern Mutual Life Insurance Company. Minutes of the Twenty-fifth Annual Meeting, July 16th and 17th, 1901* (n.p., 1901), 30–41; DJB, "The Ideal Lawyer," *Atlantic Monthly* 98 (November 1906):597; DJB [presidential address], *Official Report of the Universal Congress of Lawyers and Jurists, Held at St. Louis, Missouri, U.S.A., September 28, 29, and 30, 1904, under the Auspices of the Universal Exposition and the American Bar Association* (St. Louis: Executive Committee, 1905), 5, 7; DJB, "A Second Hague Conference. What May Be Expected from It," *Christian Endeavor World* 19 (July 6, 1905):787–788; Edward Everett Hale and DJB, *Mohonk Addresses* (Boston: Ginn and Co., 1910).

30. Hale and DJB, *Mohonk Addresses*, 98–103, 125–128.

31. Ibid., 104–115; *Proceedings of the American Society of International Law at Its First Annual Meeting, Held at Washington, D. C., April 19 and 20, 1907* (New York: American Society of International Law, 1908), 9, 23–24, 37.

32. DJB and Butler, *International Law* (New York: American Law Book Co., 1906), 4–5.

33. Hale and DJB, *Mohonk Addresses*, 120–124.

34. Ware, "D. J. Brewer," 20; DJB, *American Citizenship*, 120–121; *New York Times*, December 17, 1906 (7:2); DJB, "Why Do I Believe in Foreign Missions?" *The Envelope Series* 8 (April 1905):7–8.

35. DJB, *The Mission of the United States in the Cause of Peace* (Boston: International School of Peace, 1910), 2, 3, 13.

36. Ibid., 10–11, 15, 16, 18–20.

37. David S. Patterson, "An Interpretation of the American Peace Move-

ment," in *Peace Movements in America*, ed. by Charles Chatfield, 20–38. (New York: Schocken Books, 1973); see also Sondra R. Herman, *Eleven Against War: Studies in American International Thought, 1898–1921* (Stanford, CA: Hoover Institute Press, 1969.

38. Patterson, "An Interpretation of the American Peace Movement," 31.

39. DJB, *The Spanish War*, 13; DJB, *American Citizenship*, 51, 64.

40. DJB, "Woman Suffrage: Its Present Position and Its Future," *Ladies' World* 30 (December 1909):29.

41. Ibid., 6, 29.

42. *Kansas City Star*, June 13, 1906.

43. DJB, "Woman Suffrage," 6; DJB and Warren Van Norden, *Addresses Delivered by Justice David J. Brewer and Mr. Warren Van Norden at Lake Mohonk Mountain House on July the Fourth Nineteen Hundred Eight* (Fulton, NY: Morrill Press, n.d.), 20.

44. William H. Baldwin, "Justice Brewer and Organized Charity," *Survey* 24 (April 16, 1910):119–121.

45. DJB, "Social Service as Exemplified in the Associated Charities of the National Capital," *Charities and the Commons* 15 (March 3, 1906):813–815; Baldwin, "Justice Brewer and Organized Charity," 120.

46. *New York Times*, December 17, 1906 (7:2).

47. DJB, *Public Office in Relation to Public Opinion. An Address Delivered to the Civic Forum in Carnegie Hall, New York City, November 20, 1907* (New York: Civic Forum, 1908), 8; *New York Times*, December 17, 1906 (7:2).

48. DJB, *Yale's Relation to Public Service*, 5.

49. DJB, "Justice Brewer's Address," *Southern Workman* 35 (June 1906):361.

50. DJB, *American Citizenship*, 102; unidentified clipping, Biographical Clippings, B, 8:57, Kansas State Historical Society; DJB, "Plain Words on the Crime of Lynching," 182.

51. Westin, ed., *Autobiography of the Supreme Court*, 192–193.

52. *Topeka State Journal*, January 20, 1902.

53. *New York Times*, July 25, 1904 (6:3).

54. DJB, *American Citizenship*, 25.

55. DJB, "Obedience to Law the First Civic Duty," in *The Making of America*, 10 vols., ed. by Robert J. La Follette, 2:108–123 (Chicago: Making of America Co., 1906)2:108–123; DJB, "Woman Suffrage," 6.

56. DJB, "The Ideal Lawyer," 589–590; DJB, *Legal Ethics*, 16.

57. DJB, "Organized Wealth and the Judiciary," *Independent* 57 (August 11, 1904):301–304; DJB, "The Supreme Court," 275, 276–277, 284; DJB, "Our Highest Tribunal," in *Our National Government* (Boston: P. Mason Co., 1904), 203–204, 205, 213–214.

58. DJB, *Address to the Agents of the Northwestern Mutual Life Insurance Company, 1906*, 3; Butler, *A Century at the Bar*, 188.

59. DJB, "The Right of Appeal," *Independent* 55 (October 29, 1903):2547, 2548–2549.

60. DJB, *American Citizenship*, 65–66; DJB, "The Jury," *International Monthly* 5 (January 1902):6–7.

61. DJB, *The Spirit of Liberty: An Address by Hon. D. J. Brewer . . . at the*

Annual Meeting of the Northwestern Agents, July 20, 1904 (n.p., 1904?), 6; DJB, *The United States a Christian Nation*, 66–67.

62. DJB, "Shall George Washington's Will Be Executed?," *George Washington University Bulletin* ("Convocation Number") 4 (March 1905):8–16.

63. *Topeka State Journal*, March 21, 1906.

64. *Kansas City Star*, May 18, 1909; members of the Supreme Court of the District of Columbia to Emma M. Brewer, July 2, 1906, Brewer Papers.

65. Among those doing so were the University of Iowa (1884); Washburn College (1888); Yale (1891); the University of Wisconsin (1900); Wesleyan University (1901); the University of Vermont (1904); and Bowdoin College (1905).

66. DJB, "The Religion of a Jurist," *Outlook* 80 (June 24, 1905):536.

67. DJB, *The United States a Christian Nation*, 11, 31, 36.

68. Undated clipping, Box 3, Brewer Papers.

69. *New York Times*, November 21, 1905 (2:3); DJB to Straus, July 12, 1902, Brewer Papers; Wolf to DJB, n.d., Brewer Papers.

70. DJB, "Were Christ's Trial and Death Legal?" *Sunday School Times*, November 17, 1906, 665–666.

71. *Kansas City Journal*, March 7, 1904; *New York Times*, May 30, 1904 (5:1); "David Josiah Brewer: An Ideal American," 361; DJB, "The Young Men's Christian Association and American Solidarity," *Intercollegian* 27 (February 1905):101–103.

72. "In Memoriam," 83 Kan. viii (1911).

73. *New York Times*, June 27, 1906 (1:4); ibid., August 6, 1906 (6:1); *Kansas City Journal*, August 4, 1906.

74. DJB, *Public Office in Relation to Public Opinion*, 6.

75. "A Sunflower Solon," 23.

76. Elting E. Morrison, ed., *The Letters of Theodore Roosevelt*, 8 vols. (Cambridge: Harvard University Press, 1954)5:396–397, 7:495.

77. Mark De Wolfe Howe, ed., *Holmes-Laski Letters: The Correspondence of Mr. Justice Holmes and Harold J. Laski, 1916–1935*, 2 vols. (Cambridge: Harvard University Press, 1953)2:1270.

78. Paul T. Heffron, "Theodore Roosevelt and the Appointment of Mr. Justice Moody," *Vanderbilt Law Review* 18 (March 1965):552, 558.

79. Possibly Valentine Mott Porter, a prominent St. Louis lawyer. Roosevelt to DJB, November 5, 1906, Theodore Roosevelt Papers, ser. 2, reel 343, Presidential Papers Microfilm, Manuscript Division, Library of Congress.

80. DJB to Johnston, December 14, 1901, W. A. Johnston Papers, Kansas State Historical Society.

81. Unsigned, undated, and incomplete letter to "Dear Girls," Brewer Papers.

82. *Topeka Capital*, August 26, 1906; Pringle, *Taft* 1:334.

83. DJB to Taft (telegram), June 19, 1908, Taft Papers, Library of Congress, ser. 3, Box 172.

84. DJB, *Thirty-third Annual Meeting of the Association of Agents of the Northwestern Mutual Life Insurance Company. Address by David J. Brewer, Trustee of the Company, at the Home Office, Milwaukee, Wisconsin, Wednesday, July 21, 1909* (n.p., 1909?), 1.

238

Notes to Pages 182–187

85. *Kansas City Journal*, June 3, 1907.

86. Pringle, *Taft* 1:529–530.

87. Edwin S. Corwin, *Court Over Constitution: A Study of Judicial Review as an Instrument of Popular Government* (Princeton: Princeton University Press, 1915), 194n.

88. Butler, *A Century at the Bar*, 189; *Emporia Gazette*, March 29, 1910; *Kansas City Journal*, March 29, 1910.

89. *Topeka State Journal*, March 29, 1910.

90. *Kansas City Journal*, March 29, 1910.

91. *Proceedings of the Bar and Officers of the Supreme Court of the United States in Memory of David Josiah Brewer, April 30, 1910* (Washington: n.p., 1910).

92. "Proceedings on the Death of Mr. Justice Brewer," 218 U.S. vii–xvi (1910).

93. *Leavenworth Times*, April 3, 1910.

94. Blackmar, *Kansas*, 49; *Emporia Gazette*, April 1 and 2, 1910; *Kansas City Star*, April 2, 1910. The actual location of Mount Muncie Cemetery is Lansing, Kansas, south of Leavenworth. George A. Christensen, "Here Lies the Supreme Court: Gravesites of the Justices," *Yearbook Supreme Court Historical Society* (1983):25, 30n.

95. *Kansas City Star*, March 30, 1910.

96. *Leavenworth Times*, April 1, 1910.

97. Mark De Wolfe Howe, ed., *Holmes-Pollock Letters: The Correspondence of Mr. Justice Holmes and Sir Frederick Pollock*, 2 vols. (Cambridge: Harvard University Press, 1941)1:160.

98. Ibid.

99. Bergan, "Mr. Justice Brewer," 192; *Kansas City Journal*, March 29, 1910.

100. "David Josiah Brewer: An Ideal American," 362–363; "The Great Minds of America: III.—David J. Brewer," *North American Review* 187 (January 1908):1–6; "In Memoriam," 83 Kan. vi–x (1911); *Proceedings of the Bar and Officers of the Supreme Court*, 15, 25–27, 31–32, 37–44, 47; Ware, "D.J. Brewer," 18–19; "Death of Justice Brewer," 773–774; *Kansas City Star*, March 30, 1910.

101. "Mr. Justice Brewer," *The Outlook* 94 (April 9, 1910):785–786.

102. DJB, "Remarks by Justice David J. Brewer at the Annual Commencement Dinner, June 10, 1903," *Graduate Magazine of the University of Kansas* 1 (June 1903):345.

103. Corwin, *Court Over Constitution*, 198n.

104. Westin, ed., *Autobiography of the Supreme Court*, 122.

105. Howe, ed., *Holmes-Laski Letters* 1:428, 686, 2:1007.

106. Abraham, *Justices and Presidents*, 10–11.

107. Frankfurter, "The Supreme Court in the Mirror of Justices," *University of Pennsylvania Law Review* 105 (April 1957):788.

108. Albert P. Blaustein and Roy M. Mersky, "Rating Supreme Court Justices," *American Bar Association Journal* 58 (November 1972):1187.

109. Bergan, "Mr. Justice Brewer," and Gamer, "Justice Brewer and Due Process."

BIBLIOGRAPHY

Manuscripts

John A. Anderson Papers. Manuscripts Division. Kansas State Historical Society, Topeka.

Chester A. Arthur Papers. Presidential Papers Microfilm. Manuscript Division. Library of Congress.

Simeon Baldwin Papers. Yale University Library, New Haven, CN.

Edward A. Bowers Papers. Beinecke Library. Yale University, New Haven, CN.

David J. Brewer Papers. Yale University Library, New Haven, CN.

Grover Cleveland Papers. Presidential Papers Microfilm. Manuscript Division. Library of Congress.

Mark W. Delahay Papers. Manuscripts Division. Kansas State Historical Society, Topeka.

John Guthrie Papers. Kansas State Historical Society, Topeka.

Benjamin Harrison Papers. Presidential Papers Microfilm. Manuscript Division. Library of Congress.

W. A. Johnston Papers. Manuscripts Division. Kansas State Historical Society, Topeka.

Kansas Corporation Charters. Archives Division. Kansas State Historical Society, Topeka.

Karrick Family Collection. Yale University Library, New Haven, CN.

Lincoln and Washburn College, First Secretary's Book . . . 1865–1889 (microfilm copy). Manuscripts Division. Kansas State Historical Society, Topeka.

William McKinley Papers. Presidential Papers Microfilm. Manuscript Division. Library of Congress.

H. Miles Moore Papers. Manuscripts Division. Kansas State Historical Society, Topeka.

"Papers re Nominations, Sen. 51B–A4, Brewer, David J." Record Group 46. National Archives, Washington, D.C.

"Personnel Records of U.S. Supreme Court Justices." Record Group 60. National Archives, Washington, D.C.

Theodore Roosevelt Papers. Presidential Papers Microfilm. Manuscript Division. Library of Congress.

William Howard Taft Papers. Manuscript Division. Library of Congress.

U.S. Supreme Court Clerk's Scrapbook. Record Group 267. National Archives, Washington, D.C.

Yale Manuscripts. Yale University Library, New Haven, CN.
Yale Miscellaneous Manuscripts. Yale University Library, New Haven, CN.

Other Unpublished Material

Lardner, Lynford A. "The Constitutional Doctrines of Justice David Josiah Brewer." Ph.D. diss., Princeton University, 1938.

Newspapers and Periodicals

American Advocate of Peace, 1893
American Law Review, 1890
Beta Theta Pi Magazine, 1896
Emporia Gazette, 1910
Industrialist (Manhattan, KS), 1875–1877
Kansas City Journal, 1901–1910
Kansas City Star, 1900–1910
Kansas City Times, 1901–1910
Kansas Law Journal, 1886
Lawrence Journal, 1903
Leavenworth Times, 1859–1865, 1910
Leavenworth Times and Conservative, 1868
Minutes of the Seventh Annual Meeting of the Bar Association of the State of Kansas, 1890
New York Sun, 1907
New York Times, 1889–1906
Report of the Thirty-third Annual Meeting of the American Bar Association . . . 1910
Topeka Capital, 1883–1910
Topeka Commonwealth, 1870–1880
Topeka Mail and Breeze, 1900–1910
Topeka State Journal, 1896–1910
Washington Post, 1902
Wichita Eagle, 1904

Government Publications

Kansas

Annual Report of the Secretary of State of the State of Kansas, 1864, 1870.
In the Supreme Court of Kansas, October 4, 1937, in Memory of William Agnew Johnston. Topeka: Kansas State Printing Plant, 1937.

United States

Official Register of the United States, Containing a List of Officers and Employees in the Civil, Military, and Naval Services on the First of July, 1895. 2 vols. Washington, D.C.: Government Printing Office, 1895.
Report of the Special Commission . . . to Examine and Report upon the True Divisional Line between the Republic of Venezuela and British Guiana. 4 vols. 55th Cong., 2d sess., S. Doc. 91 (1898).

Court Cases

The Federal Reporter. Cases Argued and Determined in Circuit and District Courts of the United States, vols. 21–64 (1884–1894).
The Pacific Reporter, Containing All the Decisions of the Supreme Courts of California, Colorado, Kansas, Oregon, Nevada, Arizona, Idaho, Montana, Washington, Wyoming, Utah, and New Mexico, vols. 1–3 (1883–1884).
Reports of Cases Argued and Determined in the Supreme Court of the State of Kansas, 2d ed., vols. 1–29 (1861–1883) and 83 (1911).
United States Reports. Cases Adjudged in the Supreme Court, vols. 123–218 (1887–1910).

Books and Pamphlets

Abraham, Henry J. *Justices and Presidents: A Political History of the Appointments to the Supreme Court.* 2d ed. New York: Oxford University Press, 1985.
Bader, Robert Smith. *Prohibition in Kansas: A History.* Lawrence: University Press of Kansas, 1986.
Bates, Ernest Sutherland. *The Story of the Supreme Court.* Indianapolis: Bobbs-Merrill, 1936.
Beth, Loren P. *The Development of the American Constitution, 1877–1917.* New York: Harper & Row, 1971.
Blackmar, Frank W. *Kansas: A Cyclopedia of State History,* supplementary volume, part I. Chicago: Crane & Co., 1902.
Blakely, William Addison, ed. *American State Papers Bearing on Sunday Legislation.* Washington, D.C.: Religious Liberty Assn., 1911.
Blaustein, Albert P., and Roy M. Mersky. *The First One Hundred Justices: Statistical Studies on the Supreme Court of the United States.* Hamden, CN: Archon Books, 1978.
Brewer, David J. [Address in] *Report. Colorado Bar Association, Sixth Annual Meeting, Colorado Springs, Colorado, July 1 and 2, 1903.* N.p., 1903?
———. *Address of David J. Brewer . . . at the Dedication of the Battle*

Monument, West Point, New York, May 31, 1897. West Point?: U.S.M.A. Press and Bindery, 1897.

———. *Address of Justice David J. Brewer to the Association of Agents of the Northwestern Mutual Life Insurance Company, July 18, 1906.* N.p., 1906?

———. *Address of Justice David J. Brewer to the Association of Agents of the Northwestern Mutual Life Insurance Company, July 16, 1908.* N.p., 1908?

———. [Address to] *Association of Agents of the Northwestern Mutual Life Insurance Company. Minutes of the Twenty-fifth Annual Meeting, July 16th and 17th, 1901.* N.p., 1901.

———. [Address to] *Thirty-third Annual Meeting of the Agents of the Northwestern Mutual Life Insurance Company.* N.p., 1909.

———. *American Citizenship.* New York: C. Scribner's Sons, 1902.

———. *The Income Tax Cases. Address Delivered before the Graduating Class of the Law Department of the University of Iowa at the Annual Commencement, June 8, 1898.* N.p., n.d.

———. *Jubilee Anniversary: An Address Delivered at the Fiftieth Annual Meeting of the American Missionary Association, October 21, 1896.* N.p., n.d.

———. *Legal Ethics: Address Delivered at Commencement of Albany Law School, June First, 1904.* Albany: Union University, 1904.

———. *The Mission of the United States in the Cause of World Peace.* Boston: International School of Peace, 1910.

———. *The Movement of Coercion. An Address by Mr. Justice Brewer . . . Before the New York State Bar Association, January, 1893.* Chicago: Building Contractors' Council, n.d.

———. *The Pew to the Pulpit: Suggestions to the Ministry from the Viewpoint of a Layman.* F. H. Revell, New York, 1897.

———. *Public Office in Relation to Public Opinion. An Address Delivered to the Civic Forum in Carnegie Hall, New York City, November 20, 1907.* New York: Civic Forum, 1908.

———. *Second Annual Report of the Superintendent of Public Schools of Leavenworth City, Kansas. August 1, 1866.* Leavenworth: Clarke, Emery & Co., 1866.

———. *The Spanish War: A Prophecy or an Exception?* Buffalo: Liberal Club, 1899.

———. *The Spirit of Liberty: An Address by Hon. D. J. Brewer . . . at the Annual Meeting of the Northwestern Agents, July 20, 1904.* N.p., 1904?

———. *Third Annual Report of the Superintendent of Public Schools of Leavenworth City, Kansas. August 1, 1867.* Leavenworth: Bulletin Cooperative Printing Co., 1867.

———. *Thirty-third Annual Meeting of the Association of Agents of the Northwestern Mutual Life Insurance Company. Address by David J.*

Brewer, Trustee of the Company, at the Home Office, Milwaukee, Wisconsin, Wednesday, July 21, 1909. N.p., 1909?

———. *The Twentieth Century from Another Viewpoint.* New York: F. P. Revell, 1899.

———. *The United States a Christian Nation.* Philadelphia: J. C. Winston, 1905.

———, ed. *The World's Best Essays, from the Earliest Period to the Present Time.* 10 vols. St. Louis: Ferd. P. Kaiser, 1900.

———, ed. *The World's Best Orations, from the Earliest Period to the Present Time.* 10 vols. St. Louis: Ferd. P. Kaiser, 1899.

———. *Yale's Relation to Public Service: Address by David J. Brewer . . . at the Yale Bicentennial Celebration, New Haven, Conn., October 23, 1901.* New Haven: Tuttle, Morehouse & Taylor, 1901.

———, and Charles H. Butler. *International Law.* New York: American Law Book Co., 1906.

———, and Warren Van Norden. *Addresses Delivered by Justice David J. Brewer and Mr. Warren Van Norden at Lake Mohonk Mountain House on July the Fourth Nineteen Hundred Eight.* Fulton, NY: Morrill Press, n.d.

Brewer, F. P. *Sketch of Rev. Josiah Brewer, Missionary to the Greeks.* N.p., 1880.

Bright, John D., ed. *Kansas: The First Century.* 4 vols. New York: Lewis Historical Publishing Co., 1956.

Brodhead, Michael J. *Persevering Populist: The Life of Frank Doster.* Reno: University of Nevada Press, 1969.

Butler, Charles H. *A Century at the Bar of the Supreme Court of the United States.* New York: G. P. Putnam's Sons, 1942.

Celebration of the Twenty-fifth Anniversary of the First Congregational Church, of Washington, D.C., November 9th to 16th, 1890. Washington?: Press of H. I. Rothrock, 1891.

Collins' Business and Resident Directory of Leavenworth. Leavenworth: C. Collins, 1868.

Collins' Leavenworth Directory for 1866–1867. Leavenworth: C. Collins, 1866?

Collins, Lynch & Edge's Leavenworth City Directory and Business Mirror, for the Years 1871–1872. Leavenworth: 1871.

The Columbian University. The School of Comparative Jurisprudence and Diplomacy. Catalogue, 1899–1900. Announcements, 1900–1901. Washington, D.C.: Judd & Detweiler, n.d.

Corbett, Hoye & Co's III Annual City Directory of the . . . City of Leavenworth. Leavenworth: Commercial Steam Book and Job Printing House, 1874.

Corwin, Edwin S. *Court Over Constitution: A Study of Judicial Review as an Instrument of Popular Government.* Princeton, NJ: Princeton University Press, 1915, 1938.

Cullum, Shelby M. *Fifty Years of Public Service*. Chicago: A. C. McClurg, 1911.

Cummings, Homer, and Carl McFarland. *Federal Justice: Chapters in the History of Justice and the Federal Executive*. New York: Macmillan, 1937.

Cutler, William G., ed. *History of the State of Kansas*. Chicago: A. T. Andreas, 1883.

Depew, Chauncey M. *My Memories of Eighty Years*. New York: Charles Scribner's Sons, 1924.

Edwin Greene's City Directory of the . . . City of Leavenworth, 1885. N.p., n.d.

Eitzen, D. Stanley. *David J. Brewer, 1837–1910: A Kansan on the United States Supreme Court*. Emporia State Research Studies, vol. 12, no. 3. Emporia, KS: Kansas State Teachers College, 1964.

Eminent and Representative Men of Virginia and the District of Columbia in the Nineteenth Century. Madison, WI: Brant & Fuller, 1893.

Fairman, Charles. *Mr. Justice Miller and the Supreme Court*. Cambridge: Harvard University Press, 1939.

Field, Henry M. *The Life of David Dudley Field*. New York: Charles Scribner's Sons, 1898.

Gresham, Matilda. *Life of Walter Quintin Gresham*. 2 vols. Freeport, NY: Books for Libraries Press, 1970.

Hale, Edward Everett, and David J. Brewer. *Mohonk Addresses*. Boston: Ginn and Co., 1910.

Hall, Kermit L. *The Magic Mirror: Law in American History*. New York: Oxford University Press, 1989.

Herman, Sondra R. *Eleven Against War: Studies in American International Thought, 1898–1921*. Stanford, CA: Hoover Institute Press, 1969.

Highsaw, Robert B. *Edward Douglass White: Defender of the Conservative Faith*. Baton Rouge: Louisiana State University Press, 1981.

Hoogenboom, Ari, and Olive Hoogenboom. *A History of the ICC: From Panacea to Palliative*. New York: W. W. Norton, 1976.

Howe, Mark De Wolfe, ed. *Holmes-Laski Letters: The Correspondence of Mr. Justice Holmes and Harold J. Laski, 1916–1935*. 2 vols. Cambridge: Harvard University Press, 1953.

————, ed. *Holmes-Pollock Letters: The Correspondence of Mr. Justice Holmes and Sir Frederick Pollock*. 2 vols. Cambridge: Harvard University Press, 1941.

Hyman, Harold M., and William M. Wiecek. *Equal Justice Under Law: Constitutional Development, 1835–1875*. New York: Harper & Row, 1982.

Karrick, Henrietta Brewer. *David Josiah Brewer: A Biographical Sketch. . . .* Washington, D.C.: N.p., 1912.

Kelly, Alfred H., and Winfred A. Harbison. *The American Constitution: Its Origins and Development.* 5th ed. New York: W. W. Norton, 1976.

King, Willard L. *Melville Weston Fuller: Chief Justice of the United States, 1888–1910.* New York: Macmillan, 1950; Chicago: University of Chicago Press, Phoenix Books, 1967.

Kolko, Gabriel. *Railroads and Regulation, 1877–1916.* New York: W. W. Norton, 1965.

———. *The Triumph of Conservatism: A Reinterpretation of American History, 1900–1916.* New York: Free Press, 1963.

Kurland, Philip B. *Religion and the Law of Church and State and the Supreme Court.* Chicago: Aldine, 1962.

Leavenworth City Directory, and Business Mirror, for 1860–1861. Leavenworth: James Sutherland, 1860.

Leavenworth City Directory, and Business Mirror, for 1862–1863. Leavenworth: Buckingham and Hamilton, 1862.

Leavenworth City Directory, and Business Mirror, for 1863–64. Leavenworth: James Sutherland, 1863.

Leavenworth City Directory, and Business Mirror, for 1865–66. Leavenworth: James Sutherland, 1865.

Malin, James C. *Confounded Rot about Napoleon: Reflections upon Science and Technology, Nationalism, World Depression of the Eighteen-nineties, and Afterwards.* Lawrence, KS: The author, 1961.

Mechem, Kirk. *The Annals of Kansas, 1885–1925.* 2 vols. Topeka: Kansas State Historical Society, 1954–1956.

Merwin's Leavenworth City Directory for 1870–71. Leavenworth: Heman Merwin, 1870.

Moore, H. Miles. *Early History of Leavenworth City and County.* Leavenworth: Sam'l Dodsworth Book Co., 1906.

Morrison, Elting, ed. *The Letters of Theodore Roosevelt.* 8 vols. Cambridge: Harvard University Press, 1954.

Myers, Gustavus. *History of the Supreme Court of the United States.* Chicago: Charles H. Kerr, 1912.

Nevins, Allan. *Grover Cleveland, A Study in Courage.* New York: Dodd, Mead, 1932.

Paul, Arnold M. *Conservative Crisis and the Rule of Law: Attitudes of Bench and Bar, 1887–1895.* Ithaca: Cornell University Press, 1960.

Pearson, Jim Berry. *The Maxwell Land Grant.* Norman: University of Oklahoma Press, 1961.

Portrait and Biographical Record of Leavenworth, Douglas and Franklin Counties, Kansas. Chicago: Chapman Publ. Co., 1899.

Pringle, Henry F. *The Life and Times of William Howard Taft.* 2 vols. New York: Farrar & Rinehart, 1939.

Proceedings of the American Society of International Law at Its First Annual

Meeting, Held at Washington, D.C., April 19 and 20, 1907. New York: American Society of International Law, 1908.

Proceedings of the Bar and Officers of the Supreme Court of the United States in Memory of David Josiah Brewer, April 30. 1910. Washington: N.p., 1910.

Proceedings of the Sixty-sixth Annual Meeting of the American Home Missionary Society, Held at the First Congregational Church, Washington, D.C., May 24–26. 1892. Washington, D.C.: Gibson Bros., 1892.

Report of the First Annual Meeting of the Lake Mohonk Conference on International Arbitration. N.p., 1895.

Rout, Leslie B., Jr. *Which Way Out? A Study of the Guyana-Venezuela Boundary Dispute.* East Lansing: Latin American Studies Center, Michigan State University, 1971.

Semonche, John E. *Charting the Future: The Supreme Court Responds to a Changing Society, 1890–1920.* Westport, CN: Greenwood Press, 1978.

Shiras, George, 3rd. *Justice George Shiras of Pittsburgh.* Pittsburgh: University of Pittsburgh Press, 1953.

Sievers, Harry J. *Benjamin Harrison, Hoosier President.* Indianapolis: Bobbs-Merrill, 1968.

Swisher, Carl Brent. *Stephen J. Field: Craftsman of the Law.* Washington, D.C.: Brookings Institution, 1930.

Syrett, Harold C., ed. *The Gentleman and the Tiger: The Autobiography of George B. McClellan, Jr.* Philadelphia: J. B. Lippincott, 1956.

Taylor, Morris F. *O. P. McMains and the Maxwell Land Grant Conflict.* Tucson: University of Arizona Press, 1979.

The United States Biographical Dictionary, Kansas Volume. Chicago and Kansas City: S. Lewis & Co., 1879.

Warren, Charles. *The Supreme Court in United States History.* Rev. ed. 2 vols. Boston: Little, Brown, 1926.

Westin, Alan F., ed. *An Autobiography of the Supreme Court: Off-the-Bench Commentary by the Justices.* New York: Macmillan, 1963.

White, William Allen. *The Autobiography of William Allen White.* New York: Macmillan, 1946.

Wilder, D. W. *The Annals of Kansas, 1541–1885.* Topeka: T. Dwight Thatcher, Kansas Publishing Co., 1886.

Williams, R. Hal. *The Democratic Party and California Politics, 1880–1896.* Stanford, CA: Stanford University Press, 1973.

Articles

Apple, R. W., Jr. "The Case of the Monopolistic Railroadmen." In *Quarrels That Have Shaped the Constitution,* edited by John A. Garraty, 159–175. New York: Harper Torchbooks, 1975.

Austin, Edwin A. "The Supreme Court of the State of Kansas." *Collections of the Kansas State Historical Society* 13 (1913–1914):96–125.

Baker, Marcus. "The Anglo-Venezuelan Boundary Dispute." *National Geographic Magazine* 9 (April 1900):129–144.

———. "The Venezuela Boundary Commission and Its Work." *National Geographic Magazine* 8 (July–August 1897):194–201.

Baldwin, William H. "Justice Brewer and Organized Charity." *Survey* 24 (April 16, 1910):119–121.

Benedict, Michael Les. "Laissez-Faire and Liberty: A Re-Evaluation of the Meaning and Origins of Laissez-Faire Constitutionalism." *Law and History Review* 3 (Fall 1985):293–331.

Bergan, Francis. "Mr. Justice Brewer: Perspective of a Century." *Albany Law Review* 25 (June 1961):191–202.

Betton, Frank H. "The Genesis of a State's Metropolis." *Collections of the Kansas State Historical Society* 7 (1901–1902):114–120.

Blaustein, Albert P., and Roy M. Mersky. "Rating Supreme Court Justices." *American Bar Association Journal* 58 (November 1972):1183–1189.

Brewer, David J. "Address to the Law School." In *Commencement Annual, University of Wisconsin, June 17–21, 1900*, i-xxi. Madison: Sommers & Reynolds, n.d.

———. "A Better Education the Great Need of the Profession." *American Lawyer* 4 (January 1896):10–13.

———. "Constitutional Convention." *Western Homestead* 3 (November 1881):70–71.

———. "Dedicatory Address of Hon. D. J. Brewer . . . Delivered at Emporia, Kansas, June 16, 1880." In *Catalogue of the Officers and Students of the Kansas State Normal School, Emporia, 1879–80*, 24–30. Emporia: Rowland Bros., 1880.

———. "The Federal Judiciary." *Tenth Annual Meeting of the Bar Association of the State of Kansas*. Topeka: Crane & Co., 1893, 81–84.

———. "Government by Injunction." *National Corporation Reporter* 15 (February 24, 1898):848–850.

———. "The Green Mountain State." *The Vermonter* 1 (January 1896):125–126.

———. "Growth of the Judicial Function." In *Report of the Organization and First Annual Meeting of the Colorado Bar Association. . .* , 82–93. Denver: Smith-Brooks Printing Co., 1898.

———. "The Ideal Lawyer." *Atlantic Monthly* 98 (November 1906:587–598.

———. "Increase of Litigation.—Its Causes and Cure." *Western Homestead* 2 (January 1880):193–194.

———. "Judge Brewer on Kansas." In *Kansas Day*, edited by F. H. Barrington, 97–98. Topeka: G. W. Crane, 1892.

———. "The Jury." *International Monthly* 5 (January 1902):1–9.

———. "Justice Brewer's Address." *Southern Workman* 35 (June 1906):359–361.

———. "The Legitimate Exercise of the Police Power in the Protection of Health." *Charities and the Commons* 21 (November 7, 1908):238–241.

———. "Libel." *Minutes of the Third Annual Meeting of the Bar Association of the State of Kansas (1886)*, 55–59.

———. "The Liberty of Each Individual." *Independent* 45 (July 13, 1893):938–939.

———. "The New Profession." *Emporia News*, July 8, 1865.

———. "Obedience to Law the First Civic Duty." In *The Making of America*. 10 vols. Edited by Robert M. La Follette, 2:108–123. Chicago: Making of America Co., 1906.

———. "Organized Wealth and the Judiciary." *Independent* 57 (August 11, 1904):301–304.

———. "Our Highest Tribunal." In *Our National Government*, 201–216. Boston: P. Mason, 1904.

———. "The Patent System." *Yale Law Journal* 3 (May 1894):149–157.

———. "Plain Words on the Crime of Lynching." *Leslie's Weekly* 97 (August 20, 1903):182.

———. "Politics in the School Room." *Kansas Educational Journal* 4 (December and January, 1867–1868):173–174.

———. "Preferential Voting." *Kansas Educational Journal* 9 (August 1872):105–107.

———. [Presidential address] *Official Report of the Universal Congress of Lawyers and Jurists, Held at St. Louis, Missouri, U.S.A., September 28, 29, and 30, 1904, under the Auspices of the Universal Exposition and the American Bar Association*, 4–7. St. Louis: Executive Committee, 1905.

———. "Protection to Private Property from Public Attack." *New Englander and Yale Review* 55 (August 1891):97–110.

———. "The Religion of a Jurist." *Outlook* 80 (June 24, 1904):533–536.

———. [Remarks at dinner given for John Marshall Harlan.] *Beta Theta Pi* 18 (February–March 1891):254–256.

———. "Remarks by Justice David J. Brewer at the Annual Commencement Dinner, June 10, 1903." *Graduate Magazine of the University of Kansas* 1 (June 1903):345–348.

———. "The Right of Appeal." *Independent* 55 (October 29, 1903):2547–2550.

———. "The Scholar in Politics." In *Commencement Exercises of Washburn College, June '83*, 9–29. Manhattan, KS: College Press, E. H. Perry, 1885.

249
Bibliography

———. "A Second Hague Conference. What May Be Expected from It." *Christian Endeavor World* 19 (July 6, 1905):787–788.

———. "Shall George Washington's Will Be Executed?" *George Washington University Bulletin* 4 ("Convocation Number," March 1905):8–16.

———. "Should Teachers Engage in Politics?" *Kansas Educational Journal* 5 (August 1868):82–89.

———. "Social Service as Exemplified in the Associated Charities of the National Capital." *Charities and the Commons* 15 (March 3, 1906):813–815.

———. "Some Thoughts about Kansas." *Minutes of the Twelfth Annual Meeting of the Bar Association of the State of Kansas* (1895):61–72.

———. "The Supreme Court of the United States." *Scribner's Magazine* 33 (March 1903):273–284.

———. "The True Greatness of American Citizenship." *Beta Theta Pi Magazine* 23 (May 1896):314–320.

———. "Two Periods in the History of the Supreme Court." In *Report of the Eighteenth Annual Meeting of the Virginia State Bar Association, Held at Hot Springs, August 7th, 8th and 9th, 1906*, 133–154. Richmond: Richmond Press, 1906.

———. "Were Christ's Trial and Death Legal?" *Sunday School Times*, November 17, 1906, 665–666.

———. "Why Do I Believe in Foreign Missions?" *The Envelope Series* 8 (April 1905):7–8.

———. "The Woman of Samaria." *Kansas Educational Journal* 6 (February 1869):227–228.

———. "Woman Suffrage: Its Present Position and Its Future." *Ladies' World* 30 (December 1909):6 and 29.

———. "The Work of the Supreme Court." *Law Notes* 1 (March 1898):167–168.

———. "The Young Men's Christian Association and American Solidarity." *Intercollegian* 27 (February 1905):101–103.

Browne, Irving. "The Albany Law School." *Green Bag* 2 (April 1890):153–166.

Burr, George Lincoln. "The Guiana Boundary: A Postscript to the Work of the Commission." *American Historical Review* 6 (October 1900):49–64.

———. "The Search for the Venezuela-Guiana Boundary." *American Historical Review* 4 (April 1899):470–477.

"A Chapter of Wabash." *North American Review* 146 (February 1888):178–193.

Christensen, George A. "Here Lies the Supreme Court: Gravesites of the Justices." *Yearbook Supreme Court Historical Society* (1983):17–30.

Clarke, Ira G. "The Elephant Butte Controversy: A Chapter in the

Emergence of Federal Water Law." *Journal of American History* 61 (March 1975):1006–1033.

"David Josiah Brewer: An Ideal American." *Case and Comment* 16 (May 1910):361–363.

"The Death of Justice Brewer." *Independent* 68 (April 7, 1910):773–774.

Fairman, Charles. "The Education of a Justice: Justice Bradley and Some of His Colleagues." *Stanford Law Review* 1 (January 1949):217–255.

Fiss, Owen M. "David J. Brewer: The Judge as Missionary." In *The Fields and the Law*, 53–63. San Francisco: United States District Court for the Northern District of California Historical Society, 1986.

Frankfurter, Felix. "The Supreme Court in the Mirror of Justices." *University of Pennsylvania Law Review* 105 ((April 1957):781–796.

Gamer, Robert E. "Justice Brewer and Due Process: A Conservative Court Revisited." *Vanderbilt Law Review* 18 (March 1965):615–641.

"The Great Minds of America: III.—David J. Brewer." *North American Review* 187 (January 1908):1–6.

Hall, Kermit L. "David J. Brewer." In *Encyclopedia of the American Constitution*, edited by Leonard W. Levy et al. 4 vols. 1:152–153. New York: Macmillan, 1986.

Heffron, Paul T. "Theodore Roosevelt and the Appointment of Mr. Justice Moody." *Vanderbilt Law Review* 18 (March 1965):545–568.

Hickman, Russell K. "Lincoln College, Forerunner of Washburn University." *Kansas Historical Quarterly* 18 (May 1950):164–204.

Horton, Albert H. "David Josiah Brewer." *Green Bag* 2 (January 1890):1–2.

———. "The State Judiciary." *Kansas Law Journal* 3 (March 20, 1886):83–87.

"Judge D. J. Brewer." *Agora* 5 (December 1895):295.

Kellogg, Lyman B. "The Founding of the State Normal School." *Collections of the Kansas State Historical Society* 12 (1911–1912):88–98.

———. "The Supreme Court." *Minutes of the Third Annual Meeting of the Bar Association of the State of Kansas*. Topeka: Geo. W. Crane & Co., 1886, 44–50.

Kingman, S. A. [Untitled address] *Seventh Annual Meeting of the Bar Association of the State of Kansas* (1890):39–41.

McCurdy, Charles W. "Justice Field and the Jurisprudence of Government-Business Relations: Some Parameters of Laissez-Faire Constitutionalism." *Journal of American History* 61 (March 1975):970–1005.

———. "The Roots of 'Liberty of Contract' Reconsidered: Major Premises in the Law of Employment, 1867–1937." *Yearbook Supreme Court Historical Society* (1984):20–33.

Malin, James C. "Notes on the Writing of General Histories of Kansas," part 3. *Kansas Historical Quarterly* 21 (Spring 1955):331–378.

Martin, Albro. "The Troubled Subject of Railroad Regulation in the Gilded Age—A Reappraisal." *Journal of American History* 41 (September 1974):339–371.

Mason, James M. "The Walruff Case." *Kansas Law Journal* 3 (February 27, 1886):33–38.

Moline, Brian J. "David Josiah Brewer, Kansas Jurist." *Journal of the Kansas Bar Association* 55 (January–February 1986):7–11.

Monkkonen, Eric. "Can Nebraska or Any State Regulate Railroads?" *Nebraska History* 54 (Fall 1973):365–382.

"Mr. Justice Brewer." *Outlook* 94 (April 9, 1910):785–786.

Patterson, David S. "An Interpretation of the American Peace Movement." In *Peace Movements in America*, edited by Charles Chatfield, 20–38. New York: Schocken Books, 1973.

Paul, Arnold M. "David J. Brewer." In *The Justices of the United States Supreme Court, 1789–1979: Their Lives and Major Opinions*, edited by Leon Friedman and Fred Israel. 5 vols. 3:1515–1549. New York: Chelsea House, 1969.

Pisani, Donald J. "State vs. Nation: Federal Reclamation and Water Rights in the Progressive Era." *Pacific Historical Review* 51 (August 1982):265–282.

Pratt, Walter F. "Rhetorical Styles on the Fuller Court." *American Journal of Legal History* 24 (July 1980):189–220.

Sawyer, A. J. "History of the Incarceration of the Lincoln City Council." *Proceedings and Collections of the Nebraska State Historical Society*, 2d ser. 2 (1902):105–137.

Scott, Robert D. "*Kansas* v. *Colorado* Revisited." *American Journal of International Law* 52 (1958):432–454.

Sherow, James E. "The Contest for the 'Nile of America.'" *Great Plains Quarterly* 10 (Winter 1990):48–61.

Shoenrich, Otto. "The Venezuela-British Boundary Dispute." *American Journal of International Law* 43 (July 1949):523–530.

Stolberg, Mary M. "The Evolution of Frontier Justice: The Case of Judge Isaac Parker." *Prologue: Quarterly Journal of the National Archives* 20 (Spring 1988):7–23.

"A Sunflower Solon." *Saturday Evening Post* 182 (September 11, 1909):23.

Taylor, David G. "Boom Town Leavenworth: The Failure of a Dream." *Kansas Historical Quarterly* 38 (Winter 1972):389–415.

Unrau, William E. "Joseph G. McCoy and Federal Regulation of the Cattle Trade." *Colorado Magazine* 43 (Winter 1966):32–43.

Urofsky, Melvin I. "Myth and Reality: The Supreme Court and Protective Legislation in the Progressive Era." *Yearbook Supreme Court Historical Society* (1983):53–72.

"The Wabash Receivership Case." *American Law Review* 21 (January–February 1887):141–145.

"The Wabash Swindle." *Nation* 40 (April 16, 1885):316–317.

Ware, E. F. "D. J. Brewer." *Proceedings of the Twenty-eighth Annual Meeting of the Bar Association of the State of Kansas* (1911):17–21.

Waters, Joseph G. "Samuel A. Kingman." *Collections of the Kansas State Historical Society* 9 (1905–1906):45–54.

Watson, Warren. "David Josiah Brewer." In *Distinguished American Lawyers*, by Henry W. Scott. New York: C. L. Webster, 1891.

Wilson, Paul E. "Brown v. Board of Education Revisited." *University of Kansas Law Review* 12 (May 1964):507–524.

Woods, Randall B. "Integration, Exclusion, or Segregation? The 'Color Line' in Kansas, 1878–1900." *Western Historical Quarterly* 14 (April 1983):181–198.

Wunder, John R. "Chinese in Trouble: Criminal Law and Race on the Trans-Mississippi Frontier." *Western Historical Quarterly* 17 (January 1986):25–41.

INDEX

Abernathy, Omar, 184
Abilene, KS, 34
Adams, Franklin G., 8
Adams Express Co., 144
Addams, Jane, 176
Albany Law School, 4–5
Allen Edward A., 226n.3
Alvey, Richard H., 123
American Bar Association, 123, 131,
  136
American Bell Telephone Co., 59, 99–
  100
American Bible Society, 129
American Board of Commissioners for
  Foreign Missions, 129
American Home Missionary Society,
  128
American Law Review, 75–76
American Missionary Association, 180
American Peace Society, 122
American Railway Union, 108–9
American Society of International Law,
  173
American Tobacco Co., 185
Andover Theological Seminary, 1
Animal Industry Act, 92
Anthony, Daniel R., 13, 33
Arkansas River, 162–63
Armour Packing Co., 142
Armstrong, Samuel Chapman, 177
Arthur, Chester A., 52
Associated Charities of Washington, 176
Atchison, KS, 50
Atchison County, KS, 67

Baldwin, Simeon E., 136
Baltimore and Ohio Telegraph Co., 59
Beales land grant, 65
Beebe, Walter, 34
Bellamy, Edward, 86

Bell Telephone Co., 59, 66. *See also*
  American Bell Telephone Co.
"Berliner patent," 99
"Bill Goat" (camp cook), 134
Blatchford, Samuel, 77, 86, 88
Blue Rapids Township (KS), 28
B'nai B'rith, 180
Borah, William E., 183
Boston Female Society for the Promotion
  of Christianity among the Jews, 1
Boxer Rebellion, 129
Bradley, Joseph P., 77, 82, 104, 122
Bradley (saloon owner), 67
Brandeis, Louis D, 153–54
Brewer, David Josiah: addresses by, 18,
  48–50, 50–51, 70, 117–23, 126–31, 133,
  135, 137–38, 169, 170, 172, 173, 174, 176,
  177, 179–80, 183, 184; antisemitism, accused of, 180; and antitrust cases (federal), 96–97, 145–47; and antitrust
  cases (state) 147; antiwar views of,
  14, 50, 126–27; on appeals, 131, 166,
  178–79; appearance, 81–82; appointed
  to Supreme Court, 72–74; on arbitration of international disputes, 122–23,
  173; Bible class teacher, 9, 128, 168;
  birth, 2; and blacks, 14, 43–44, 104–
  5, 107–8; board of education of District of Columbia, member of, 177,
  179; on bond issues, 26–28, 29–30,
  82; on bond issues to subsidize railroads and other private interests, 26–
  28, 29, 58, 101–2; on centralized
  power, xiii, 49–50, 54, 120, 140, 164,
  172, 185, 187; and charities, xii, 176;
  and child custody cases, 39–41; and
  Chinese, xiii, 105–8, 121, 158–59, 176–
  77; and "Christian nation" doctrine,
  110–11, 180, 225n.23; and cigar smoking, 8–9, 134; on collusive suits, 166;

and commerce power, 67–68, 91–93, 98, 103, 140, 150; commissioner of the federal circuit court, 9, 13; Circuit Court, U.S. Eighth, appointed judge of, 52; as circuit justice, 77, 88–89, 102–3; confirmation of appointment to the Supreme Court, 74–75; constitution of Kansas, advocates new, 47; and contracts and the contract clause, 98–99, 149–50; on corporate privileges and immunities, 31; on corporate wrongdoing, 170–72; corruption, accused of, 61–62; as county attorney, 19–20, 24; on county seat disputes, 32–33; courts, dignity and sanctity of, 46, 64, 69; courts, on misuse of, 113; on creditors and debtors, 44–45; on crime, 3, 11, 34–35, 111–13, 164–66; criminal court of Leavenworth County, judge of, 11–12; on damages awards, 30–31, 57; death of, 182–83; dissents on Supreme Court, number of, 80; district court judge, 13–15; divorce cases, 41–42, 43; on due process, 67–68 (*see also* Substantive due process; Fourteenth Amendment); education of, 3–5; education, support of, 15, 17–18, 179, 185; on election fraud, 29–30, 32–33; on eminent domain, 31; eulogies of, 185; evaluations of, 184–87; on *ex post facto* laws, 112; family relations of, 39, 46–47, 70, 133; on fencing laws, 26; and freedom of expression, 165; funeral and burial of, 183–84; grandchildren of, 169; and habeas corpus, 166; health, decline of, 181, 182; honorary degrees, 179, 237n.65; humor of, 46, 81, 185; hunting trips of, 134–35; on immigration, 178; and imperialism, 127–28, 161–62, 175; on income tax, 95–96, 119–20; and Indians, 43, 121–22, 159–60; individual, his concern for the, xii, xiii, 4, 38, 49, 150, 177, 185, 187; on inheritances, 117; on injunctions, 119; interviews of, 114–15, 116, 173, 174, 180; ju-

dicial background of, xi; on judicial infallibility, 178; on judicial reform, 47–48; on the judiciary, independence of, 119; jurisprudence of, 150, 187; on the jury system, 179; on Kansas Central Relief Committee, 29; Kansas State Teachers' Association, president of, 18; Kansas Supreme Court, election to, 22; and labor cases, 62–64, 108–10, 151–55; on labor unions, 118, 171–72; and land cases, 64–65, 100–101; as a lawyer in Leavenworth, 7–8, 20; on legal education, 131–32; on legal ethics, 45–46, 69, 113, 167, 178; as a legislative candidate, 10; on lynching, 177, 178–79; marriages of, 9, 168; memorial and obituaries, 183, 185; and militia duty, 9–10; and missionary activity, 129; and monopoly, 56, 86; on obedience to the law, 178; obstinacy of, 82–83; opinions, length of, 140; opinions, number of, 167; opinions, writing of, 213; on oral arguments, 166; as orator, 116, 185, 186; patent cases and patent law, 65–66, 99–100, 130–31; as peace advocate, xii, 122–23, 126–28, 173–75, 185; on petty offenses, 165, 233n.68; poetry of, 5–6, 8–9, 19, 47, 106–7, 136, 137, 208n.22; and police power, 25–26, 38, 58, 91–92, 97, 103, 110, 117, 120, 140, 147, 154, 165, 165–66, 172–73; political activities of, 133; political views of, 132, 180–81; on Populist movement, 121; on preferential voting, 48; as presidential prospect, 132; as probate judge, 10, 11; on prohibition and temperance, 35, 36–38, 66–67, 121; and property rights, xii, 25, 35, 38, 42–43, 44, 59, 64, 66–67, 85, 86, 91, 103, 117–18, 146, 150, 158, 185, 187; and "public interest" doctrine, 24–25, 55, 84, 86, 118, 143; on publicizing corporate wrongdoing, 170–71; public visibility of, 116; on reapportionment, 34; on rebates, 141–42; receivership cases of,

Northern Securities Co., 145–46
Northwestern Mutual Life Insurance Co., 170
North Yakima, WA, 87–88
Norway and Sweden, King of, 124

Ogden, C. W., 133
Old South Church, Boston, 179
Oleomargarine Act, 165
Olney, Richard, 123
Omaha, NE, 169
"Original package" doctrine, 91–92
Orinoco River, 125
Oswego Norman School, 168
"Our Judge" (cigar), 134
Outlook, 179, 185–86

Panama Canal and Canal Zone, 162
Paris, Treaty of, 160
Parker, Amasa J., 5
Parker, Isaac C., 53, 111–12, 164
Parrott, Marcus J., 8
Paul, Arnold M., 222n.10
Peckham, Rufus W., xii, 77, 90, 181, 186; in agreement with DJB, 110, 142, 151, 152, 155, 158, 161, 166; death of, 139; disagrees with DJB, 97, 112, 144, 148, 159; and *Employers' Liability Cases,* 155; and *Northern Securities* case, 145; response to reform, 140
Peithologian (literary society), 3
Pendery, John L., 20
People's party. *See* Populist party
Philippine Islands, 127, 160, 161
Philips, John F., 54
Phillips Academy, 1
Pierce, C. B., 9
Pierce, Franklin, 5
Pike's Peak gold rush, 6
Piper, Elizabeth, 7
Plumb, Preston B., 52, 72, 73–74, 75
Police power, 86, 142, 144, 151, 152. *See also* Brewer, David Josiah: and police power
Pollock, Frederick, 184
Pope, John, 13–14

Populist party, 88, 89, 121, 147
Porter (Valentine Mott?), 181
Price, Sterling, 10
Prizes of war, 113
Progressive Era, 139
Prohibitionists: opposed to DJB's appointment to the U.S. Supreme Court, 74, 76
Puerto Rico, 127, 160
Pullman, George M., 133
Pullman boycott, 108–9, 119, 133
Pullman Palace Car Co., 59, 108

Quantrill, William C., 10, 12

Railroads: Atchison, Topeka, and Santa Fe, 25, 31, 58; Atlantic and Pacific, 101; Baltimore and Ohio, 91; Chicago Great Western, 141; Chicago, Rock Island, and Pacific, 83; Denver and Rio Grande, 57, 63–64; Great Northern, 146; Illinois Central, 93; Kansas Pacific, 24, 31; Missouri, Kansas, and Texas ("Katy"), 57, 61–62; Missouri Pacific, 31; Northern Pacific, 154, 87–88; Southern Pacific, 101; Texas and Pacific, 102; Union Pacific, 57, 102–3, 135, 140; Wabash, St. Louis, and Pacific, 60–61, 62–63
Reed, Thomas B., 114
Removal Act of 1875, 54–55
Rice, John T., 12
Roosevelt, Theodore, 145, 156, 162, 177, 181; on DJB, 181, 186; foreign policies of, 174; and trusts, 146–47. *See also* Brewer, David Josiah: on Theodore Roosevelt
Ruggles, R. M., 22
Russell, W. H., 6
Russell of Killowen, Lord Chief Justice, 124
Ryan, Archbishop Patrick John, 129

Safford, Jacob, 22
St. John, John P., 52
St. Louis, MO, 93

Michael J. Brodhead is an archivist at the National Archives–Central Plains Region, Kansas City, and professor emeritus of history at the University of Nevada, Reno. He has taught courses in nineteenth- and twentieth-century America and constitutional history. Among his publications are *Persevering Populist: The Life of Frank Doster, Elliott Coues: Naturalist and Frontier Historian* (with Paul Russell Cutright), *Brushwork Diary: Watercolors of Early Nevada* (with James C. McCormick), and *A Naturalist in Indian Territory: The Journals of S. W. Woodhouse* (edited, with John S. Tomer). His current research interests are naturalists of the nineteenth century and military history.